DONGSHAN'S FIVE RANKS

DONGSHAN'S
FIVE
RANKS

KEYS TO ENLIGHTENMENT

Ross Bolleter

WISDOM PUBLICATIONS · BOSTON

Wisdom Publications
199 Elm Street
Somerville MA 02144 USA
www.wisdompubs.org

Library of Congress Cataloging-in-Publication Data
Bolleter, Ross, author.
  Dongshan's Five Ranks : Keys to Enlightenment / Ross Bolleter.
    pages cm
  Includes bibliographical references and index.
  Includes translations from Chinese.
  ISBN 978-0-86171-530-5 — ISBN 0-86171-530-6 (pbk. : alk. paper) — ISBN 978-1-61429-131-2 (eBook)
  1. Liangjie, 807–869. Wu wei. 2. Caodong (Sect)—Doctrines. 3. Enlightenment (Buddhism) I. Liangjie, 807–869. Wu wei. English. II. Title. III. Title: Keys to Enlightenment.
  BQ9449.L524W8833 2014
  294.3'85—dc23
                        2013043113

18 17 16 15 14
5 4 3 2 1

Cover and interior design by Gopa&Ted2, Inc.
Set in Sabon LT Pro 10.25/15.

Wisdom Publications' books are printed on acid-free paper and meet the guidelines for permanence and durability of the Production Guidelines for Book Longevity of the Council on Library Resources.

Printed in the United States of America.

This book was produced with environmental mindfulness. We have elected to print this title on 30% PCW recycled paper. As a result, we have saved the following resources: 12 trees, 5 million BTUs of energy, 1,010 lbs. of greenhouse gases, 5,479 gallons of water, and 367 lbs. of solid waste. For more information, please visit our website, www.wisdompubs.org. This paper is also FSC® certified. For more information, please visit www.fscus.org.

for Amanda and Julian

Contents

THE FIVE MODES IN DETAIL

THE CYCLE OF MERIT

THE LITERARY HERITAGE OF THE FIVE RANKS

III. Coda to the Five Ranks

Appendices

Preface

M Y LIFE AS A MUSICIAN has been informed and shaped by Zen practice. In fact, much of the music that I have created would have been unthinkable without it. In saying this, I speak for the power and virtue of zazen, whose effects are incalculable. Beyond that, metaphors of the Way have often been an inspiration for the structures and procedures in my compositions.

I discovered Beethoven's Piano Sonata no. 30, op. 109, in the midst of the squalor and emotional chaos of my teen years, and I found in it a luminous principle of order: a music that carried me into a deeper life and gave me my first remembered experience of timelessness. Years later I discovered John Cage's book *Silence* with its Zen influenced account of sound as silence. Under the spell of his *Sonatas and Interludes for Prepared Piano* in the early 1980s I prepared a piano, inserting a variety of objects such as guitar jacks, postcards, fishing sinkers, combs, clothes pegs, and erasers between and around the strings to alter the sound of the piano in unheard of ways. By the end of the morning it sounded, to my joy, like a demented gamelan orchestra. Later, when I was making a cup of tea at lunchtime, I accidentally knocked the kettle against the stovetop—brang!—and found myself in a state of confused joy. It was somehow no longer "me" darkly stumbling about, unrestricted.

The sound of the kettle striking the stove evoked my yearning and stirred something deeper than thought. I trusted my experience and proceeded on trust. I had to, for, in the ordinary sense what I was getting into couldn't be known in advance, or even known at all. Through koan work, over time and with persistent effort, I came to appreciate that words themselves, even as they retain their conventional sense, are at the same time beyond considerations of sense and meaning. In this they convey the Way no less than the caroling of magpies and the low hum of the fan with its periodic gathering of harmonics, reminiscent of a slow hymn played over and over on an old electronic organ. The genesis of this book on Dongshan's Five Ranks lies in these experiences.

My interest in the Five Ranks has also been furthered by my explorations of ruined piano as a composer and improviser. A piano is said to be ruined (rather than neglected or devastated) when it has been abandoned to all weathers with the result that few or none of its notes sound like those of an even-tempered upright piano. It raises the question, "What is a piano?" When I discovered a ruined piano in a tractor shed on a West Australian sheep station, my passion for prepared piano and its contrivances gave way to one for pianos prepared by nature: by searing heat, flash floods, and by how far off the stars are.

For me "ruined piano" belongs with those other dead-end metaphors for emptiness: the stringless lute, the iron flute with no holes. The ruined piano may be evocative of emptiness, but each ruined piano is, at the same time, utterly unique with respect to action and tuning (if we can talk of tuning at all). An F# one-and-a-half octaves above middle C on a West Australian ruined piano in a semidesert environment differs radically from the same note on a flooded piano in a studio four floors below pavement level in Prague.

The ruined piano, abandoned in nature, becomes intimate with its environment. As its sound board opens wider to show the cloudless sky, and a dusty wisteria clambers over its broken hammers, the piano that is no longer a piano is so open at the edges that everything and everyone can come through, can come in. And they do—yapping sheep dogs, trucks revving up, sheep-station owners complaining about the drought, roosters crowing in some out-of-joint time—all of them singing the 108,000 tongues of the Buddha through the empty, dilapidated window of a single long-ringing ruined note. Taking this all together, we can discern three aspects of ruined piano: no-self, uniqueness, and intimate inclusiveness, three characteristics that connect the ruined piano into the feed-stream of the Five Ranks.

In this book I take two approaches to the Five Ranks. The first is straightforwardly descriptive. I employ this approach in the first exploration of the five modes of the essential and the contingent as well as in the history and context for the Five Ranks. Elsewhere, especially in the more detailed treatment of the Ranks, I draw freely on koans, especially in the extended exploration of Dongshan's profound and subtle verses.

In terms of how to read the book, the book is as it is read. My recommendation is to jump into the middle of things and to explore from there. Memorizing the verses and meditating on them is also surely helpful for coming to terms with the Five Ranks. My hope is that, with persistent meditation and study, the Five Ranks will become familiar. In J. M. Coetzee's novel, *The Childhood of Christ*, an immigrant worker on the docks apologizes to the senior stevedore about his poor command of the local language. The stevedore responds, "As for your Spanish, persist. One day it will cease to feel like a language, it will become the way things are."

*A NOTE ON THE TRANSLATIONS

Peter Wong Yih-Jiun and I have aimed for a clear, fairly literal translation that hopefully presents Dongshan's Dharma without being overly interpretative, and without unnecessary adornment. I hope we have been able to provide a clear source where there has been much obfuscation and guesswork. While we have both exercised care, any errors are entirely mine.

Ross Bolleter

Southern Spring, 2013

Acknowledgments

BACK IN 1986, John Tarrant gave me a copy of Robert Aitken's monograph "The Five Modes of Tung-shan." Over the years this unpublished typewritten manuscript became an inspiration for my practice. I came to love Robert Aitken's exquisite translations of Dongshan's verses, and I memorized them walking through the streets and along the riverbank near my home.

Aitken's commentary was my first map of Five Ranks territory. I worked that country most intensively with John Tarrant at the end of koan study in 1992. I'm deeply grateful to him for his generous and brilliant account of the Ranks, which he passed on to me, sitting on a blanket amid the spring wildflowers at Mount Helena, Western Australia.

I've been inspired to write on the Five Ranks as a way of trying to requite the generosity of my teachers, Robert Aitken and John Tarrant, and as a way of returning the inspiration I got from working the Five Ranks country with my students (now teachers) Ian Sweetman, Susan Murphy, Glenn Wallis, Bob Joyner, Mary Jaksch, Mari Rhydwen, and Arthur Wells. Their enthusiasm has kindled my own.

I am deeply grateful to Peter Wong Yih-Jiun for his unstinting work and support in the collaborative project of translating Dongshan, Caoshan, Shitou, Linji, and others, and for the research that he has done for this book. His patience, kindness, and painstaking care throughout the course of this work of more than seven years has enabled me to understand the Five Ranks in new ways, and has been an immeasurable help in writing this book. I am also grateful to Peter for giving me relevant books and articles on the Five Ranks, as well as other works, both musical and literary, which have inspired my work.

My thanks to Nelson Foster for recommending that Peter collaborate with me in producing the translations.

I am grateful to Korin Charlie Pokorny for his exemplary Jewel Mirror Translation Study, which has been an invaluable resource during the writing of this book. Charlie made his scholarship freely available to me, and his labor of love introduced me to a plethora of distinct approaches to the Five Ranks and the "Song of the Precious Mirror Samadhi." My thanks to Charlie for his generous responses to my questions on a variety of aspects of Caodong scholarship and for supplying me with relevant research articles.

Thanks to Andy Ferguson for translating the Ranks for me, and for providing me with a helpful commentary on them. His translations from the Foguang Dictionary were invaluable and assisted me in coming to terms with the Cycle of Merit, in particular.

I owe a debt of gratitude to Glenn Wallis, who read parts of the manuscript and offered his feedback and encouragement. He also engaged with me in weekly dialogues on the Ranks and the "Song of the Precious Mirror Samadhi." I found our exchanges to be helpful and invigorating, and I have included some of his cogent responses to the koan aspects of the "Song of the Precious Mirror Samadhi."

I extend my thanks to Ian Sweetman, who lent me half his library over the course of writing this book and offered his unstinting encouragement, and to Arthur Wells for reading part of the manuscript and for his feedback and encouragement at every stage of the process.

My heartfelt thanks to Susan Murphy for her loving encouragement, for her cogent advice and support throughout the long process of writing the book, and for her invaluable suggestions that helped to shape the second draft of this book.

Mari Rhydwen and Arthur Wells contributed important stories, which I have quoted. I am grateful for their contributions.

I was also kept moving by the warm encouragement of Kathy Shiels, who read the book in manuscript form and offered invaluable suggestions, and by Mary Heath, who read the book and gave me important feedback on it. Joe Harding urged this project on to completion when my energy flagged. I am grateful to him for his support over many years now. I am most appreciative for the transcription, editing, and compilation work done by Mary Jaksch, Kathy Shiels, Mary Heath, Bob Joyner, Judy Peppard, Brigid Lowry, and David Kotlowy.

My thanks to Joe Harding, for computer typing the manuscript in its early form, and to Glenn Wallis, who negotiated the ever-unfurling faxes that I kept sending and managed the project into its early stages—ten talks all elegantly packed side by side in a Winzip file. Thanks, also, to Glenn and the Dunedin Zen Group for providing a bach for me at Purakaunui, where I was able to do the bulk of writing and revision on the early drafts of this work.

I acknowledge my children (now brilliant adults), Amanda and Julian Bolleter, and their mother, Glenys Davies, for their enduring love, support, and encouragement as I wrote. My thanks are due to Amanda who read the first draft, made invaluable suggestions, and encouraged me. And to Julian for his unstinting encouragement and suggestions on reading the first draft, and for providing me with a second computer screen to facilitate the final draft of the book.

My thanks and appreciation to Josh Bartok, senior editor for Wisdom Publications, who helped me shape the rewrite of this book from 2011 to 2012, and to Andy Francis, another Wisdom editor, for his labors in restructuring the book into its most recent form, and thereby giving it scope and enabling it to breathe deeper. Discussion with friends also shaped the writing of this book. I am grateful to Eric Harrison for his friendship, generosity, and wisdom over many years, and for his invaluable suggestions regarding writing style and approach. I am also grateful to Anthony Cormican for his friendship and unstinting encouragement of my work over the last decade and more.

Finally, I extend my deepest gratitude to Antoinette Carrier—who is in a class of her own—for her love, support, and patience through the protracted final stages of writing.

Ross Bolleter
Southern Spring, 2013

DONGSHAN'S
FIVE RANKS

GATHA OF THE FIVE POSITIONS
OF RULER AND MINISTER[1]

The master composed the Gatha on the Five Positions of Ruler and
Minister,[2] which says:

The Contingent within the Essential[3]
At the beginning of the third watch, before moonrise,
don't be surprised if there is meeting without recognition;
one still vaguely harbors the elegance of former days.

The Essential within the Contingent[4]
Having overslept, an old woman encounters the ancient mirror.
This is clearly meeting face-to-face—only then is it genuine.
Don't lose your head by validating shadows.

Arriving within the Essential[5]
In nothingness there is a road apart from the dust.
If you don't break the taboo on mentioning the Emperor's name
you will surpass the eloquence of the previous dynasty's
    worthies, who cut off tongues.

Approaching from the Contingent[6]
No need to dodge when blades are crossed.
The skillful one is like a lotus in the midst of fire.
Seemingly, you yourself possess the aspiration to soar to
    the heavens.

Arriving at Concurrence[7]
Who would presume to join their voice with someone
who has surpassed "there is" and "there is not"?
Everyone longs to leave the mundane stream, yet finally
you return to sit in the charcoal heap.

The Five Stages of Merit[8]

Orientation[9]

Sage rulers have always modeled themselves on Emperor Yao.

Treating others with propriety, you bend your dragon waist.

At times, passing through the thick of the bustling market,

you find it civilized throughout and the august dynasty
  celebrated.

Service[10]

For whom have you washed off your splendid makeup?

The cuckoo's call urges you to return.

The hundred flowers have fallen, yet the call is unending,

moving deeper and still deeper into jumbled peaks.

Merit[11]

A withered tree blossoms in timeless spring.

You ride a jade elephant backwards, chasing the unicorn.

Now, as you dwell hidden high among the thousand distant
  peaks—

a white moon, a cool breeze, an auspicious day.

Merit in Common[12]

The many beings and buddhas do not intrude on each other.

Mountains are high of themselves; waters are deep of
  themselves.

What do the myriad differences and distinctions clarify?
Where the partridge calls, the hundred flowers bloom afresh.

Merit upon Merit[13]
If horns sprout on your head, that's unbearable;
If you rouse your mind to seek Buddha, that's shameful.
In the vastness of the empty kalpa there is no one who knows—
Why go to the South to interview the fifty-three sages?

I.

Overture to the Five Ranks

1. Dongshan and the Five Ranks

Dongshan: A Brief Biographical Sketch

DONGSHAN LIANGJIE (807–869) was a great teacher among great teachers during the flowering of Chan (Zen) Buddhism in the Tang dynasty. He was the thirty-eighth ancestor in the lineage that comes down from the Buddha and in the eleventh generation of the grand masters of ancient China. He and his successor Caoshan Benji (840–901) are revered as the founders of the Caodong lineage (known in Japanese as *Sōtō*), the name of which is a portmanteau of Cao and Dong, the mountains on which these two masters lived and taught.

Dongshan went on pilgrimage as a young man and engaged with some of the foremost teachers of his era, including Nanquan Puyuan (748–835) and Guishan Lingyou (771–853). Dongshan finally settled with Yunyan Tansheng (784–841), under whom he had his initial awakening. Eventually, Dongshan established his own center on "Cave Mountain" (*dong shan*) in Hungzhou. He had twenty-six successors, the principal ones being Caoshan Benji and Yunju Daoying (835?–902). The latter's line endured for about eight hundred years in China, disappearing in the seventeenth century. Eihei Dogen (1200–1253) brought the Caodong line to Japan in the thirteenth century, and it has persisted there as Soto, one of the major streams of Zen that comes down to us today, the other being the Linji (*Rinzai* in Japanese).[14]

Dongshan's style of teaching was often dark, elliptical, and subtle. His enigmatic expressions gave his students little to cling to, but nonetheless nourished generations of disciples. His wry, sardonic humor and aloofness from ordinary human concerns are readily evident in the following account of his death.

The story goes that when Dongshan knew that he was about to die, he changed his clothes, struck the bell, and announced the fact to his assembly. He then sat in zazen and began to pass away. Because he was much loved and respected, his disciples wept and wailed.

Annoyed by the disturbance, Dongshan opened his eyes and said, "Those who travel the Buddha Way should have a mind unattached to life and death. People struggle to live and are confounded by death, but what's the use of lamenting?"

He then ordered the temple manager to make arrangements for a delusion banquet. The prospect of this banquet didn't alleviate his students' feeling of bereavement, so preparations were prolonged for seven days.

In order to urge the preparations along, Dongshan joined in, grumbling, "You monks have made a great commotion over nothing. This time when you see me dying, don't make a noisy fuss."

Then, probably expecting more grief, he retired to his room, sat in zazen, and died.[15]

The poetic work widely known as the Five Ranks—a pair of esoteric five-verse summations of Chan teachings—is traditionally attributed to Dongshan. I accept the traditional attribution, although we cannot be certain who in fact authored the work. The two cycles that comprise the Five Ranks, and the poem "Song of the Precious Mirror Samadhi," appear near the end of the Record of Dongshan. The Record appears to be loosely chronological, but even if it is not, the two cycles and the Precious Mirror certainly feel "late," in the way that Bach's "Art of the Fugue"—unfinished at his death—does. Bach crystallized insights gained from a lifetime of writing fugues and emulating the contrapuntal techniques of his forbears. Just as with Bach's masterwork, there is nothing crabbed in Dongshan's Five Ranks, in which he draws on a long tradition of skillful means and teaching devices that go back to the Buddha.

Also, both of Dongshan's cycles feel "composed" and are strikingly different from the mostly brief responses to questions that are recorded in his Record. The following is typical:

A monk asked, "When a dying monk passes away,
    where does he go?"
"After the fire, a single reed stem," Dongshan replied.[16]

Brief, but plenty and enough.

In the Five Ranks, Dongshan uses a dialectical formulation to present the Buddha Way. Over the centuries since its appearance, the cryptic dialectic of the Five Ranks has captured the imagination and inspired the practice of countless teachers and students of the Way.

Dongshan arranges the perspectives of the Five Ranks in two closely related cycles. The first of these focuses on enlightenment itself and is composed of five perspectives on the great matter: awakening, its expression, its embodiment and integration into our life, and finally the transcending of steps and stages. The second cycle presents enlightenment in terms of the stages on the journey to awakening, followed by the stages beyond. Each cycle focuses in a different way on the relationship between the timeless, inexpressible realm of our essential nature and the contingent realm of life and death, where myriad beings, things, and events appear as separate and unique.

Although study of, and meditation on, the Five Ranks are a peerless means to undertake the quest for awakening and a means to confirm that awakening, the text encourages us not to take seeing into our true nature as the final destination of practice, for there is so much more to be discovered and lived. Seeing into our true nature is only the beginning. Study and practice of the Five Ranks push us beyond the one-sided partiality of our little stories to realize the timeless immensity present in even the least of our experiences. When we awaken to that immensity, we live it in even the mundane moments of our lives. Unerringly pointing us beyond naïve individualism, the Five Ranks encourage us to take care of the world, and of each other.

Still, the Five Ranks are not merely teachings or instructions on how to walk the Way, although it is possible to infer such teachings from them. They also intimate what can't be taught, employing a matchless combination of poetry and koans. Expression of the inexpressible thus becomes one of the central themes of the Five Ranks. Dongshan employs the music of poetry—which through the power of allusion and suggestion is capable of expressing much more than the content of its words—to point the reader's mind toward the ineffable.

As I follow the precedent of attributing the Five Ranks to Dongshan that was set in the Record of Dongshan Liangjie, I do likewise for the poem "Song of the Precious Mirror Samadhi," in which we find configured the same themes encountered in the Five Ranks. It is possible that the Five Ranks and the "Song of the Precious Mirror Samadhi" were composed during the Song dynasty, after Dongshan's time. Whatever the case may be, subsequent to their appearance, the Five Ranks entered the transmission streams that would become the Soto and Rinzai schools in Japan, where, although their popularity has waxed and waned over the centuries, they remain important works to this day.

*A NOTE REGARDING THE TERM "RANKS"

Because I feel that the term "ranks" seems unduly hierarchical, I use the terms *positions*, *modes*, or *stages* to refer broadly to the five distinct phases treated within each of the two cycles. I use the word "position" to refer to the particular relationship between the essential and the contingent, as expressed by the verse caption alone. I use the word "mode" to refer to the caption and verse taken together, and to the mood and spirit they evoke. I use the word "stage" to refer to any of the progressive "positions" of the second cycle, the Cycle of Merit. Finally, I use the expression "Five Ranks" to refer to the two cycles taken together as a complete work or to acknowledge the traditional translation of the title into English, and on occasion to refer to Dongshan's cycle of the essential and the contingent when other options seem to involve undue hair-splitting.

The title of Dongshan's first cycle is "Gatha of the Five Positions of Ruler and Minister" (*Wuwei junchen song*; Jap. *Henshō Gōi Shō*). The Chinese phrase *wuwei* has traditionally been translated into English as "five ranks," but I prefer to translate it as "five positions"—a translation that takes into account that the Chinese sense of *wei* is not always evocative of hierarchy. I also choose to use the word "position" to translate *wei* because it captures the dual meaning of "a point in relation to others" or "a perspective on reality," as in "having a position" on an ethical or political issue. The positions enumerated in the first cycle of the Five Ranks depict the relationship between the essential and the contingent—the relationship between, among other things, the universe and ourselves.

The Two Cycles of the Five Ranks

Dongshan's Five Ranks consists of two cycles: the Cycle of the Essential and the Contingent, and the Cycle of Merit. I use the term "cycle" to mean a completed series of events (or positions, or stages)—in keeping with the way this term is used with literary or musical cycles, such as the Arthurian Cycle or Wagner's Ring Cycle. This definition gives us an overview of the Five Ranks as comprised of two series, each consisting of five "events"—five perspectives on awakened mind and five perspectives on the progress of the Way—rather than a cyclic account of reality that constantly returns to its starting point. These two cycles run broadly in parallel, like two great mountain ranges. I will very generally introduce the two cycles here, providing a brief sketch of each of them.

THE CYCLE OF THE ESSENTIAL AND THE CONTINGENT

In the first cycle, five perspectives on enlightenment are conveyed by Dongshan's captions, or titles, that precede each of his verses:

1. The Contingent within the Essential
2. The Essential within the Contingent
3. Arriving within the Essential
4. Approaching from the Contingent
5. Arriving at Concurrence

These five statements express the varying relations between the timeless, inexpressible realm of our essential nature and the contingent realm of life and death, where myriad beings and events appear as separate and unique. Each of these five positions evokes the most profound and far-reaching considerations concerning the relationship between the universe and ourselves, as well as other beings, sentient and nonsentient alike; at the same time our experience of them is utterly intimate and personal. We can say that these five statements express profound enlightenment considered from five perspectives.

Although Dongshan's presentation of this cycle of perspectives on enlightenment may seem novel, the technique of teaching by means of such paradigms did not originate with him. The Huayan masters, in particular, had already developed a similar way of teaching the nature of reality from the perspective of enlightened mind under the rubric of the four *dharmadhatu* with its interacting realms of principle and phenomena, as well as in their elaborations of that doctrine. The dialectic between essential and contingent in Dongshan's five positions is likely a distillation, or even a simplification, of the Huayan dialectic of principle and phenomena, and particularly of a Huayan doctrine called Ten Approaches to the Second Discernment, which will be discussed below.

Yet, though Dongshan's verse captions clearly seem to have been influenced by Huayan dialectics, the verses themselves overflow with the unmistakable spirit of Chan (Zen)—allusive, playful, and challenging. The way in which Dongshan composed verses to accompany each of the five positions, as identified by the captions, often counterpoints or subverts them, wittily exploring, enriching, and deepening their implications. Dongshan conjures vivid and memorable imagery in his verses—an old woman oversleeping at daybreak, a withered tree blooming in timeless spring, a lotus in the midst of fire. The Five Ranks deftly evoke the Huayan legacy even as they transcend it.

Even though the Five Ranks owe a debt to Huayan formulations, they aren't reducible to them. The Five Ranks stand out from their historical background and influences for their capacity to synthesize the experience of awakened mind in memorable images and koans. In this, they are much more than the sum of their influences. Rather like Bach, Dongshan transformed whatever he inherited and gave it not only the eyes of profound insight but also poetry that moistens and enlivens what otherwise might have been dry and abstract.

THE CYCLE OF MERIT

In his second cycle, the Cycle of Merit, Dongshan summarizes the manner and means of living the positions of the first cycle. The second cycle is more concerned with the how of the Way: how we are to lay the ground for awakening, and once awakened, how we deepen that awakening in our lives.

Here are the five stages of merit, literally "the five positions of merit and honor" (*Wuwei gong xun*; Jap. *Kōkun Gōi*), as set out in the captions that precede the verses:

1. Orientation
2. Service
3. Merit
4. Merit in Common
5. Merit upon Merit

Each of these captions presents a stage on our journey to maturity on the bodhisattva path. Although the path is laid out in stages, the entire journey is implicit in our dawning curiosity and our first hesitant step. Importantly, each stage—including the first two, which apparently precede awakening—is an expression of enlightened mind. Moreover, each stage opens to eternity, even as it occurs in time. Thus considered, the five stages of merit show the progressive path from an enlightened perspective: orientation as the full expression of our timeless essential nature, service as the full expression of our Buddha nature, and similarly for each of the subsequent stages taken in turn.

The five stages of merit are cumulative; they take time. In this regard, each stage represents a level of maturation that serves as a basis for the next one. As long as we continue to practice, the earlier stages are not lost, but remain like the growth rings of an ancient tree. From this perspective, there is no shortcut to maturity.

2. The Philosophical Heritage of the Five Ranks

Nagarjuna and the Two Truths

NAGARJUNA, a pioneering philosopher of ancient Mahayana Buddhism, proposed that the Buddha's teachings could be classified as revealing one or the other of two types of truth: a truth of worldly convention or an ultimate truth. Truth of worldly convention is truth that can be spoken, while ultimate truth is inexpressible. Truth of worldly convention is conveyed through the medium of language, taken at face value, which makes available to us knowledge of time, space, karma, love, and compassion. On the other hand, there are no words with which we might encompass, or even touch, the ground of ultimate truth.

Chekhov's story "In the Ravine" beautifully captures the sense of these two types of truth as they interrelate with one another. In the story, a young girl and her mother grieve the disastrous marriage the girl has unwittingly entered. Chekhov writes:

> However much evil existed in the world, the night was still calm and beautiful, and there was, and always would be, truth in God's universe, a truth that was just as calm and beautiful. The whole earth was only waiting to merge with that truth, just as the moonlight blended into the night.[17]

Chekhov's words express the entangled heart's yearning for union with vastness. Beneath our experience of the knowable world we have an inkling of the unknowable, just beyond the scope of word and thought. That very longing for union with the unknowable vastness is what draws us to the Way and finds pointed expression in Nagarjuna's notion of the Two Truths.

We know almost nothing of Nagarjuna's life. Stephen Batchelor, in his book *Verses from the Center*, teases out its protean, mythic strands and weaves poetry from them. He writes that Nagarjuna was born a Brahmin, and that he is supposed to have appeared at different moments in history as a monk, the founder of Mahayana Buddhism, the first Madhyamika philosopher, a tantric adept, an alchemist, and as a Nepalese trader. It seems that a minor hill in the Himalayas was named after him, and that at some point he was regarded as god of the millet crop. Such are his myths.

The Nagarjuna that is more familiarly known is the one found in that luminous work of philosophical poetry, the Mulamadyamakakarika, or Fundamental Verses on the Middle Way. His Two Truths doctrine, developed in that work, shows him to have been not only the preeminent poet of emptiness, as Batchelor terms him, but also to have been a superb dialectician.

Since Kumarajiva (344–413) first translated Nagarjuna's work into Chinese, the Two Truths doctrine has had a rich and complex history in China. I won't address the convoluted development of the doctrine through its many twists and turns over the centuries in China, but will instead confine myself to drawing a brief comparison between Nagarjuna's account of the Two Truths doctrine and Dongshan's dialectical first cycle, with its five positions of the essential and the contingent. The comparison will not only be useful for clarifying the meaning of terms employed in the dialectic of the first cycle, but an introduction to Nagarjuna's thought will also enrich our understanding of key themes that will be explored later in the book.

Nagarjuna presents the Two Truths doctrine as dialectic, with its seemingly irreconcilable polarities being the ultimate and conventional classes of truth. The fact that the Two Truths doctrine is arranged dialectically makes for an apt comparison with Dongshan's dialectical first cycle, which is itself comprised of the seemingly irreconcilable polarities of the essential and the contingent. One of the unique features of Chan, particularly as expressed in Dongshan's first cycle, is that it closes an assumed gap between the Two Truths by demonstrating that conventional words and language, for all their inherent duality, can in fact evoke the ultimate. But before we begin to explore the ways in which Chan plays with the Two Truths, let us first consider the Two Truths on their own merits.

The following three propositions supplied by Nagarjuna in his Mulamadyamakakarika, or Fundamental Verses on the Middle Way, present a concise statement of Nagarjuna's Two Truths doctrine:

> The Buddha's teaching of the Dharma is based on two truths: a truth of worldly convention and an ultimate truth.
>
> Those who do not understand that distinction drawn between these two truths do not understand the Buddha's profound truth.
>
> Without a foundation in the conventional truth, the significance of the ultimate cannot be taught. Without understanding the significance of the ultimate, liberation is not achieved. [18]

Conventional or mundane truth belongs to the realm of everyday discourse. It is the truth of the world we know intimately, the truth of cause and effect, birth and death, time, karma, compassion, and expediency. It is the variegated field of experience in which we recognize, discern, and distinguish discreet events and objects, verify and adjudicate meaning, and determine the whys and wherefores of our lives. Conventional truths are true as opposed to false. Ultimate truth, on the other hand, is beyond conception, and beyond the dualities of words and language, being precisely that which cannot be imagined or talked about. In these respects, ultimate truth has no "opposite."

Although conventional and ultimate truths are readily distinguishable from each other, they are also mutually dependent. To speak of one is to evoke the other. The Two Truths do not represent different realities. Rather, they provide differing perspectives on reality. With his doctrine of the Two Truths, Nagarjuna is saying that you must understand conventional truth, on one hand, and ultimate truth, on the other, as distinct viewpoints from which one reality is seen. Moreover, we cannot apprehend the profound significance of the ultimate except through the conventional apprehension of time and space, coming and going, birth and death, and so on. The ultimate truth is to be found within the very same mundane experiences immediately familiar to us. For this reason, although the Buddha's awakening was inexpressible, Buddha took recourse to words and language in order to convey the experience and guide others along the Way to awakening. So realization of the ultimate and essential depends upon, and is grounded in, the conventional and contingent. If we fail to get this, and seek the ultimate as isolated from our mundane lives, we entirely miss the Way of liberation.

What is the Way of liberation? When it is hot I turn on the fan. When I'm tired in the afternoon, I take a nap. At night the stars come out; at dawn they fade. That is the Way in its grand sufficiency. It cannot be sought apart from our ordinary, but inexpressibly unique, days and nights. Because conventional and ultimate truths are mutually dependent—inseparable, yet distinct—Nagarjuna's dialectic is said to be an expression of the Middle Way. This is also precisely the case concerning Dongshan's first cycle, for the essential and the contingent—at each point—are mutually dependent. The essential may conceal the contingent or vice versa, but when either is revealed, the other is implicitly present. This is similar to knowing the dark of the moon when viewing its brightness.

In terms of the middle way, we don't need to seek out mystery, or extraordinary inner spaces—the kinds of experiences we associate with deep samadhi—rather, we should dwell within the moment-to-moment weave of our lives. The mystery unfolds as the life we live: ultimate truth finds its expression precisely as our life in its unfolding. That is the Buddha's profound truth.

In a subsequent verse, Nagarjuna warns of the danger of seeking the ultimate as something isolated from our lives. He calls such seeking "a misperception of emptiness."

> By a misperception of emptiness,
> a person of little intelligence is destroyed.
> Like a snake incorrectly seized,
> or like a spell incorrectly cast.[19]

Nagarjuna's warning rings true for the Five Ranks as well, which offers us many opportunities to mishandle snakes. It is fatally easy to reify emptiness.

As we shall see in our study of the Five Ranks, a word can reveal the universe, no less than a flower. Words and language—even with all their conceptual traps and snares—convey the timeless essential realm, even when they purport to describe it, as Nagarjuna does when he clarifies the distinction between types of truth.

After his great enlightenment, the Buddha could have remained silent. However, he finally chose to teach others. With this decision came the problem of how to express his enlightenment in words. The question thus becomes: "How can you express what is beyond words through conventional language, which is inherently dualistic, and the source of innumerable conceptual traps and snares?"

Chan resolves this question by collapsing the gap between the Two Truths. It brings "the discourse of the inexpressible" and "the discourse that can be expressed in words" into something closer than mere contact, and the result is fireworks.

Here is a classical Chan dialogue that indicates more clearly and playfully the art of going beyond the Two Truths.

> Changqing once said, "It is better to say that the Arhats have the three poisons than to say the Tathagata has two kinds of words. I don't say the Tathagata has no words. I only say he does not have two kinds of words."
> Baofu asked, "What are the words of the Tathagata?"
> Changqing said, "How can a deaf man hear?"

Baofu said, "I understand. You are speaking on the second level."

Changqing said, "Well, what are the words of the Tathagata?"

Baofu said, "Have some tea."[20]

"Two kinds of words" can be understood as a lighthearted reference to Nagarjuna's Two Truths, and "to speak on the second level" can be understood as speaking from the ground of ultimate truth. The Sanskrit term *tathagata* is used as an epithet for the Buddha, but its significance is surely deeper than this. When the Buddha awakened upon seeing the Morning Star, he is supposed to have said, "Now I see that all beings are tathagata—are just this person." His exclamation upon enlightenment is one example of "the words of the Tathagata." More generally, the Buddha referred to himself as "tathagata" instead of making use of pronouns such as "I," "me," or "myself." This suggests that the teaching is being delivered from a transcendent place, beyond the duality of self and other, and beyond conventional speech and language with its dualisms. The foregoing gives a literal account of "the words of the Tathagata." However, we must surpass the literal and ultimately discover our own words—free of all levels and ranks—to be "words of the Tathagata."

Changqing's opening gambit playfully denies the Two Truths, and in response, Baofu challenges Changqing—and all of us—to speak the words of the Tathagata. Both Baofu and Changqing, when challenged by the other, oblige by uttering such words in all their purity, which is to say that their words evoke the inchoate and the inexpressible, even as they retain their ordinary meaning and orderliness. Baofu's comment, "I understand. You are speaking on the second level," shows us that even the jargon of the Two Truths, so lightly evoked here, can be just such a limpid expression of the inexpressible.

The decisive expression within the dialogue, however, is "Have some tea." These utterly ordinary words, in their naked simplicity and purity, are a vehicle for the inexpressible, and they collapse the dichotomy between ultimate and conventional truths. Such words, more intimate than our beating heart, are the miracle of Chan. The dialogue between Changqing and Baofu illustrates the means by which pure words can expresses the timeless, essential Way, transcending categories, such as "levels of truth." Concepts of truth and matters to be understood are important themes in the Two Truths doctrine. But these are entirely up for grabs in Chan, where we neither seek truth nor avoid fantasy. In Chan, "truths" and "matters to be understood" are like ever-shifting reflections in water.

Nagarjuna's Two Truths imply a path whereby ordinary, even explanatory, expression can convey the ultimate. The Chan tradition later broadened the path paved by Nagarjuna, taking full advantage of the ambiguity, beauty, and evocativeness of language to express in myriad ways the ultimate concealed as the mundane. But Nagarjuna's doctrine of the Two Truths was not the only influence that shaped the dialectic at work in the Five Ranks. Dongshan likely inherited Nagarjuna's legacy through the Huayan dialectic of principle and phenomena.

Huayan Thought

The model for the dialectical captions that Dongshan employs in both cycles of the Five Ranks was most probably the Huayan dialectics of principle and phenomena, especially as they are developed in the doctrine of the four dharmadhatu and its elaborations. The four dharmadhatu, themselves, provide four extensive perspectives on the nature of reality. These range from the commonsense realm of phenomena viewed from the perspective of conventional truth in the first dharmadhatu, to the realm of perfectly interpenetrating phenomena and phenomena, where conventional truth completely embodies and enacts ultimate truth, in the fourth. In terms of their scope and grandeur of conception they are certainly comparable to Dongshan's Five Ranks, and, as noted, they were a likely model for the creation of the Five Ranks.

THE FOUR DHARMADHATU

Behind the Five Ranks, and the Huayan categories that anticipate them, stands the towering Avatamsaka Sutra. Highly esteemed as perhaps the grandest and most elaborate of Buddhist sutras, it is one of the world's great religious masterworks. Written in stages, beginning some five hundred years after the death of the Buddha, translation of the Avatamsaka Sutra into Chinese was completed by the early eighth century. From the time of the mid-seventh century, commentaries inspired by the Avatamsaka Sutra, the best known being the Discernments of the Dharmadhatu, a work attributed to Dushun (557–640), and the celebrated essay "On the Golden Lion" by Fazang (643–712), began to arouse widespread interest within Chinese schools of Buddhism, especially within the emerging Chan schools.[21]

The fundamental idea espoused in the Avatamsaka Sutra is that of *dharmadhatu*. Chang Chung-Yuan captures the sense of this central Huayan concept in his book, *Original Teachings of Ch'an Buddhism*:

> [Dharmadhatu] is the unimpeded mutual solution of all particularities, where each particularity, besides being itself, penetrates all other particularities and is in turn penetrated by them. This harmonious interplay between particularities and also between each particularity and universality creates a luminous universe, free from spatial and temporal limitations and yet no less the world of daily affairs. This is called dharmadhatu. In it, the boundaries of each particularity melt away, and the reality of each becomes infinitely interfused with every other being.[22]

This is a profoundly inclusive vision of reality, full of eros—all that radiant union with the vastness, and with each other—with nothing and no one left out. Dharmadhatu is clearly rich in implications for our lives, for the study of, and meditation on, these themes inspires us to take up the bodhisattva way of freeing ourselves from self-preoccupation and discovering our intimate connection with countless sentient beings, which include us, and which we likewise include. Deep reflection on the dharmadhatu leads to the cultivation of care, tenderness, and respect for those we encounter, and encourages us to cooperate, rather than to compete, with others. The vision that dharmadhatu provides also has profound ecological implications, for if, in this multidimensional universe, each phenomenon is inclusive of and included within all others, what we do to the planet and its creatures so clearly matters.

Dharmadhatu entails, at the bare minimum, that each and every phenomenon in its uniqueness perfectly reflects, contains, and is interfused with all other phenomena. This theme with its several variations informs the Five Ranks. The polarities of "principle" and "phenomenon" (translated as "universality" and "particularity" in the foregoing account of dharmadhatu) are mutually dependent, just as are the essential and contingent used in Dongshan's first cycle. "Principle and phenomenon," as well as "essential and contingent," are two dialectical formulations whose polarities are mutually dependent. There can't be one polarity without the other. Like Dongshan's essential and contingent, Huayan's relationship of principle and phenomena is thus also an expression of the Middle Way, and an extension of Nagarjuna's legacy.

Huayan presentations of dharmadhatu are delivered from the perspective of enlightenment. Instead of laying out the steps that would lead one from a state of ignorance to enlightenment, Huayan's dharmadhatu presents the world as perceived through enlightened eyes. As noted earlier, this is a vision free from spatial and temporal limitations. Such freedom from temporal limitations is aptly encapsulated in the Avatamsaka Sutra's statement: "In this one instant, infinite numbers of eons are realized." So, in the light of Huayan's presentation of the Way in its all-at-onceness, with all sequence gone, to enter the path toward final enlightenment is, in an important sense, to already have manifested it.

One can easily recognize the general imprint of Huayan thought in Dongshan's Five Ranks, where reality is presented as an expression of enlightened mind, even as it appears, especially in the second cycle, the Cycle of Merit, in steps and stages. And where—even when a step-by-step path to enlightenment that unfolds over time is acknowledged—each step on the Way is considered to be timeless. Let's now turn from these broad comparisons to consider more specifically the Huayan influences on Dongshan's work.

We begin with the Huayan dialectical terms "phenomena" and "principle," and their use in the celebrated formulation of the fourfold dharmadhatu, which is enumerated as follows:

1. the dharmadhatu of phenomena
2. the dharmadhatu of principle
3. the dharmadhatu of perfectly interpenetrating phenomena and principle
4. the dharmadhatu of perfectly interpenetrating phenomena and phenomena

The term "phenomena" (*shi* in Chinese) encompasses within its semantic field objects and events: White clouds at evening, bright stars cutting through them; customers clambering into a cab outside a restaurant; the humidity of the night air. Phenomena make up the typically felt experience of daily life. The realm of phenomena corresponds to the first dharmadhatu, where reality is presented in terms of what is discrete, separate, and individual.

In terms of our study of the Two Truths in the preceding section, the dharmadhatu of phenomena corresponds to the realm of conventional truth.

The term "principle" (*li* in Chinese) carries a rich and diverse range of meanings, but for our purposes here, we can take it to mean "a fundamental order of reality," as well as the means employed to elucidate such order. "Principle"—understood here in its sense of a fundamental order of reality—can correspondingly mean emptiness, considered as an expression of the Middle Way. On these terms, the second dharmadhatu—the realm of principle—is the realm of emptiness, where phenomena are understood to lack inherent existence. This realm corresponds to Nagarjuna's ultimate truth.

To give a vivid sense to principle, I would say that—drawing on our example for phenomena from earlier—white clouds at evening, as well as the bright stars cutting through them, are completely empty, which is to say that they are without enduring self-identity. This absence of self-identity does not leave a void but rather enables the gathering of the universe itself—in the guise of those white clouds at dusk, of the couple gazing into the park with its soft lamps illuminating the Moreton Bay fig trees, their elephantine roots buckling the pavement.

So we can say that the second dharmadhatu—the realm of principle—is one where the absence of enduring self in phenomena "enables" the participation of the universe. We call that universal participation "principle." While the clouds, the stars, the couple, the lamps, the trees represent phenomena, each, and any one, of these involves the participating universe. It is no accident that it is has been awkward to discuss principle without invoking phenomena. They are completely interdependent—you can't have one without the other—and their interdependence is expressive of the Middle Way. Such mutuality invokes the third dharmadhatu: the realm of perfectly interpenetrating phenomena and principle. "Perfectly" means "totally," in the sense of "nothing left over." This means that the interpenetration of the phenomenon and principle is complete, with nothing left out. Another implication of perfect is "mutual." Not only does principle penetrate phenomena, but, equivalently, phenomena penetrate principle. In this way, to extend the imagery of the restaurant, the park and the couple—a compliment over dinner carries the universe, while the universe, correspondingly and unerringly, finds its expression in the returning compliment, "You look beautiful tonight." Nothing is left over; nothing is left out.

The fourth dharmadhatu—the dharmadhatu of perfectly interpenetrating phenomena and phenomena—refers to the interpenetration or dynamic interrelationship of phenomena and phenomena. I will speak in more detail about the fourth dharmadhatu below. For now, I would say only that this is the realm where conventional truth completely embodies and enacts ultimate truth: which is to say, our ordinary words express the timeless inexpressible realm of the ultimate, without remainder.

The formula of the fourfold dharmadhatu was a likely starting point and inspiration for both cycles of Dongshan's Five Ranks, but at the same time the latter's positions and stages cannot be simply reduced to these four categories. While "principle" and "phenomena" are akin to, and in many ways parallel the "essential" and "contingent" of Dongshan's first cycle, the two sets of terms are not synonyms for each other, nor are they interchangeable.

The second cycle of the Five Ranks, the Cycle of Merit, relates more closely to the fourfold dharmadhatu than does the first cycle of the essential and the contingent. The first two stages of the Cycle of Merit, Orientation and Service, can be understood as broadly analogous to the first dharmadhatu: the world of phenomena. The third stage, Merit, or personal awakening, aligns with the second dharmadhatu: the world of principle. The fourth and fifth stages, Merit in Common and Merit upon Merit, correspond broadly to the third and fourth dharmadhatu: the world of perfectly interpenetrating phenomena and principle, and the world of perfectly interpenetrating phenomena and phenomena.

Dongshan alludes to the Huayan in his concluding verse of the Cycle of Merit, where he asks, "Why go to the South to interview the fifty-three sages?" This question is made in reference to the Entry into the Realm of Reality chapter of the Avatamsaka Sutra, in which the pilgrim Sudhana visits fifty-three teachers over the course of his pilgrimage. By closing his work with this allusion Dongshan acknowledges the Avatamsaka Sutra, and implicitly Huayan, as the background against which his Five Ranks have been formulated. His concluding question is also perhaps a bit of a subtle championing of the path afforded in the Five Ranks.

THE THREE LEVELS OF DISCERNMENT AND THE TEN APPROACHES

The Huayan formula that aligns more closely with Dongshan's Cycle of the Essential and the Contingent is found within expositions of the third and fourth dharmadhatus: the dharmadhatu of perfectly inter-penetrating phenomena and principle, and the dharmadhatu of perfectly interpenetrating phenomena and phenomena. It is in those two realms that we find a more precise correlation between the dharma-dhatu doctrine and the dialectical positions developed by Dongshan in his first cycle. In particular, a stronger correlation can be drawn between the first four positions of essential and contingent and four of "the Ten Approaches to the second and third of the Three Levels of Discernment" as laid out in the Discernments of the Dharmadhatu (*Huayan Fajie Guanmen*), a work attributed to Dushun (557–640), the first patriarch of Huayan.[23]

Dushun's text is a meditation on dharmadhatu, composed to reveal the richly diverse relationships between principle and phenomena. He sees dharmadhatu as a single continuous reality that can be plumbed to three degrees of depth. He calls these three levels (literally "layers" or "tiers") the three levels of discernment. They are:

1. discernment of true emptiness
2. discernment of the mutual nonobstruction of principle and phenomena
3. discernment of total pervasion and accommodation.

The three levels of discernment represent awakening to the second, third, and fourth dharmadhatu, respectively. Dushun's Guanmen outlines ten approaches to the Second Discernment (of the mutual nonobstruction of principle and phenomena). The Ten Approaches open up an astonishing array of possible relationships between phenomena and principle. If we imagine the dharmadhatu as white light, it is as though Dushun passes it through a prism, revealing all the colors of the rainbow hidden within it. Due to their profusion, it is easy to forget that these ten approaches are themes for meditation, which reflect aspects of the Buddha's enlightenment that we can bring into lived experience, despite their high level of abstraction.

The Ten Approaches to the Second Discernment are enumerated as follows:

1. Principle pervades phenomena.
2. Each phenomenon pervades principle.
3. Phenomena are formed by principle.
4. Phenomena can reveal principle.

5. Phenomena are sublated (subsumed, cancelled, or negated) by principle.

6. Phenomena can conceal principle.

7. True principle is identical with phenomena.

8. Each phenomenon is identical with principle.

9. True principle is not a phenomenon.

10. Phenomena are not principle.

The formative influence of Huayan on the dialectical captions of Dongshan's first cycle is found primarily in these approaches, rather than in the more general formulation of the four dharmadhatu. We can see from the outset that the relations between essential and contingent outlined in Dongshan's first cycle are austere when compared to Dushun's more elaborate Ten Approaches. In comparing the Ten Approaches to the Second Discernment with the dialectical positions of Donsghan's first cycle, we find the following correspondences:

1. The First Approach, principle pervades phenomena, corresponds to Dongshan's second position, the Essential within the Contingent.

2. The Second Approach, each phenomenon pervades principle, corresponds to Dongshan's first position, the Contingent within the Essential.

3. The Fifth Approach, phenomena are sublated by principle, corresponds to Dongshan's third position, Arriving within the Essential.

4. The Sixth Approach, phenomena can conceal principle, corresponds to Dongshan's fourth position, Approaching from the Contingent.

5. Dongshan's fifth and final position, Arriving at Concurrence, corresponds to the fourth dharmadhatu: the dharmadhatu of perfectly interpenetrating phenomenon and phenomenon.

In both Dongshan's final mode and Dushun's fourth dharmadhatu, the realm of worldly affairs is finally affirmed without appeal to principle, which—from that ultimate perspective—we at last completely embody, manifest, and enact in the world through our ordinary lives. With arriving at concurrence, all that we have regarded on the one hand as essential and on the other as contingent are regarded as none other than each other. With this, our enlightenment is none other than our daily life. Thus, Dongshan's account of concurrence broadly aligns with Dushun's account of the fourth dharmadhatu.[24]

Having noted that four of the Ten Discernments correspond closely to and may have anticipated the dialectical captions of the first four of Dongshan's five positions of essential and contingent, I feel compelled to point out that although these four dovetail fairly well with one another, their connections with Dongshan's five positions of the essential and the contingent should not be drawn too tightly or in too deterministic a manner. Huayan's interfusion of principle and phenomena surely inspired the enterprise of Dongshan's Five Ranks, but the dialectic of the latter crystallized (and simplified!) the baroque formulations it inherited from Huayan philosophy.

Overall, I imagine the influence of the four dharmadhatu on the five modes to have been rather like that of Bach's Goldberg Variations on the wonderful set of six variations that conclude Beethoven's Piano Sonata no. 30, op. 109. Beethoven clearly knew Bach's magnificent set well, and allowed it to influence his own work. However, regardless of that influence, each work stands alone in its own greatness. The Huayan dialectical formulation of the four dharmadhatu and its elaborations and Dongshan's two cycles of the Five Ranks share a similar relationship.

The array of relationships between principle and phenomena outlined in the Huayan system discussed above also represents an elaborate development of Nagarjuna's Two Truths doctrine, with the Chinese term "principle" broadly corresponding to "ultimate truth" and "phenomena" corresponding to "conventional truth." In this regard, we can also view the Huayan categories as the conduit through which the Two Truths, in a highly elaborated form, entered Dongshan's Five Ranks.

The Huayan dharmadhatu laid the groundwork for what Chan came to call "the further step." The notion of the further step was encapsulated in the image of climbing the hundred-foot pole, a Chan metaphor for mastering Huayan thought. Gaining mastery of the Huayan system was likened to climbing a hundred-foot pole, the pinnacle of which represents the experience of emptiness. After experiencing emptiness, however, one must take the dizzying step from the top of the pole and risk plunging back into life in all its vitality and pain. Changsha Jingcen (d. 868) expressed the metaphor memorably in his verse:

> The enlightened person sits at the top
>   of a hundred-foot pole;
> She has entered the way, but is not yet genuine.
> She must take a step from the top of a hundred-foot pole,
> and the worlds of the ten directions will be
>   her complete body.[25]

When we take that further step, dimensionless multidimensional realms sit down to drink coffee, or go to pick up the cat from the vet. With that step, we enter the extraordinary ordinary realm of helping and being helped, of heartbreak and forgiveness, where our limitations and failings are, at the same time, the intimate expression of the empty world. Dongshan's Five Ranks are an expression of that further step taken and an indication of where we need to be heading.

Experiencing emptiness is not enough. Stepping clear of emptiness is not enough. The Five Ranks show us that—regardless of what we think we may have realized—there are yet unrealized modes of awakening in which the world and our selves move into ever-deeper intimacy.

The I Ching and Its Influence on the Five Ranks

The hexagrams of the I Ching (*Yijing*) were a shaping influence on Shitou's Accord and are an important presence in Dongshan's poem "Song of the Precious Mirror Samadhi," most particularly the Li hexagram (the Illumination Hexagram) with its imagery of intertwined fire and darkness. Within Li four other hexagrams are configured, with the five hexagrams thus formed corresponding to the five positions of Dongshan's first cycle of the Five Ranks. Although the I Ching hexagrams have six lines, and Dongshan's first cycle has only five positions, the notion of "positions" may have been influenced by the I Ching hexagrams, with their hierarchies indicated by the positions of lines within a given hexagram.

In the light of the I Ching's significance in Chinese culture, where so much that is of cultural importance has taken its inspiration from the I Ching, it is no surprise that Chan masters, including Shitou and Dongshan, sought to communicate the Buddha Dharma by means of it. Connecting Chan with the ancient native Chinese cosmology in which Confucianism and Taoism are grounded was a way to validate a Chinese expression of the Buddha Dharma. By so doing, Chan masters such as Shitou and Dongshan transformed the traditions they inherited and made them accessible and attractive to Chinese teachers and students of the Way. I sense that the same can be said of Dongshan's choice of folk style forms in composing his verses.

Shitou Xiqian's Accord and Dongshan's Five Modes

It's appropriate at this point that we briefly refer to Shitou Xiqian's poem "Accord on Investigating Diversity and Wholeness" (Cantongqi; Jap: Sandōkai), for it encapsulates aspects of Huayan thought, as well as drawing on a variety of I Ching associations, both in its title and in its imagery. The Accord is also an important influence on Dongshan's first cycle, as well as being an even more direct influence on its containing poem, the "Song of the Precious Mirror Samadhi," composed at least a century and a half later. Below, we will explore a variety of correspondences between the Accord and Dongshan's cycle of the essential and the contingent, and clarify the influence of the Accord on Dongshan's poem. For the present, I will touch briefly on the imagery of dark and bright as it appears in both poems. We can see this imagery in common as evidence that the Accord influenced Dongshan's first cycle—indeed the two poems are deeply entwined—but beyond this consideration, such imagery provides us with a memorable poetic representation of the five positions, which will enable us to bring its formulations readily to mind in the course of this book.

In his "Accord on Investigating Diversity and Wholeness," Shitou
wrote the following beautiful lines that express the Middle Way in
terms of the meeting of bright and dark:

> There is dark within the bright, but do not meet it as dark.
> Within the dark there is bright, but do not view it as bright.
> Bright and dark mutually correspond, like front and
>   back foot walking.

Here we can take "bright" as evocative of contingency, the variegated
world of color and form, and "dark" as suggestive of the mysterious,
undifferentiated realm of the essential. The correspondence of bright
and dark with the contingent and the essential allows us to read the
Accord as an encapsulation of the intimate meeting between them. The
above lines also anticipate the themes of the essential and the contingent explored in the positions of Dongshan's first cycle. If we play out
the correspondences between the Accord's imagery of bright and dark
and the first cycle's dialectic of the essential and the contingent, we
can produce the following synthesis of the two, a snapshot in black
and white:

1. the bright within the dark
2. the dark within the bright
3. just the dark
4. just the bright
5. the dark as the bright

I find it helpful to use this representation of Dongshan's first cycle
positions as an aide-mémoire, especially as the caption titles for this
cycle are rather abstract and hard to bring to mind.

In terms of the imagery of dark and bright, when we examine the
verses for the first cycle of the modes of the essential and the contingent, we notice their alternation throughout the cycle. The first mode
plunges us into the darkness of the third watch; then we encounter, in
turn, the dawn of the second mode; the implicit darkness of the third
mode of emptiness alone, the blaze of the lotus in the midst of fire of

the fourth mode, and finally the darkness of the charcoal heap in the fifth and concluding mode.

Beyond these alternations of dark and bright, we notice that, through the verses, Dongshan's images evolve and recur—darkness, the moon, the bloom and fade of flowers; a lotus in the midst of fire transforming to a charcoal heap in which we return to sit. Finally, the imagery of dark and bright evokes the entwined fire and darkness of the Li hexagram—the emblematic core of the "Song of the Precious Mirror Samadhi"—with the five positions of the essential and the contingent arrayed within it.

The Legacy of the Five Ranks

In composing the Five Ranks, it seems reasonable to imagine that Dongshan wanted to further develop and refine what he had inherited from his forbears, and to pass this on in a succinct form to future generations. The Five Ranks feel like the encapsulation of generations of reflection, practice, and teaching the Buddha Way.

Legend has it that Dongshan, as a token of transmission, passed on the Five Ranks to his student Caoshan Benji, concealed within the "Song of the Precious Mirror Samadhi." Caoshan, in turn, developed Dongshan's legacy, composing his own verses and commentaries on the Five Ranks, thereby ensuring that they became part of the teaching arsenal of the developing Chan tradition. Fenyang Shanzhao (947–1024) introduced the Five Ranks into the Linji (Rinzai) School and composed his own verses on them.[26] Later, the Caodong master Hongzhi Zhengjue (1091–1157) integrated the Five Ranks into the practice of Silent Illumination in his Manual on Sitting in Meditation, in which he emphasized seeing into the interfusion of the essential and the contingent, and the identity of the bright and the dark in the sphere of practice, and not just at the level of metaphysical speculation.

Korin Charlie Pokorny, in his Notes on Chinese Buddhist Philosophy, indicates that Chan masters absorbed Huayan teachings, even as they subverted the kind of philosophical expositions that Huayan was renowned for. The Chan tradition criticized the Five Ranks as conceptual elaboration, while at the same time continuing to develop the teachings of the Five Ranks in various ways leading to a complex nest of variations. Attempting to sort through these complications was repeatedly criticized as a waste of time. The Five Ranks were thus revisited repeatedly but were also an object of scorn.

Subsequently, the Five Ranks entered the Soto and Rinzai streams of Zen in Japan, where, although they have gone in and out of fashion over the centuries, they retain their importance in contemporary Soto and Rinzai: especially in the latter, where they are used for final checking at the conclusion of koan study.

The Five Ranks are a background presence in the writings of Dogen Kigen (1200–1253). When he mentions them, it is primarily to dismiss the way they have been misused by teachers and students. This is especially the case when the Five Ranks are seen as "the kernel of Dongshan's teaching." Dogen was scathingly critical of people who indulged in this view.

Japanese Soto masters, such as Gasan Joseki (1275–1366), encouraged students to take up the Five Ranks as teachings for everyday life, by treating the second cycle, the five stages of merit, as a practical application of the first cycle, the five modes of the essential and the contingent.[27] But it is really Hakuin Ekaku (1689–1769) who can be credited with rescuing the Five Ranks from centuries of neglect and misunderstanding by giving them a prominent place in his own practice and teaching.

Hakuin's commentary on the Five Ranks in his *Keisō Dokuzui*[28] has provided an important introduction for contemporary students and practitioners of the Way and has been an inspiration for my own practice and teaching. Hakuin treats Dongshan's first cycle of the Five Ranks dynamically, transforming it into a ladder to transcendence and beyond. He does this by treating Dongshan's captions and verses as a hierarchy of stages, or "ranks." At each stage of training, the spirit is "not enough, not yet enough, never enough," to borrow Linji's words. Hakuin uses Dongshan's ranks to inspire and challenge us, and to propel us onward. When a particular "rank" is realized and integrated, the next one looms.

The tension found between the approaches taken by Hakuin and Gasan has been an important influence on the writing of this book. While I will stress the importance of approaching the Five Ranks from a koan perspective, I will make a special point of drawing out their implications as they bear on everyday life and will give weight to the Cycle of Merit, which, to my knowledge, Hakuin does not deal with. The themes of this book can also nourish shikantaza practice.

Regarding the Five Ranks and its role in Zen training, Hakuin wrote:

> What I received from Shoju Rojin forty years ago, I now offer as a donation of teaching to genuine students of the mystery who have experienced the great death. This should be handed on privately, because it was not set up for people of middling and lesser potential. Make sure not to take it too lightly![29]

So we have been warned. My hope is that if you aren't yet a genuine student of the mystery who has experienced the great death you will take Hakuin's warning as a challenge to awaken and will use this book to begin to walk the koan path, deepening and refining your insight amid the challenging circumstances of your life.

3. Working with the Five Ranks

Practice of the Five Ranks

WHILE THE FIVE RANKS are an inspiration to walk the Way, they may also be misused as a measuring stick for progress on the path. We might become obsessed with trying "to get somewhere," so that we tick off the stages and miss the richness that lies so close to hand. This is already the tendency for many students. Underlying this concern with progress is the assumption that the Way must lead somewhere and that we must be able to gauge our position in relation to a destination. We want to know what we are getting into, where it will lead us, and how far we have left to go.

However, preoccupation with the process of the Way can militate against our becoming immersed in it and thereby awakening to it. Rather than waste our time trying to work out where we are on some imaginary spiritual scale, it would be better simply to make a commitment to meditation, stick with it until we awaken, and then deepen our awakening through further meditation.

The real relationship to experience of the positions and stages described in the Five Ranks is like that between the sign that stands on the cliffs at Cape Leeuwin on the Southwestern tip of Australia and the ocean below. The rusty sign has an arrow pointing west with the words "Indian Ocean" scrawled on it and an arrow pointing east with the shaky words "Southern Ocean" likewise scrawled on it. You look down, and there is boundless churning ocean whichever way you look, stretching to the horizon. Although maps and guideposts of positions and stages can be helpful in locating oneself in our journey in Zen, it's important not to confuse the signpost for the ocean, or the map for the reality. So it is good to keep in mind that, while the notion of walking the Way in terms of steps and stages is a helpful device that allows us to simplify and easily reflect on that process as it unfolds, the steps and stages themselves are merely expedient means and should not be blindly clung to.

Study of the Five Ranks

With regard to the study of Dongshan's Five Ranks, analysis should be no barrier to love. I remember getting to know the late period Beethoven piano sonatas by analyzing their themes in great detail in order to establish how the disparate sections of those works were unified. Minute and penetrating analysis never diminished my love of Beethoven's sonatas or compromised my appreciation of their splendor. I feel that the same holds true for the Five Ranks.

The Five Ranks are rather philosophical in orientation, but to settle for them as a philosophical system, and to remain there, would be to opt for the menu rather than the meal. The Five Ranks can get us interested in the Way and inspire our practice. Like the Huayan dharmadhatu and its elaborations, the Five Ranks are valuable as themes for meditation. At the end of koan study the Five Ranks also serve as an effective means of reviewing the path traveled and, if you are working with a teacher, for final checking.

Although memorization is unfashionable these days, I have found it helpful to memorize the ten brief verses of the Five Ranks, so as to carry them with me. I have found, as well, that chanting the verses—treating them as a song—has allowed me to more readily bring them to mind as themes for meditation.

Music and the Five Ranks

In terms of the musical aspects of the Five Ranks, we can note that the Chinese word *song* is used in Buddhist literature to translate the Sanskrit word *gatha*, which means "verse," "speech," and coincidentally "song." One could, therefore, translate the Chinese word *song* in the title of Dongshan's first cycle "Wuwei junchen song" as "song." As a musician, I was naturally drawn to this translation.

The English word "song" evokes the joy and gratitude that we feel when we encounter our true nature. "Song" aligns Dongshan's "'Song' of the Five Positions of Ruler and Minister" with his "Song of the Precious Mirror Samadhi," the poem from which the five positions are drawn. "Song" also strikes an accord with other great Dharma songs, such as Hakuin's "Song of Zazen," or with old, popular love songs, which are in their own right Dharma songs—"Night and day, you are the one. Only you beneath the moon and under the sun." Finally, translating the Chinese word *song* as "song" brings to mind the luminous "songs"—those slow arioso movements—that we find in the late Beethoven piano sonatas and string quartets. One such example is the third movement from Beethoven's String Quartet no. 15, op.132, composed after he had been desperately ill in the winter of 1824–1825. It is a sublimely beautiful movement that the composer identified as "A Song of Gratitude for his recovery offered to the Divinity, in the Lydian Mode." Beethoven's employment of the ancient Lydian Mode— one of the traditional church modes used especially by medieval and renaissance composers of sacred music—in alternation with contemporary resources pioneered in part by him, broadly parallels Dongshan's pairing of traditional Huayan resources in his verse captions with his Chan-inspired verses. All this said, for reasons I will set out below, I have retained the traditional Sanskrit term *gatha* in translating Dongshan's title for the first cycle—"Gatha of the Five Positions of Ruler and Minister."

Poetry and the Five Ranks

Robert Aitken once said to me, "The Way is founded in true experience and poetry." The Way is fertile and breeds fertility. The need to clarify the Way for oneself, and to find ways of conveying it to others, inspires poetry. In these regards, the poetry of great teachers such as Jianzhi Sengcan (d. 606), whose poem "Faith in Mind" influenced much of subsequent Chan literature, or Yongjia Xuanjue (665–713), whose

"Song of Enlightenment" proved equally influential, stands witness to the importance of poetry in Zen. Poetry, with its vivid imagery and rhythms, can moisten the Way and open our hearts and minds to it. Finally—and this observation is at the core of our enterprise with the Five Ranks—because words don't cut it, there is poetry.

DONGSHAN'S VERSES AS *GATHA*

The themes of Dongshan's verses are lofty, but the verses are composed in a folksong style popular with poets of the middle and later Tang dynasty. Each verse consists of three lines, with each line consisting of seven characters. Or, if one counts the titles, each verse consists of four lines, with the first line containing only three characters. Dongshan's employment of folk-song form in his profound verses is reminiscent of Bach's employment of two traditional German folk song melodies, including the light-hearted (even mildly bawdy) "I haven't been with you for so long" and "Cabbage and turnips," in creating the Quodlibet, the concluding variation and final summit of his Goldberg Variations.

As mentioned above, I have used the Sanskrit term *gatha* to translate the Chinese word *song* in my rendering of Dongshan's title for the first cycle, "Gatha of the Five Positions of Ruler and Minister." I have done so because the term *gatha* bears on how Dongshan may have wished us to understand the verses of the Five Ranks. The Sanskrit word *gatha* has a field of meaning that includes "verse," "speech," and "song." In Buddhist canonical literature *gatha* refers to a versified portion of a sutra. There are, for instance, 140 mindfulness gathas in the chapter on purifying practice in the Avatamsaka Sutra. The following can serve as an example:

> Seeing a well I wish
> that all beings have the power
> to elucidate reality.[30]

In the hands of Dongshan and others the notion of gatha was developed into that of *toujijie*.[31] Toujijie is a compound, formed of the words *touji*, which generally means "getting along well with" but in this context means "intimate meeting with buddha-mind," and *jie*, an abbreviation of the Chinese transliteration of gatha. Therefore, we can translate tou-jijie as "a gatha of intimate meeting with buddha-mind."[32] Toujijie were written to mark experiences of awakening. Dongshan composed just such a poem on the occasion of his own awakening when he glimpsed his face reflected in a stream as he crossed it.

> Taking heed not to seek it elsewhere,
> as if it were distant from myself,
> I now go on alone,
> yet I meet him everywhere.
> He is now exactly me,
> but I am not now him.
> You should meet in this way,
> for only then can you realize thus.

Dongshan vividly and memorably conveys intimacy with buddha-mind in his Stream Gatha. His opening line tells us not to seek buddha-mind as if it were separate from ourselves. The "him" to which the middle lines refer is simultaneously Dongshan's teacher, Yunyan, and the timeless dimensionless nature of buddha-mind. Dongshan sets up the seeming paradox at the heart of intimate meeting with buddha-mind: its vastness is none other than ourselves, even as we are unique and as readily differentiable from it as we are from each other. He concludes by telling us that we need to have just such an intimate meeting—complete with its implicit contraries—for our awakening experience to be genuine. If we understand the verses of the cycle of the essential and the contingent to be five interlinked toujijie, the title "Gatha of the Five Positions of Ruler and Minister" suggests five ways of intimately encountering buddha-mind; which is to say, five ways in which we encounter our true nature.

The five modes of the essential and the contingent are themselves configured within the Stream Gatha. By means of this configuration, Dongshan has created gathas within a gatha—five modes of realization within a containing poem of intimate meeting with buddha-mind. This gives the sense that with profound awakening—as when the Buddha saw the Morning Star, or when Dongshan glimpsed his face reflected in the stream—five aspects of enlightened mind are implicitly present, mirrored within the vastness. Dongshan returns to this theme in great depth in his "Song of the Precious Mirror Samadhi," where he unfolds the five modes of the essential and the contingent within the larger Song, revealing them to be dark and brilliant facets of the Buddha's awakening.

EXPRESSING THE INEXPRESSIBLE

An important theme of this book is expressibility. The Five Ranks intimate what can't be expressed, and through a matchless combination of poetry and koans, they open a window onto the mysterious and ever-changing landscape of the enlightened Way.

As we shall see, at the core of the theme of expressing the inexpressible is the emptiness of words and language. Although, in the familiar way of the Zen caution, we are enjoined not to speak of enlightenment—in Caoshan's terms not to transgress the center—yet when we awaken to the emptiness of words and language we discover that even talk of enlightenment can manifest its realm. I hope that the reader may extend such a consideration to the words and language of this book.

Finally, because awakening is seamless and inexpressible, to try to understand it in terms of positions and perspectives runs the risk of violating its spirit. However, as we shall see, formulations, such as "the five positions"—and indeed the Five Ranks' apparatus of terms and categories—can eventually find its home as an expression of awakened mind. This is a central theme of this book, and we will explore it in depth and detail below.

Working with Koans

In the Diamond Sangha tradition in which I teach, working with the Five Ranks presupposes a long and arduous journey with koans. In terms of that journey, the Five Ranks are used for final checking of the student's insight, and to give the student an overview of the koan path they have traveled thus far. This is a view from the mountain, where having traveled the long path from the early struggle with the dharmakaya, or first barrier koans, through the koans of differentiation; having awakened to those concerned with the mystery of words, then struggled with the many koans that are difficult to pass through; the student arrives at the final stage—the Five Ranks themselves.

The hierarchy just indicated reflects the paradigm developed by Hakuin and his heirs as a means to organizing koan study. There are five levels to their system corresponding to the five positions of Dongshan's cycle, the last of these levels being the five modes of the essential and the contingent, themselves.[33]

Broadly speaking, the order of Dongshan's first cycle positions, as it has been widely adopted by Hakuin and others, accords with my own experience of the unfolding of the Way, both as a student and teacher. From Dongshan's ordering we can infer a credible account of how we deepen in the Way through koan study. The koan path encourages us not to stay within the small lit circle of what we may have realized, but, rather, trusting the Way as it is evoked through both of Dongshan's cycles, we commit to the steps and stages of the koan path, and finally to the Five Ranks themselves in order to come to fuller awakening.

WORKING WITH THE FIRST KOAN

Koans widely considered suitable for working with in order to awaken to our essential nature include Zhaozhou's "Mu," Hakuin Zenji's "What is the Sound of One Hand?", and Bassui Zenji's "Who is hearing that sound?" and "Who am I?" When we work with the first koan, we find that our most deeply embedded concepts of self and other, and of existence and nonexistence—vital for making sense of, and for making sense in, the world—are exposed as insubstantial. After a time, we are no longer aware of the soft avalanche of notions we once held dear. Eventually we reach a place where we are blocked, and can neither advance nor retreat. In that place, we just renew our questioning. It's like being in a dark ravine, a mysterious valley. It's as if we are pregnant, but we can't give birth. Everything waits, in a dark pause, aching to be breathed out into life. We feel edgeless, looking into a mirror that reflects only darkness. The night moves on little feet, or big feet, depending.

Over time, waiting wears itself out. We come to expect nothing. It is like walking out on a long jetty at night without being able to see hand in front of face, and hearing the sound of water lapping in the darkness. The deeper into a koan we go, the more we leave behind; the more we leave behind, the deeper in we go. This goes on beyond reason. The Way gathers in darkness; it gathers as we struggle to return to our koan, with sleep closing in. For the most part, we don't notice it gathering. Most of the time we feel a bit desperate, and we may even wonder why we've undertaken such an unreasonable, impossible practice. If we're questioned concerning our koan, we don't know. When we aren't being questioned, we still don't know. It's important to settle into that not knowing, which should not be confused with the dumb blankness of ignorance. Rather, it is a profound mystery that has not found its tongue. In its own good time, the moon rises and reflects in the water. Meanwhile, we come up to the gate a thousand times. When our time is ripe, under cover of darkness, we go through.

WORKING WITH KOANS BEYOND THE FIRST BARRIER

When we walk the koan path beyond the first awakening we are discovering, embodying, learning how to express and finally forget the relation between the universe and ourselves. We could frame this journey, theoretically, as one where we work with the changing positions of the essential and the contingent. However, when we are actually up against it in one or another of the hundreds of koans that we must pass through, we never mention or entertain such matters. The teacher discourages the student from speculating on process and progress. Instead, at the coal-face of our effort, each koan must fill the frame of our attention completely. Transformation takes place insensibly in the depths of absorption in a particular koan, and in the engulfment of the next. We emerge transformed, but find it difficult to say where we have been, or how we have traveled.

Through this silent way, we enable the secret core of fire and darkness to settle at deeper and deeper levels, completely out of reach of the conceptualizing mind. Like this, the Way comes to convey itself innocently through our ordinary words, and we unreflectively embody it in our everyday activity.

Shikantaza and the Five Ranks

Over the years of teaching I have noticed that students who practice shikantaza—the practice of "just sitting"—describe their relationship to the environment, and the environment to them, in terms that sometimes reflect Dongshan's first-cycle positions. The stages of the merit cycle also play out in devoted shikantaza practice. The language of the Five Ranks is also a valuable resource for communicating insights that occur in shikantaza. Although the themes of the Five Ranks are not taken up as themes for meditation in shikantaza—that is not the nature of the practice—study of the Five Ranks literature, and dialogue on it, is surely valuable for inspiring and deepening the shikantaza path.

Socrates said, "Truly it is through beauty that we come at wisdom." Through meditation, study, and translation, I have come to love Dongshan's verses. I find in them a well of inspiration for practice and teaching. Poetry may not save the world, but I believe that Dongshan's poem, when one grows wholly familiar with it, will change the way one sees the world and, as a result of that, how we may act in it.

I hope that this book on the Five Ranks might serve as a rough mud-map of the trackless Way, and that it might illuminate a little the country traveled.

II.

Movements of the Five Ranks

THE CYCLE OF THE ESSENTIAL AND THE CONTINGENT

4. An Overview of the Cycle of the Essential and the Contingent

The Essential and the Contingent

Dongshan's Five Ranks consists of two cycles: the Cycle of the Essential and the Contingent, and the Cycle of Merit. In this chapter I will give an overview of the first of these cycles, focusing primarily on its dialectic. This is the business end of our exploration, a base-camp operation that precedes the ascent occasioned by Dongshan's verses. That said, the dialectic of the first cycle is the backbone of our enterprise, and when its terms are clarified, I hope to show that it brings its own power for the Way.

In this first cycle Dongshan offers us five perspectives on awakened mind. Each of these perspectives provides a different view of the relationship between our timeless essential natures and our lives as they pass in time. The five perspectives expressed in Dongshan's first cycle are as follows:

1. The Contingent within the Essential
2. The Essential within the Contingent
3. Arriving within the Essential
4. Approaching from the Contingent
5. Arriving at Concurrence

*A NOTE ON THE TERMS "ESSENTIAL" AND "CONTINGENT"

Before I begin an in-depth explanation of each of these perspectives, I must discuss the terms "essential" and "contingent," which I have used to translate the Chinese terms *zheng* and *pian*. Our reading will be enriched if we first unpack and clarify the meaning and context of these multivalent Chinese terms.

Rendered as literally as possible, the word *zheng* means "straight," or "upright," while the word *pian* means "slant" or "askew." These are also important terms in the ritual writings of Confucianism. In the context of Confucian social ritual, *zheng* would mean "main," which is to say, "dominant" or "central." *Pian*, on the other hand, would correspondingly mean "minor," which is to say, "subordinate" or "peripheral." More specifically, in terms of marital status, the main wife is zheng, and the concubines are pian. Therefore, the main wife was referred to as the "Zheng chamber," while a concubine was referred to as the "Pian chamber."[34]

The terms *zheng* and *pian* are intimately related to the imagery of ruler and minister as it appears in the title for this cycle: "Gatha of the Five Positions of Ruler and Minister" (*wuwei junchen song*). It is possible to view zheng and pian as positions in a ritual setting. In the ritual sense, *zheng*—evoking the image of the ruler—means main or dominant, while *pian*—evoking the image of the minister—means minor or subordinate. Correspondingly, *zheng* refers to the position in a ritual setting that is occupied by the person who is either host, elder, or honored guest, while, on the other hand, *pian* refers to the humbler positions occupied by others. In this regard the main seat at the table is zheng, while the seats to the sides are pian. These positions are present in ordinary day-to-day interpersonal interactions, such as the seating arrangement assumed when having a meal at home. This idea is not foreign to Western culture either, with its notion of "head of the table."

So we can understand that zheng and pian represent dominant and subordinate positions when used in the context of ritual or social formality. This observation allows us to appreciate the resonance that zheng and pian share with the imagery of "ruler" and "minister" captured in Dongshan's title for this first cycle.

However, it should not be assumed that "ruler" and "minister" are static roles associated with particular persons. To do so would be to drastically oversimplify Dongshan's intended meaning, depriving it of any nuance. The complex matrix in which social rituals unfold is subtle and always shifting. Dominant and subordinate roles must therefore be determined according to their context. Because it is difficult to fully convey the social and political nuances implicit in the terms *zheng* and *pian* without conjuring an image of imperial status and authority, as well as likely invoking a particularly sharp dualistic image when the terms are translated literally, I have chosen to avoid rendering them in that way.

Instead, I have opted for a less literal, less narrowly specific translation of zheng and pian, by using the more abstract terms "essential" and "contingent" to render them. It is my hope that by allowing the degree of abstraction that "essential" and "contingent" confer, I will gain greater flexibility when it comes to presenting Dongshan's subtle dialectic in a variety of contexts without importing too much hierarchy or, as it turns out, metaphysical baggage.

I use "essential" as a metaphor for our timeless essential natures and "contingent" to evoke the image of our lives as they pass in time. I must note that choosing the English word "essential" to translate the Chinese term *zheng* comes at a semantic cost, although the same is true of any of the paired opposites that have been tried in English—including absolute and relative, real and apparent, and universal and particular, to name but three pairs.

The cost associated with choosing "essential" is that it imports the notion of essence and its potential metaphysical baggage. "Essence" is used in Western metaphysics and theology to refer to "being," "soul," and other entities imagined to be concealed behind the veil of birth and death. But in Chinese Buddhism there exists no such veil to be lifted, no concealed mystery dwelling within. In the Five Ranks the mystery is as clear as a spring day, with its warm sun and deafening sparrow song.

Most importantly, the terms *essential* and *contingent* do not refer to separate realms. Properly understood, they indicate five diverse perspectives on the same indivisible reality. There are myriad agents for our awakening to indivisible reality: the sound of wind, a computer's hum, church bells. The gate of sound is vast, as are the gates of touch, sight, smell, taste, and even those of thought and language. There are innumerable opportunities to awaken; far more than there are perspectives or positions. Any moment is up for it. But, in terms of perspectives, five is fine, generous, and magical.

The Middle Way Dialectic of the Essential and the Contingent

Awakening is seamless and indivisible and you can't think your way there. Awakening—the experience of the ultimate—cannot be conveyed by words and language. After his great enlightenment, the Buddha could have honored its essence and remained silent. Yet he ultimately chose to teach, and with that decision came the problem of how to express what is inexpressible through the dualisms of ordinary speech and language.

From that compassionate impulse to express the incommunicable beginning with the Buddha, teachers of the Way have used dialectic as an expedient means to express the nature of reality, and to prepare the mind for awakening—if not to trigger it.

"Existence and nonexistence" in the Kaccayanagotta Sutta, "form and emptiness" in the Heart Sutra, "conventional truth and ultimate truth" in the works of Nagarjuna, and "principle and phenomena" in Huayan philosophy are examples of but a few of the dialectical pairs that have been developed by Buddhists down through the ages to convey the incommunicable. Such dialectical constructions use the play of polarities—of complementary, interdependent opposites—to suggest a reality beyond the paradoxes that such dialectical constructions entail.

Unlike many of the dialectics developed by others, Dongshan does not develop his in the form of a dialogue or as a treatise on the weighty matter of reality. Rather, he arrays a constellation of five positions, each of which is a presentation of awakened mind. These positions choreograph the changing relations between "essential" and "contingent," whose dance—now together, now apart, now as none other than each other—shows the intimate dance of the universe with each of us. Or to state things more comprehensively, Dongshan's dialectic choreographs the relationship between the universe and any particular phenomenon or event, for this is not just a human matter and concern.

The source and taproot of the Five Ranks dialectic is the legend of the Buddha's awakening. After his long night of meditation, Shakyamuni looked up and saw the Morning Star and exclaimed, "Now I see that all beings are tathagata—are just this person—only their delusions and attachments prevent them from seeing it."

Marvelous!

Reflecting on the Buddha's first words following his awakening, we find the play of opposites that characterize Buddhist dialectics. How could the immensity of the cosmos, manifested as that flickering star, be that exhausted, elated man? Or any of us? For that is the implication. At the heart of the Buddha's exclamation lies an impasse. It is the same impasse intrinsic to the Heart Sutra's paradoxical "form and emptiness" dialectic, and to the dialectic of the Five Ranks. Dongshan's dialectic of essential and the contingent is similarly an expression of the Middle Way, where the essential and the contingent appear as opposites, even as they depend on each other: without the contingent, the essential is absent from the realm of daily affairs; without the contingencies of speech, silence and eternity cannot be evoked.

From the middle way perspective we don't take either the polarity of the essential or that of the contingent as an exclusive account of reality. If we treat the essential as exclusive, we reify emptiness and set up our life in luminous denial of our place in the world, and of our faults and virtues. If we treat the contingent as the whole story, we are at the mercy of our karmic view and may thereby shut out the possibilities of awakening and transformation.

However, Dongshan's dialectic isn't simply the finding of a mean between the essential and the contingent. It offers instead a radical path, through which the play of essential and contingent—complementary opposites—evokes the ultimate. The dialectical tension between those complementary opposites is resolved in a manner that finds its expression as our daily lives lived as the Way. Like this, we live what is timeless and transcendent through the unique details of our daily lives. Indeed, we live it as them.

The Five Positions

Here is a diagram showing the interrelationships between the five posi-
tions of the essential and the contingent, adapted from *Preliminary
Notes on Henshō Gōi and Kokun Gōi*, an unpublished manuscript by
Yamada Koun and Robert Aitken used within the Diamond Sangha.

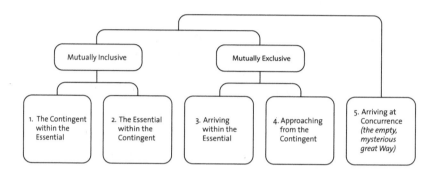

We notice that in the first two positions, the essential and the contingent
are "within" each other, so that these two positions form one group-
ing characterized by the mutual inclusiveness of the essential and the
contingent. The third and fourth positions constitute a second group-
ing, characterized by the mutual exclusiveness of the essential and the
contingent. Finally the essential and the contingent are regarded as
concurrent—that is to say, they occupy the same place at the same time.

In our first investigation into the nature of the cycle of the essential
and the contingent I make use of this three-part division of the five
modes, because it is formally elegant and clearly exposes important
relationships between the five positions. If we choose to regard our
passing from position to position as a journey, then the fifth position
can be regarded as our destination, and some of its various senses derive
from that consideration. More importantly, however, the fifth position
is expressive of the empty, mysterious great Way. In this it corresponds
to the profound enlightenment of the Buddha and is thus prior to any
position, number, division, or sequence.

The concurrent is fundamentally present within, and as, each position. At the same time, each position is fundamentally an aspect of the concurrent in its profound inclusiveness. Each position, because it is fundamentally the concurrent, includes the other four. Understood thus, the essential and the contingent and their relationships, as well as their means of expression, are completely empty. This latter point regarding the emptiness of expression has far-reaching implications for how we understand the Five Ranks and is a central theme of this book.

The essential and the contingent can't be permanently identified with particular persons, places, or events, for they are in ever-shifting relation to one another—now mutually pervasive, now apparently separate, now none other than each other. Like this, there is no particular corner of experience that can be permanently identified as "the essential"—that is to say, none that can be conceived of as a distinct realm of enlightenment. And none, for that matter, that can be permanently identified with "the contingent"—that is to say, none that can be conceived of as a distinct realm of samsara, irretrievably sunk in delusion and suffering. Integrating and transcending the opposing polarities of the essential and the contingent is the great koan at the heart of our investigation of the first cycle of the Five Ranks, and indeed of traveling the Way in our lives. We will return to this theme in its various developments throughout this book.

Progress in the First Cycle

The positions in this first cycle aren't inherently progressive. However, it is possible to infer a progression, as follows: In the first mode, the contingent within the essential, we embark and realize emptiness. In the second mode, the essential within the contingent, we realize that whatever appears—sky, red flower, the cat like sun and shadow running—is no other than our true nature. In the third, arriving within the essential, we deepen our experience of emptiness and realize the subtle nature of words and language. In the fourth, approaching from the contingent, letting go of any preoccupation with hidden understandings, we step into the vivid life where each thing, person, and event is experienced as unique, even as it encodes the whole. There, up to our ears in conflict and passionate attachment, we awaken others and ourselves. Finally, in the fifth mode, arriving at concurrence, having forgotten all the previous stages, we live enlightenment—without remainder—as our daily activity.

This pilgrim's progress unfolds in time, even as each step opens to eternity. When we walk the path, we are discovering, embodying, and learning how to express and convey the relation between the universe and ourselves. Although this involves a journey that is sometimes expressed in terms of the shifting positions of essential and contingent, it is best not to get entangled in conceptualizing the moves in the dialectic, but rather to trust the raw experience of awakening to our true nature, and live it to the best of our ability in our daily lives. It is important to note that the five modes of the essential and the contingent—beyond all abstraction—are modes of experience.

Given the various schemata, and the wielding of categories—deft or otherwise—it is easy to forget that we are dealing with human experience, and the most intimate and subtle personal experience at that. It is easy to kill the spirit through a kind of schematoid arthritis of the mind, and I am trying to be on my guard against it, even as the expedient categories that we are using to refine our understanding of the Way proliferate. Living experience of the essential is spontaneous and generous. It freely reflects the world emerging as us, and we as it. In the heart's wide clarity, all things gather, but the heart is never overcrowded.

5. The First and Second Modes Paired: Encountering the Ancient Mirror

The Contingent within the Essential
At the beginning of the third watch, before moonrise,
don't be surprised if there is meeting without recognition;
one still vaguely harbors the elegance of former days.

The Essential within the Contingent
Having overslept, an old woman encounters the ancient mirror.
This is clearly meeting face-to-face—only then is it genuine.
Don't lose your head by validating shadows.

LET'S BEGIN TO unpack the first cycle by briefly exploring the themes of the first two modes—the Contingent within the Essential, and the Essential within the Contingent—as a pair. In terms of the dialectical choreography of Dongshan's first cycle, these two modes share the theme of mutual inclusiveness and are complementary. The sense of the contingent being "within" the essential, rather than strictly identical to it—as in formulations like the Heart Sutra's "Form is exactly emptiness, emptiness exactly form"—would seem to be a legacy from Huayan categorizations that connect principle and phenomena through modalities such as pervasion, sublation, and concealment.

The Contingent within the Essential

> If you release a blackbird at night, it flies clothed in
>   snow.
> —Keizan Jokin

The mode of the contingent within the essential is our point of embarkation, the first step on our journey into awakening and beyond. At the
same time, this mode is enlightenment itself, with the journey and its
stages contained within it. The caption of this first mode indicates that
you and me, the hibiscus, the stars, and the sky are all within emptiness. "Within" is rather soft and noncommittal, but it implies that
the realm of the contingent—birth, death, the seasons, the passage of
time—is empty.

As we venture into this mode, we increasingly find that there is no
one to "own" our experience, and we sense that whatever this self may
be, it is insubstantial and finally nothing at all. When we experience self
as nothing at all, at least momentarily, the clouding and unclouding
skies are our mind, and our heart is the night of turning stars. Opening
to that immensity, we are released from the cramping, confining attitudes that close off our heart and close us down. With this experience of
self as nothing at all, we find that we are traveling the path of liberation,
which, in the words of the "Song of the Precious Mirror Samadhi," is
"fully illuminated at midnight, yet hidden at daybreak."

This journey challenges our commonsense views about who we are
and our place in the scheme of things. At the same time it brings a
sense of wonder and awe to our setting out. Though this mode is the
first, and may appear embryonic, it is not less than enlightenment itself.

In the verse that follows, Dongshan deepens and extends the formal
considerations evoked by its title, "The Contingent within the Essential," revealing the time before we awaken, our awakening, and our
clinging to awakening each to be timelessly empty, like ever-changing
reflections in dark water.

At the beginning of the third watch, before moonrise . . .

In old China, the period between sunset and sunrise was divided into
five two-hour watches. The third watch began roughly at midnight,
and it carries the spirit of vigil. In this sense, it evokes the image of
Buddha's long night of meditation, which ended when he awakened
upon seeing the Morning Star. The third watch is suggestive of our own

time before enlightenment, when awakening is nascent. Moonrise, on the other hand, evokes enlightenment, which has no season or date.

Dongshan calls our sticking with our practice in the vigil that precedes awakening "treading the darkling path," paying tribute to the gathering obscurity as we open our eyes at deeper levels. For him, to tread the darkling path is to persevere in practice. Perseverance, apart from renewing the koan, means to allow each circumstance—aching knee, the taste of the fruit salad, the sound of a truck being unloaded—to bring us home. Each of these is home. The Zen teacher Mari Rhydwen, who sailed around the Indian Ocean in a small boat with the man she was married to at that time, vividly captures the sense of vigil in the middle of sailing at night as "natural and unavoidable shikantaza."

> Ah, the midnight to 3:00 am watch, struggling out of sleep and a warm bunk to sit alone in the middle of the big dark ocean. Sometimes full of stars (I'd try to identify the constellations in my book using a little torch); sometimes full of moon (easy as daylight turned mysterious); sometimes cloudy, wet and dark. Those nights were the hardest, storm and heaving seas and I'd have to wake Allen so we could reef sails. Like birth and death, the biggest storms come in the darkest hours.
>
> Zazen? What else could I call it? It was natural and unavoidable shikantaza. Every hour I'd break to go and plot my course on the chart, compass and pencil in hand. Sometimes make a cup of tea. Never below for more than ten minutes, which is how long it takes a big ship to cross the horizon and get close by. Even thinking of it fills me with that strange feeling of tired and lonely, calm, dogged and totally alive.[35]

Her "tired and lonely, calm, dogged and totally alive" unerringly conveys the third watch of late-night sitting. It also indicates the need to stay attentive, even though that big ship crossing the horizon might just be your longed-for catastrophe.

. . . don't be surprised if there is meeting without recognition . . .

Meanwhile, we encounter our true nature, without recognizing it. We see raindrops flashing on the leaves. We meet it—as our face in the mirror, as the long ringing bell that opens us up the way an airplane opens up the sky. "Meeting without recognition" is at the same time awakening to the emptiness of our self. We don't recognize the vastness of our true and essential nature, because we are it and it is us, without remainder.

When Dongshan writes, "Don't be surprised if there is meeting without recognition," he is very delicately and equivocally presenting just such an encounter. His expression here, as well as elsewhere in the Five Ranks discourse, embodies a spirit of "not transgressing the center," that is, of not naming enlightenment. Yet, regardless of how we express it, when we genuinely encounter the darkened mirror of our essential nature we are changed in our depths.

The foregoing is difficult to convey descriptively, but I will return to explore the encounter with the darkened mirror at greater length below, in the context of the story of Longtan blowing out the candle and awakening Deshan. Such a story takes us where words cannot readily go, and for me it remains an exemplary means of conveying the spirit of this mode.

. . . one still vaguely harbors the elegance of former days.

Awakening to emptiness feels ancient. In Zen teacher Arthur Wells' words, with the experience of emptiness "there is a sense of ancestral presence, and although you can't say how, your experience keeps grand company." There is the sense that it has always been thus, and so—that we share this experience with those who have gone before us, and have awakened like this. Wumen Huikai (1183–1260) expressed our intimacy with the old teachers as "the hair of your eyebrows entangled with theirs; seeing with the same eyes, hearing with the same ears."[36]

This line on harboring the elegance of former days is rich in implications—including the sense that we tend to cling to an experience of awakening and need to move on from it.

In his verse on the Contingent within the Essential, Dongshan discloses three perspectives on the Way: the vigil that precedes awakening, meeting our true nature without recognizing it, and harboring the experience of awakening. Each of these perspectives is empty. We see, and see through, each perspective with eyes of emptiness.

The Essential within the Contingent

> If you want to know the miracle, how wind can polish
> a mirror,
> Look, the shining glass grows green in spring.
> —Mirza Ghalib

What was unrecognized in the preceding mode is now as clear as this cold day of blue sky and red flame blossom. In the first mode we met the void without recognition. Now the darkness lifts and we recognize the flame blossom as our deepest nature. The world steps in and takes up lodgings, where it already has long-term tenancy. This is the intimacy of true meeting, captured in an account of personal experience of intimacy that my friend Arthur Wells shared in correspondence.

> I think I was twenty-seven years old (now nearly sixty-five), so nearly forty years ago, journeying by train from Christchurch to Dunedin, the clackety-clack of the rails and the swaying of the carriage put me into a strangely receptive mood. . . . Suddenly we came out beside the wide tidal flats of Blueskin Bay near Dunedin and I was transfixed by seeing a grey heron stalking its prey in a tidal shallow. It was walking slowly, lifting each foot out of the water and putting it back very quietly so as not to disturb any fish, as it slowly turned its head from side to side and craned its neck as it peered into the water. I felt in an ecstatic, illogical way that I was the bird looking for its food. As the train moved on

I came back to myself, but I continued to feel sure that the bird's conscious awareness was of the same nature as my own, and this filled me with warmth and joy. Like the mess of the backyards we'd been traveling past, this example of "nature red in tooth and claw," which I'd never felt reconciled to (perhaps because it aroused my own fear of death), was now acceptable and felt completely alright. From that time I stopped feeling so resentful and fearful of the way things are in the natural world. Something of the tenderness of that experience, and sympathy for the struggle of all living things to survive, has never left me since that day.

That grey heron was such a welcome invasion of privacy. Arthur speaks of the changes that his experience wrought in his life. Although we don't have control over this, the hope is that an awakening such as Arthur's will touch our lives and make changes for the better in how we relate to the world and to each other.

In terms of the bright mirror of this mode, the world—in the guise of heron, or star, or the sound of chiming clock—steps into our life as our life. This is intimacy. Here, intimacy includes friendship and love, but is also clearly more than them. We encounter intimacy without fear or favor: intimacy with ocean, star, earth, fire, with those we can't stand, as well as with those we love. Such intimacy is unlooked for. We move toward it not so much by our own agency but because it is the deep down condition of things, with an undertow deeper than our own designs.

The experience of intimacy is an encounter with the ancient mirror of our genuine nature. The mirror isn't actually a mirror, limited in time and space, but is timeless, dimensionless reality in the guise of the warm river goose-bumped with rain, or the noisy plumbing in the old house. With respect to this ancient mirror, eyes and seeing are just the treetops and their twenty shades of rustling green. Whatever we encounter is our true nature. And this is so, not just generally in terms of humans and sentient beings, but also for stones, clouds, dust, and atoms.

As for the lived experience of this mode, the timeless and dimensionless find their expression in the ordinary. As William Blake says in his poem, "Auguries of Innocence":

> To see the world in a grain of sand,
> And a heaven in a wild flower,
> Hold infinity in the palm of your hand,
> And eternity in an hour.

A grain of sand is the world's means to appear; an hour is eternity's. In this way, when you extend your hand everything and everyone comes along. When you sing old blues in the style of Bessie Smith, that's all the ages singing as you. Your reflections on time and aging are timeless, and the eternal gets to ponder the loss of those it loves. Elsewhere—and still vividly conveying this mode—Blake wrote, "Eternity is in love with the productions of time." This is a fine koan. How do you respond?

If it weren't for the transient—a wild flower, the palm of your hand, an hour—the eternal would have no means to express itself. The Zen teacher Glenn Wallis says that "the universe is searingly impartial in its flourish of you."

Having overslept, an old woman encounters the ancient mirror.

Encountering the ancient mirror is Dongshan's metaphor for awakening to our essential nature. Here, the timeless meeting takes place in the country of half-awakeness, where what is merely vague rubs shoulders with genuine not-knowing. In this inchoate realm, it's hard to tell our muddle-headedness from the shadowy, lackluster dawn—a fruitful confusion.

When we are least focused on awakening—stumbling about, our eyes full of sleep—we are most vulnerable. The moment of grace often arrives unexpectedly. When we are ripe, any moment can be the occasion for true meeting, and with that, we awaken to what has always been the case, even as it is for the first time.

This is clearly meeting face-to-face—only then is it genuine.

The old woman's experience, and ours if it is genuine, is the same as the Buddha's when he looked up and saw the Morning Star, or as Dongshan's when he awakened upon seeing his face reflected in the stream he was crossing. The occasions differ, but the sense of true encounter—the world being none other than our self, even as we are clearly distinguishable from it—is shared in common.

When we awaken to our essential nature, we awaken in our own way, and that experience is unique to each of us. From Dongshan's perspective, for that awakening to be genuine it needs to accord with the timeless immensity of Buddha mind manifesting here and now as you.

Don't lose your head by validating shadows.

The Surangama Sutra tells the story of the madman Yajnadatta of Sravasti, who delighted in watching himself in the mirror. One morning—and this is like a parody of encountering the ancient mirror—Yajnadatta looked in the mirror and failed to see his head. He rushed around in great consternation, and no one could convince him that his head was on his shoulders. Eventually, one of his friends gave him a thump on his skull, and Yajnadatta felt his head as never before. Now, each morning, Yajnadatta gazes into the mirror, enjoying his smiling image, and preening himself: all's right with the world.[37]

"Losing your head while validating shadows" means (at the very least) mulling over the experience of awakening to emptiness and trying to recreate it, which doesn't work. When we do this, we don't get that our experience is properly vested in head, heart, and hands. Trying to recreate our awakening, we're like Yajnadatta, trapped in emptiness, seeking his missing head. After awakening, we need to let go of the experience of awakening and invest the love and energy that flow from it into how we treat the world, and how we work with our own karmic tendencies.

We may come to the practice of Zen in order to realize our true nature, but if we stay, it is for the years of hard work with our own difficulties. This isn't a way of beating ourselves up for our faults and failings. If we stay the course, we can grow our life down little by little into the world. Some of the pain we feel is growing pain. It's confronting, but we are doing what we must do.

We may awaken in an instant. But in terms of allowing light to penetrate, and to really come to know ourselves, we have to take the time it takes. Making changes takes time. Ultimately, we discover that when we open to the bony structures of our defensiveness and resistance—to the ribcage of our fear—we are also encountering in that boniness a face that is no other than our own. Over time, we get to know the lineaments of that face.

A Summary of the First Two Modes of the Essential and the Contingent

Both of the first two modes, the Contingent within Essential and the Essential within Contingent, are about our encounter with the ancient mirror of our essential nature in its differing aspects. In the first mode we encountered the darkened mirror: an encounter with our timeless, vast, and undifferentiated nature, which is none other than the nature of Buddha. In the second mode, we encountered the clear, bright mirror of reality and experienced intimacy with the universe, in the guise of a star, a bell, or a flight of birds. This overview of the first two modes has concentrated on the aspect of intimacy with the whole. It is important to note, however, that the second mode may also be viewed from the perspective of differentiation. I will explore that perspective below, when I discuss each mode individually.

The modes of the first cycle resemble St. Paul's words from his Epistle to the Corinthians: "Now we see through a glass darkly; but then face to face. Now I know in part; but then shall I know, even as also I am known" (I Corinthians, 13:12). The four phrases employed by St. Paul in this verse constitute four koans, which are well worth taking up alongside the five modes of the essential and the contingent. His words suggest a journey into intimacy with our essential and timeless nature, and resonate with Dongshan's account. The lines "Now we see through a glass darkly; but then face-to-face" correspond closely to the first two modes as we have explored them here, as well as to the movement between them—being the movement from darkness to light.

6. The Third and Fourth Modes Paired: Solitary and Exquisite

Arriving within the Essential
In nothingness there is a road apart from the dust.
If you don't break the taboo on mentioning the Emperor's name
you will surpass the eloquence of the previous dynasty's worthies,
    who cut off tongues.

Approaching from the Contingent
No need to dodge when blades are crossed.
The skillful one is like a lotus in the midst of fire.
Seemingly, you yourself possess the aspiration to soar to the
    heavens.

LET'S CONTINUE our unpacking of the themes of the first cycle with an exploration of the third and fourth modes, Arriving within the Essential and Approaching from the Contingent. In the last chapter we saw that, with regard to the first two modes, Dongshan choreographed the essential and the contingent as being mutually inclusive. With the second pair of modes, Dongshan treats the essential and the contingent as mutually exclusive—which is to say that each polarity keeps its own place. Accordingly, we will explore the essential in isolation from the contingent in the third mode, and the contingent in isolation from essential in the fourth.

This strategy may appear to violate the spirit of the middle way, where, as we have seen, the essential has no reality apart from the contingent, and the contingent is likewise meaningless without the essential. However, although they play out at the extremes, these two modes, being complementary, are mutually corrective. This means that when you raise the essential, the contingent "comes along," or is at least implicitly present. And when you raise the contingent, the essential is implied. To give this a Huayan spin, we can say that in the third mode the essential "conceals" the contingent, and in the fourth the contingent "conceals" the essential. In each case, the mode that is concealed is nonetheless implicit.

The advantage of focusing on one polarity and then on the other is that we manage a fuller engagement with each. When we focus exclusively on the essential, as we do in the third mode, we are encouraged to realize at deeper levels and to open beyond our cramping attitudes and stories. Also, by treating emptiness as a sole topic of consideration, the way is opened for Dongshan to deal undistractedly with the subtle matter of the emptiness of words and language.

When we plunge into contingency alone in the fourth mode, we forget the essential realm, facing up to challenges and difficulties without taking refuge in emptiness to ward off what we dislike or fear. Out of such practice the genuine person emerges: you emerge in your true colors.

Arriving within the Essential

Now we turn to the empty realm without the reassuring traction of the contingent, which, however, remains implicit. In this mode of Arriving within the Essential, we open to emptiness in more thoroughgoing and subtle ways.

Regarding the experience of emptiness: when that pristine timeless source is, we are not. We cannot turn and look back into it, for that would be like the sun trying to shine on itself, or like the eye trying to see itself. The radiant darkness informs—closer than breathing—our lying down at night and our walking over the wet lawn to pick up the newspaper in the morning. Its subversion can be soft, like waking from a dream and finding that the boundaries imposed by a limited view of who we are have dispersed. It brings joy and equanimity where there is no one to receive such blessings. Although it cannot be prolonged by will, it pervades our lives. Grief and pain are carried differently, if we can speak of their being carried at all, and the world walks through our heart, as our heart.

There are no words for it. To call it "nothingness" is to defame it; to call it "somethingness" is to lie. What will you call it? Dongshan's addresses this very question with his verse.

In nothingness there is a road apart from the dust.

In traditional Buddhist terms, "dust" is a metaphor for phenomena as we experience them through the senses. A road apart from the dust conjures the image of emptiness in isolation from phenomena. It is a position of lopsided purity, like riding a seesaw to the high position with no one on the other end: there is no way but down. The "downward path" is encountered in the next mode, Approaching from the Contingent.

Here, the road apart from the dust is the Way of emptiness. The road apart from the dust specifically indicates a path where words and language, including the dialectic and imagery of the Five Ranks, are empty. Realizing this, truly awake to this, we find that we are walking the path of liberation. We awaken to the mystery of words, and find that a word encloses the universe, no less than a flower. With our awakening to the mystery of words, we are, ideally, not tossed about in the currents of abuse and gossip, for these—along with blandishments and endearments, and indeed the torrent of media chatter—are the pure expression of the Way, and our means of liberation, no less than birdsong and the sound of the bell.

In the light of the foregoing, the Five Ranks are not simply expedient teachings. They are a direct presentation of the inexpressible, essential Way. It is true that this is the default mode for all language and communication, but, especially with regard to the Five Ranks, I feel that Dongshan consciously and deliberately crafted them to focus, and as far as possible, to directly present the timeless essential realm. The essential cannot be expressed in words; rather, it is expressed as words. What is timeless and essential reveals itself as the dialectic and poetry of the Five Ranks.

If you don't break the taboo on mentioning the Emperor's name . . .

When you try to describe enlightenment, or to use Dongshan's phrase, "to mention the Emperor's name," you run the risk of separating from his or her radiance. However, if you remain silent concerning the matter, that hermetic seal will encourage your practice to mature in silence and darkness. This is why it's good not to spill the beans about any insight you've had to your friends and companions on the Way. It's unseemly, and the common experience is that afterward you feel that you've betrayed yourself and your practice, which may well be the case.

NOT MENTIONING THE EMPEROR'S NAME: SILENCE

> It speaks in silence; in speech you hear its silence.
> —Yongjia Xuanjue

There are no words that can adequately convey emptiness. So, understandably, silence represents a way of expressing it. Silence is inscrutable. It can be an expression of profound not knowing, or it can simply indicate that we don't know how to respond. It can be hauteur designed to wound or an indication that we carry suffering and horror too great to express.

It is also a time-honored way of presenting the essential. I remember a student who, whenever I asked regarding her koan, always placed her finger to her lips. The following poem is expressive of her Dharma:

> Like Vimalakirti
> she shuts her mouth,
> following the old way.
> All day long, she sits within the gate.
> She does not tell anyone her inner treasure.

> When she sees the Blue Mountain
> through the veranda, and recognizes it,
> she feels she has spoken too much.

In Chan traditions, silence speaks for the empty realm *as* it. Consider this koan:

> A philosopher asked the World-Honored One, "I do not ask for the spoken; I do not ask for the unspoken."
>
> The World-Honored One just sat still.
>
> The philosopher praised him, saying, "The World-Honored One with his great compassion and mercy has opened the clouds of my delusion and enabled me to enter the Way."[38]

The Buddha could have given a wordy discourse. Instead, his silent presence cleared away the obstacles of words and no words—a conception evocative of Nagarjuna's conventional and ultimate truth—opening the Way for the philosopher. We could say that the Buddha's silence, in the spirit of Dongshan's concluding line, "surpassed all eloquence."

NOT MENTIONING THE EMPEROR'S NAME: DISCRETION

For the first few centuries after the Buddha died there were no images made of him. If he had to be depicted at all, it was as a wheel, a tree, or a footprint. This deference subtly recalls his radiance, and yours. You answer to a name, but in the vast country of "I don't know," you have no name. It is written in the stars, or in blown grass.

Caoshan wrote regarding this Cycle of the Essential and the Contingent, "The reason for using the imagery of ruler and minister and essential and contingent is to avoid transgressing the center." By this he means that the imagery of the ruler and the minister is a detour to avoid naming or describing the ultimate. His own use of the term "the center" also evokes but does not name the ultimate: the timeless, undifferentiated essential. In this way, our discretion in not referring directly to the ultimate becomes its very expression, as does any attempt to explain it, although the latter might be harder to appreciate.

Thus far, we have understood the taboo on mentioning the Emperor's name—that is, on speaking of enlightenment—in terms of silence. Now, in taking the taboo on mentioning the Emperor's name in terms of discretion, the deeper point is made that even discussion of enlightenment does not transgress the center, because such discussion can be itself a presentation of the timeless essential. In this regard, the words and imagery of the Five Ranks avoids the problem of breaking the taboo on mentioning the Emperor's name, because their very means of communicating and elucidating the Way—bright words, the play of bright and dark—are completely empty.

> **. . . you will surpass the eloquence of the previous dynasty's worthies, who cut off tongues.**

When we awaken to the empty path of words and language, even our unthinking "good morning" surpasses the words of old teachers whose eloquence—shouts, blows, poems, snatches of song—gave their students nowhere to stand and nothing to say. Thus deprived, students awakened to their timeless essential nature. When we surpass this, that is when we speak from the same depths, our ordinary words similarly express the timeless essential.

Mari Rhydwen, Glenn Wallis, Arthur Wells, and I were giving an evening of short talks for students in Glenn Wallis's dojo in Dunedin after sesshin. I gave one on gratitude, which was warmed by the fact that I had mislaid my wallet several times that day—and found it again. Each time I had it back in my hand I'd mumble, "Thank you, universe." I continued, "I'm sure there must be a better way to express that." Mari chimed in, "Thank you."

We come to hear the world's chatter, mundane or sublime, as a song of the Way. Over time, and with deepening in the koan path, we also learn to convey the inexpressible. Then even our simplest "Good morning. How are you doing?" shines with the first light of the world, and our silences leave all poetic loquacity for dead.

Approaching from the Contingent

Whereas the preceding mode demonstrated awakening to emptiness, to the emptiness of words and language in particular, the mode of

Approaching from the Contingent shows us enlightenment emerging from contingency. Whereas the contingent was backgrounded in the preceding mode, here emptiness is backgrounded, although it remains everywhere implicit. In this mode, it is as though we see the bright side of the moon, while knowing full well that the dark side is there.

"Approaching from the Contingent" means that we come back into the light: into the realm of uniqueness and differentiation. This is the necessary antidote to hiding out in the darkness of the empty realm. Coming back into the light? Rain falls at the precise angle of the roof's zinc corrugations; a cat glides through tall grass; the sun goes down; the stars come out. Nothing is hidden. The honest solidities of this long day here show you who you are, even as they show you who you are not. Such experiences are as unmistakable as the taste of blood in the mouth, and as candid as the face of death.

If our experience of emptiness has been genuine, it informs our engagement with the differentiated world. As the experience of emptiness fades, we don't attempt to recreate it. Instead we enter our life fully, uniting with circumstance and facing up to challenges as they inevitably present themselves. This is the realm where we deepen our awakening through our engagement with others in the midst of a suffering world.

No need to dodge when blades are crossed.

The crossed swords correspond to the realms of essential and contingent, understood here as separate and yet to be integrated. We have realized the dark "essential," but now reencounter the world of harsh contingency, which may feel opposed to our experience of the void, not least because of our doubts and fears, which cannot be lost overnight, if at all.

Given the impossibility of advance or retreat, we stay put, opening to our lives where we are. This is what is meant by "not dodging." We now undertake, or rather continue, the training that enables us to engage difficulty, and face up to natural differences and adverse circumstance. We forget emptiness, and treat differences and difficulties as all there is. When we do this, unknowingly, we bring our awakening into the world.

The skillful one is like a lotus in the midst of fire.

The Vimalakirti Sutra lists the bodhisattva's protean resources for awakening suffering beings. One of these is her meditation, which is described as being like a lotus blossoming in a scorching fire. The blossoming lotus is a metaphor for becoming enlightened and enlightening others, while fire is a metaphor for desire. Dongshan broadens the metaphor to include both a bodhisattva's meditation and activity, not only in the midst of desire, but in the suffering world at large.

We awaken and deepen our awakening in the midst of our own troubles and confusion. There is no perfect environment, and we don't have to be perfect. We work with the life that is mysteriously ours, with its unique weave of love and pain—the difficult parent, the sterile relationship, the pain of abandonment. Any or all of these are the perfect ground for awakening. When you commit to meditation in the midst of your difficulties, you become like the lotus blossoming in the midst of fire: you enlighten yourself and others in the midst of challenges and troubles.

Seemingly, you yourself possess the aspiration to soar to the heavens.

We forget about the sublime; we're oblivious to paradise. We encounter the broken world and our own brokenness. Over time we grow to be able to include more of both. Dongshan acknowledges us when we undertake to go the distance, saying, "Seemingly, you yourself possess the aspiration to soar to the heavens." His estimation of our capacities is a cautious one. Praise can drain away aspiration. Uplifted by such parsimony, we ascend the heavens as we step down deeper into our lives.

A Summary of the Third and Fourth Modes of Essential and Contingent

Having briefly examined the third and fourth modes, we see how both are aspects of the same path of liberation, despite their apparent opposition. With regard to Arriving within the Essential, we saw how silence and even words and language can convey the empty realm. With Approaching from the Contingent, we saw that it is necessary for us to move on from experiences of emptiness to engage the complexity of our real lives. The bodhisattva path of liberating others and oneself, indicated with the metaphor of a lotus blossoming in the midst of fire, is an important theme in this, the fourth mode.

In terms of the overall sequence of modes in the Cycle of the Essential and the Contingent, the third, Arriving within the Essential, is central, which means that it expresses the pure essential: the radiant darkness of the empty realm where all expressive means are completely empty. The third mode's emphasis on the emptiness of words and language is applied by extension to all five modes, including itself. So the third mode is not only central in the sense of marking the mid point among the five modes but is central in a thematic sense as well.

7. The Final Mode: Homecoming

Arriving at Concurrence
**Who would presume to join their voice with someone
who has surpassed "there is" and "there is not"?
Everyone longs to leave the mundane stream, yet finally you
return to sit in the charcoal heap.**

L OOKING BACK over the path traveled, in the first two modes of the essential and the contingent we awaken to emptiness and experience the world as intimate with us. With the third mode of Arriving within the Essential, we awakened to the mystery of words and language, while in the fourth mode we embodied our deepening insight within a variety of challenging circumstances and found grace and compassion there.

As a result of long training we are now able to express and embody the Way in measure. We find a degree of ease in the world with its challenges, and we realize that our difficulties—including our faults and manifest failings, our vexations and passions—are not less than enlightenment itself.

Arriving at Concurrence

"Concurrence" means that the complementary opposites of the essential and the contingent, those shifting degrees of light and dark that had been in intimate dialectic, converge; that the essential and contingent simultaneously occupy the same space. It may seem as if we are trying to square the circle, but in terms of our experience, essential and contingent, far from being mutually resistant, yield to one another. And this is the lightest, most delicate matter.

With concurrence, we live awakening as our daily lives, with their rituals of love and work—shopping for gifts in the morning, having a nap in the afternoon. It's a relief to let go of the conceptual frames of the five modes of the essential and the contingent, and to ride the great bike of the Tao without the training wheels of categories and terms.

By now we've forgotten any attainments. "What were they, again?" What previously was effortful is now, after much travail, lighter. The path is endless. It seems absurd to continue to travel it, yet we do. Foolish and forgetful sages gather to encourage us and caution us about taking ourselves too seriously.

Grey clouds gathering, doves on the wet boughs, and the cat asleep in front of the heater. This is the everyday miracle of concurrence. When we experience it, we understand that it has always been so, and that it has always been us.

Who would presume to join their voice with someone who has surpassed "there is" and "there is not"?

This is the only question that Dongshan asks in the Cycle of the Essential and the Contingent, and so we ought to take it to heart. We can read this question as an invitation to harmonize with the one who has stepped beyond the polarities of existence and nonexistence, to sing the clear ancient song of the Way unhindered by dialectical complexities and snares. Dongshan's question has roots in the dialectic of existence and nonexistence, which we have seen expressed in the Kaccayanagotta Sutta. There the Buddha posits "Everything exists," as one extreme, and "Everything does not exist," as the other. He goes on to say that the Tathagata teaches the Dharma by means of the middle way, meaning, in that context, that he doesn't veer to either extreme.

But the middle way being discussed here is not merely a middle course or an average between polarities. Rather, we are invited to sing the song of the Way beyond existence and nonexistence, and by extension, beyond contingent and essential. We are invited to transcend the terms of the dialectic of this very cycle. Chan is radical and playful. Although the dialectic of the Cycle of the Essential and the Contingent has a long history behind it, including the sophisticated Huayan concepts that informed it, we are personally being asked to do something new. Our initiative is required.

Everyone longs to leave the mundane stream . . .

The "mundane stream" is the stream of birth and death, within which all things pass away. Few of us live in the places where we were brought up. Our early loves are gone, or live on only in our hearts. Our children grow and move away. When loved ones die and pass out of this life, we see ourselves going the same way. Trapped within currents of change, we are compelled to attempt more and more with ever lessening time. We scramble to finish our tasks, to bring our enterprises home, knowing that, finally, everything gets ploughed under.

We long to leave the mundane stream because we suffer there. So we attempt to bulwark our lives against change: a folly, which is itself a source of further suffering. Longing to step out of the stream of samsara is, therefore, a profound impulse for seeking the Way. However, as we shall see, there is no way out of the stream but in.

. . . yet finally you return to sit in the charcoal heap.

Charcoal is made when wood is burned with reduced oxygen. When charcoal itself is burned, it radiates a steady warmth and light. Here, "charcoal" suggests a transformation emerging from persistent practice, wherein the fire of each koan burns away any residue of dualistic thought.

Although there is nothing in the Chinese expression for "charcoal heap" that directly correspond to the skandhas and their metaphorical "heaps" of form, sensation, and so on, for me the "charcoal heap" evokes the traditional Buddhist notion of the five skandhas, or "heaps," that constitute the basis onto which the self is projected: form, sensation, perception, mental formation, and consciousness. The Heart

Sutra clearly states that the five "heaps" or "aggregates" are imperma-
nent and completely empty. "Returning to sit in the charcoal heap"
may sound austere, ascetic, even rueful—and to a Christian ear may
conjure an image of repentance amid the ashes. But in Zen, "returning
to the charcoal heap" suggests a return to emptiness.

We may wish to leave the mundane stream, and to experience the
timeless. Yet, in Dongshan's terms, we do so by fully inhabiting and
focusing on our lives of constant change. When we return to the charcoal heap, we find that change itself—the loss of a love, the sundering
of a friendship—is the timeless reality we sought when we tried to leave
the mundane stream. Even our longing to leave the mundane stream is
like this. Longing evokes time and duration, but longing is, in the same
breath, the timeless immensity in its gathering.

A Summary of the Fifth Mode

With our arrival at concurrence we transcend the polarities of the
essential and the contingent, letting go of the terms and categories of
the five modes of the essential and the contingent. With this we live
the great life of the Way as our humanity, expressed through love
and work. Although this mode is the last and may seem to announce
an end to practice in some marvelous realm of changeless perfection,
in fact the path of practice and transformation goes on indefinitely.
Truly the charcoal heap is the place where we struggle to improve the
lot of those who suffer deprivation and injustice, as well as working
to redeem our own karmic inheritance. The charcoal heap is a place
where you get dirty.

Through the five modes of essential and contingent we have discovered that, although we awaken in very individual ways, we can broadly
discern staging posts on the path. As we have explored these matters up
to this point, we can say that, initially, we experience emptiness, and
begin a lifetime's work of embodying it. We awaken to our intimate
connection to all that is, realize the subtlety of words, and then letting
go of any preoccupation with hidden understandings, we awaken ourselves, and others, in the thick of the world and its suffering. Finally,

we emerge transformed, but find it difficult to say where we have been, or how we have traveled. We live our life—with its give and take, joy and sorrow, increase and decline—as the Way.

THE FIVE MODES IN DETAIL

8. The Darkened Mirror: The Contingent within the Essential

At the beginning of the third watch, before moonrise,
don't be surprised if there is meeting without recognition;
one still vaguely harbors the elegance of former days.

> I feel a peace fall in the heart
> of the winds, and a clear dusk settle
> somewhere far in me.
> —Christopher Brennan

WHEN WE AWAKEN to this mode of the contingent within the essential, we die to our isolation from stars and earth into the radiant darkness of nothing at all, as it. Each thing is and all things are obliviously and helplessly us, as they have always been. Although this experience is personal, it isn't just our matter—the cat, an earthworm, even a clump of wild oats is thus.

When we realize that the source of our being is no source at all, grief and pain are carried differently, if indeed it is proper to speak of "being carried" at all. Awakening to emptiness, we are released a little, or a lot, from the confining stories that close us down. Everything breathes a little deeper, and we find a measure of spaciousness and ease.

An old evocative line associated with awakening to the contingent within the essential reads:

> The branches of the apricot trees in the orchard part at
> your approach.

The twisted branches, bursting with fruit, are precisely you: lone, inalienable, and indivisible. In the words of old master Wumen Huikai (1183–1260), "When you pass through the gateless barrier, you walk the universe alone."[39] Not only do you walk the universe alone, you sleep it, wake it, and die it alone; and each of these in grand sufficiency. This is the spirit of the contingent within the essential.

Let us now turn to Dongshan's mysterious verse, which we will explore in detail, bringing stories and koans to bear on it as appropriate.

At the beginning of the third watch, before moonrise . . .

The very first line of the Five Ranks announces the themes of time, and implicitly timelessness, that will unfold within both cycles. As noted above, in old China the night was divided into five two-hour watches, the third of which began at midnight. Midnight marks the transition of our days under cover of darkness—a dark, middle moment. Each moment of our life is the middle moment. There is no point of change-over from middle moment to middle moment, for each is timeless and dimensionless. We live each moment of our life like this: the middle moment of joy, the middle moment of sky sluiced clear by rain.

In terms of the dialectic of contingent and essential, we can say that time is fleeting, and the middle moment, timeless. We know all too well that time is fleeting; we know that on our pulses. Awakening to this mode, we open to the immensity of each moment: the moment of remembering, the moment of recognition, the moment of anticipation.

The Spirit of Vigil: Working with a Koan

The darkness of the third watch is a vigil in anticipation of the rising moon, which is Dongshan's image for awakening. The vigil of the third watch takes place before awakening, even as its moonlight illuminates our arduous journey filled with yearning, questioning, and a continuous struggle to return to the koan. Dongshan's image of the third watch evokes all-night sitting on the last night of Rohatsu sesshin—

when students and teachers meditate all night to emulate Shakyamuni Buddha, who after his long night of meditation awakened when he looked up and saw the Morning Star. Rohatsu sesshin is held in early December and concludes on the morning of December 8, celebrated in the Zen Buddhist calendar as Buddha's Enlightenment Day.

This particular mode of the essential and the contingent has been associated with the hexagram fifty-seven of the I Ching, called *Xun* (gentle; penetrating; wind). The title of the hexagram suggests a way to practice, like a gentle wind that blows unceasingly, getting in everywhere. We may ask, "Who am I?" and get lost in thought. After struggling to find our way back, we get lost all over again. Yet, although the results may seem inconspicuous, like a gentle wind that blows persistently in one direction, our steadfast practice enduring over time makes its changes. And with each return to the koan we develop strength of concentration and build the vessel of practice.

With persistent practice, we're disabused of our cherished notions and opinions about the world and ourselves. We allow ourselves to be cut and shaped by the stream of the Way. This is a necessary simplification—a stilling, a darkening. We encounter our doubt too. Doubt about whether we deserve the Way when there is so much suffering in the world; or if we're enlightened from the beginning, why we have to sweat and struggle like this. In some instances, such doubt can be traced to our fear of failure. However, attending the specter of failure at this early stage of the journey doesn't pay. It is wise as well to guard against being led about by the idea of the great sea change we're undergoing. Later we will be able to examine such preoccupations in the light of the full moon and uncover their root systems with the cultivation that continues after enlightenment.

The moon rises and is reflected in the water in its own good time. Meanwhile, you come up to the gate a thousand times. When your time is ripe, under cover of darkness, you go through.

. . . don't be surprised if there is meeting without recognition . . .

We've explored the notion of "meeting without recognition" above. We found that such meeting is still true meeting, even without recognition. In this regard, we meet the empty realm without recognizing it, because it is none other than us.

But enough of this maneuvering in the dark! The metaphor of meeting without recognition is best conveyed through story, and the following tale of Deshan Xuanjiang (819-914) encountering the darkened mirror is exemplary in this regard.

Deshan lived in ninth century China. When he was young, he was a scholar who specialized in the Diamond Sutra. So preoccupied with the sutra was he, and such an authority on it, that he earned the nickname "Diamond Zhou." He was proud of his hard-earned knowledge, as experts sometimes are, and could be arrogant and overbearing. Whenever any talk arose regarding his area of expertise, his unvarying response was, "I know." Others fell silent in his presence.

When he heard that the Southern School was teaching that the Way was not established on words and letters, and that transmission occurred independently of scripture (including the Diamond Sutra), Deshan responded vehemently, "How dare those southern devils say that just by pointing at the human mind one can see self-nature and attain buddhahood? I'll drag them from their caves and exterminate their ilk, and thus repay the kindness of Buddha!"

Packing bundled commentaries on the Diamond Sutra—evidence for the prosecution—into a cart, Deshan set off on the long road to the south. Having reached the vicinity of "southern devils," he paused for refreshment at a roadside teahouse run by an old woman. Curious about this aloof young fellow, the old woman asked him what he had in his cart. Deshan replied stiffly that the bundles were notes and commentaries on the Diamond Sutra.

Her face lighting up, the old woman spoke, "I have a question for you. If you can answer correctly you can have my dim sum for free. If you cannot, you'll have to pay."

Deshan was a bit taken aback by what seemed an attempt to play a flippant game with his revered sutra, but being tired and hungry, he agreed to play.

The old woman asked, "In the Diamond Sutra it says, 'Past mind cannot be grasped, neither can present mind, nor future mind.' Which mind does Your Reverence aim to grasp?"

Deshan was unable to reply.

Finding a measure of humility, he asked the old woman, "Is there a Zen teacher in the area?" poignantly unaware of the Zen teacher who stood before him.

"Longtan lives just up the hill," she replied.

The story of Deshan shows that we are dangerous when we think we have truth on our side. What we so arrogantly condemn in others is often at work in us in the form of our own doubt and uncertainty. We may try to quarantine our doubt, even as it is already at work undermining our carefully thought out positions. Being blind-sighted to our doubt sets us up for a disillusioning fall.

Finally being brought down from our high horse provides a path back into life, beyond the painful rigidity of our fixed views. When the tea lady's question landed neatly within Deshan's field of obsessive expertise and he was unable to respond, he was forced to confront the limits of his "knowledge." In his moment of defeat, Deshan came face to face with a matter that he hadn't resolved.

The old woman's challenge involves a play on the word "dim sum," which most typically means "small snack." But the phrase can also mean "grasping," "touching," or "refreshing the mind." The line from the Diamond Sutra that the old woman quotes appears in a passage in which the Buddha explains to his disciple Subhuti, "What the Tathagata calls different mentalities are not in fact different mentalities. That is why they are called different mentalities." Sensing his disciple's confusion, the Buddha continues, "Past mind cannot be grasped, neither can present mind, nor future mind."[40]

These "minds" cannot be grasped because they are completely empty. This is also why they can be called "past mind," "present mind," and "future mind"—these being precisely differentiated names for the timeless realm where there are no names at all. The Buddha spilled koans in this sutra like they were going out of fashion. The point about the emptiness of past, present, and future was made only in passing in Deshan's story, yet it reflects this mode of the Contingent within the Essential, which treats the future, the present, and the past as empty. More generally, it reflects the dialectic of the temporal and the timeless encountered throughout the Five Ranks.

> After his failure to answer her question, the old woman directed Deshan to Longtan Chongxin (n.d), who lived just up the hill, and was probably her master. Having climbed the hill, Deshan sincerely questioned Longtan far into the night.
>
> Worn out from Deshan's eager questioning, Longtan finally said, "It is getting late. Why don't you get some sleep?"
>
> Deshan made his bows and lifted the bamboo blind to withdraw, but was met by darkness. Turning back he said, "It is dark outside."
>
> Longtan lit a taper and handed it to Deshan. As Deshan was about to take it, Longtan blew it out. At this, Deshan had sudden realization and made bows.
>
> Longtan asked, "What truth did you discern?"
>
> Deshan replied, "From now on I will not doubt the words of an old priest who is renowned everywhere under the sun." [41]

Deshan doesn't answer Longtan's question either. Or rather, he does so only obliquely, with his grateful, enigmatic, "From now on I will not doubt the words of an old priest who is renowned everywhere under the sun." The lacuna says it all. The truth that Deshan has discerned has knocked him flat and stolen his tongue. He is spoken for, and his life course is now set.

Deshan honors Longtan, no longer a contemptible southern (sudden!) devil, but someone renowned beyond consideration of North and South. He attributes to Longtan his own experience of timeless, dimensionless nature. Deshan's praise of Longtan also reveals his change of heart, full of gratitude and admiration. His old judgment has been upended, and Longtan is now his teacher.

Such an awakening moves us profoundly, and can ease our fear of living and dying. It can impart to us confidence, equanimity, and joy—at least for a time. It can also open a window for us onto the old koans and stories. Such experiences are not the end of the matter, however. Traditional wisdom holds that our practice only begins with them. There are immeasurable distances, as mapped in the remaining modes, for us to travel in order to express, to embody, to convey, and finally to forget this experience.

After such an awakening, we may be inclined to feel that the "small beer" (to borrow an expression from Shakespeare) of our lives and that of others doesn't matter. But that's not it. Because all of it is empty, and we can experience the freedom that that brings, we take minute care of the small and fleeting, and we treat the world with tenderness and respect. Otherwise, it is as if your left hand were caught in a rabbit trap and your right hand were to say, "I have business elsewhere. There's nothing I can do to help you."

Next morning, before his assembly, Longtan predicted that Deshan would become a great teacher. In front of the Dharma Hall Deshan burned up all his notes on the Diamond Sutra, and indeed he went on to fulfill Longtan's prediction, fashioning at least a couple of great descendants, Xuefeng Yicun (822–908) and Yantou Quanhuo (828–887). We will meet these two luminaries in dialogue below.

. . . one still vaguely harbors the elegance of former days.

Dongshan's beautiful concluding line renews the theme of time. In the first line of his verse, "At the beginning of the third watch, before moonrise," the phrase "before moonrise" carries the sense of before awakening, of "not yet." The phrase "meeting without recognition" in the subsequent line conveys "awakening to the timeless realm." Here, "harbors the elegance of former days" evokes an image of the past lingering within the present, and carries the sense of "still, yet."

Each of these perspectives is empty, and in the spirit of the Five Ranks, we see through each perspective with eyes of emptiness. Correspondingly, we can regard each perspective as a koan. When we awaken, we know that we've embarked where the ancestors of the Way have gone before us. In this way, we encounter our true contemporaries, not only those who are contemporaneous, but the old teachers with whom we share timeless, dimensionless mind.

Yamada Koun (1907–1989) reads other implications into this line, writing:

> We still remember the beauty of the old days; even though we have realized that every ordinary activity is no other than essential nature itself, still it seems to us that in our deepest consciousness something which may be called essential nature exists, other than ordinary activity.[42]

No matter how deeply we realize, we yearn for greater depth. This "beauty of the old days" that lies deep within encourages us to journey into the vastness that is each of us. Our incompleteness calls for deeper connection, for fuller life. At the same time, that very incompletion and our yearning is, without remainder, the vastness of our essential nature.

I find it useful to regard Yamada Koun's "ordinary activity" to include dream, reflection, reverie, and artistic creation, along with the usual standing, sitting, eating when hungry, and sleeping when tired. Our ordinary activities—even the innermost expressions of our humanity, musically and poetically expressed—are lit by the moon.

The Zen teacher Bob Joyner, commenting on this line, wrote to me that there is always something deeper that we want to clarify after realization. He calls it "a trace." The death of a loved one and the birth of a child can be "traces" that call for clarification. Concluding his letter, Bob wrote, "This is what draws me deeper and will continue to do so. Maybe this is what kept Zhaozhou wandering for all those years in old China, seeking out masters to engage with." Bob's words convey the spirit of harboring the elegance of former days. Even after a deep realization, we feel that it is not enough. Actually, that is a measure of its depth: the deeper the realization, the deeper the sense that it is not enough.

"Harboring the elegance of former days" can also refer to our tendency to cling to the experience of emptiness after awakening, like someone waking from sleep but still being in the spell of a dream. Clinging to emptiness is understandable. I've known people who have wept at the receding of the experience. But if we cling to the experience of emptiness, it ossifies into our thinking about it. Under the spell of our "achievement," we cannot move on, and our practice, and indeed our life, stagnates. And yet, clinging—even that stultified condition itself—is an expression of the timeless eternal realm, too. Although we may regard an experience of awakening to emptiness as complete, it is at the same time only a first step on the path. It is important to let go of whatever experiences we may have had, and to open ourselves to uncertainty again, leaving behind any knowledge of the Way we think we may have acquired.

Heraclitus, describing soul, says that she is so vast that you could journey many days without reaching the end of her. For days, let's read years or decades. The undertaking of coming to know who you are, and your deep connection to all that is, is endless. The darkened mirror of the first mode yearns for the clear, bright mirror of the second. At each stage of the Way it is "Not enough. Not yet enough. Never enough." And this is the deepest encouragement of all.

9. The Dawn Mirror:
The Essential within the Contingent

Having overslept, an old woman encounters the ancient mirror.
This is clearly meeting face-to-face—only then is it genuine.
Don't lose your head by validating shadows.

> There is no person without a world.
> —Anne Carson

NOW LET US develop the themes of intimacy and true meeting associated with the mode of the Essential within the Contingent that we briefly touched on above, using stories to more fully convey the koan perspective. In the previous chapter on the mode of the Contingent within the Essential, we explored the image of encountering the darkened mirror as a metaphor for awakening to the emptiness of the self, and by extension, of the world. Dongshan referred to this encounter as "a meeting without recognition." In this mode of the Essential within the Contingent, darkness lifts from the mirror, and we recognize the world as our deepest nature.

The story of Irina Harford illustrates this aptly. Irina sat with the Zen Group of Western Australia for many years, until her death in 2003. She took part in most of the group's activities, wrote haiku, and was interested in quantum physics and its implications for the Way. Even when her ovarian cancer was advanced, and she was in a lot of pain, she still climbed the wooden steps to the zendo. When Irina was very close to death, she asked me if she could take up another koan. I gave her the following verse, part of Case 36 of *The Iron Flute*:

True intimacy transcends friendship and alienation;
Between meeting and not meeting, there is no difference.
On the old plum tree, fully blossomed,
the southern branch owns the whole Spring,
as also does the northern branch.[43]

Irina was not expected to live a fortnight. As I was leaving to fly to
New Zealand, I came to the hospital to say goodbye to her. When I
invited her to present her koan, she sat up with great effort and silently
raised her withered arms. That was how she conveyed the intimacy
of the universe (in the guise of the old plum tree) with herself. Irina's
response beautifully captures the spirit of the mode of the Essential
within the Contingent.

Having overslept, an old woman encounters the ancient mirror.

Dongshan uses the old woman's encounter with the ancient mirror as
a metaphor for her awakening to her essential nature. But, unfortu-
nately, we must acknowledge that Dongshan likely chose the image
of an old woman encountering the ancient mirror to illustrate the fact
that awakening comes even to those with the weakest faculties and
intelligence. We might understand his intended message in the verse as
being, "Even an old muddle-headed woman can encounter the ancient
mirror. So why can't you?"

Having acknowledged the metaphorical use of the old woman in this
way, it is important to point out that although women have historically
gone largely unacknowledged in Chan and Zen traditions, many, old
and young alike, have in fact awakened. Awakened women, no less
than their male counterparts, have passed the light of the Way on to
others. We recall the Zen granny in Deshan's story, who had a hand
in his awakening with her koan-like questioning. And here, as well,
in the service of illustrating the theme of intimacy, which characterizes the mode of the Essential within the Contingent, we turn to the
story of another woman, Asan of Shinano, and her encounter with
the ancient mirror.[44]

Asan of Shinano lived in Japan in the eighteenth century. She was a sincere student who meditated assiduously. One morning, drifting in and out of sleep, and struggling to stay present to her koan, she heard a rooster crow.

Her mind suddenly opened, and she exclaimed, "The fields, the mountains, the flowers, and my body, too, are the voice of the bird. What is left that could be said to hear?"

Asan and everything else vanished into that rooster's crow. That raucous invasion of her privacy cleared things up for her. It set her on her feet.

Such experiences are incontrovertible. Still, it is wise to have them examined by a master. In this regard, Asan set her standards high. To test her realization, she visited the greatest Zen teacher of that era, Hakuin, when he came to Shinano.

From Xuedou Chongxian's "A single palm does not make a sound in vain," Hakuin had forged the koan "What is the sound of one hand?" and had pioneered the use of it with his monks. When Asan met him, he challenged her with it.

She replied, "Better than the sound of one hand is to clap both hands and do business."

Hakuin, who was a consummate artist and calligrapher, immediately drew Asan a broom.

Unfazed, Asan shot back, "Sweeping away all the bad teachers in Japan, starting with Hakuin!"

Hakuin roared with laughter.[45]

It may seem as if Asan failed to engage with the koan. Not at all. The sound of one hand does business, like it goes shopping and tidies up. She's saying to Hakuin, "Don't bother me with those smelly checking questions that you inflict on your monks. Let's get down to brass tacks." Hakuin drew Asan a broom—that's his presentation of the sound of one hand! Perhaps he's teasing her: "Here's a broom to help you sweep away your delusion." Asan's radiant gust of abuse made Hakuin roar with laughter. Drawing a broom, abuse, laughter—each unerringly conveys the sound of one hand, even as it blasts contrivances such as "the sound of one hand" away. Hakuin's laugh is expressive of Asan's and his kinship in the Way, and it implicitly acknowledges her insight.

Encountering the Ancient Mirror: True Meeting
as It Unfolds in Your Life

With an awakening such as Asan's, we realize that the wind that moves the branches, no less than the smell of petrol, is our genuine nature, and that the face of the stranger is no other than our own. A young man reaches out to touch his teacher's beard, and the shock of its wiriness jolts him out of exile. He finds that the whole world walks through his heart—as his heart—and he feels overwhelming love for his wife and his children. This meeting is older than the night sky and is beyond our agency.

Don't get carried away, though. Sun, moon, and stars are that for the earthworm or a clump of grass, and vice versa. We don't have to try to make this so, it's simply given. We don't have to deserve it either, any more than we have to deserve our lives: it is the rising of the sun, the returning to life after obligatory death; it is the vastness—alive and glinting in the wetness of your eyes and in the angles of your irony.

"Still wandering in your mind?" I asked a student.

"You bet."

"What's there?"

"Oh, grey sky, the sun on the salmon gums."

After the shock and joy of true meeting come confidence and equanimity, in their time. Something has opened that is alive and at ease. Its power and energy surface from unknowable depths, animating our action in the world. We are enlivened, and we move others. We preach vigorously with our simple "Good morning," and with our laughter quickened by wind and sunshine. Our simplest acts—picking up a cup, listening attentively—touch and enliven others.

Encountering the Ancient Mirror: True Meeting
as the Play of Mirrors

Hakuin, after many awakening experiences, could give teisho all day. He was alive for whoever came before him, and he had creativity to burn. Here is his open-throttle account of the ancient mirror as awakened life:

> All the myriad phenomena before his eyes—the old and
> the young, the honorable and the base, halls and pavilions,
> verandas and corridors, plants and trees, mountains and
> rivers—he regards as his own original, true, and pure aspect.
> It is just like looking into a bright mirror and seeing his own
> face in it. If he continues for a long time to observe every-
> thing everywhere with this radiant insight, all appearances,
> of themselves, become the jeweled mirror of his own house,
> and he becomes the jeweled mirror of their houses as well.[46]

The mutuality of the jewel mirror is entirely given, and always has been. Rain roars at the back door. The dog howls for its owner. The green bus curves out of traffic toward us, *as* us. There's not one of these that doesn't radiantly convey us. There's not one of these that is not our original face.

We are not aware of our role in this, either. That's perhaps the strangest and least suspected angle—our appearing as the original aspect of others: the true face of an earthworm, the true face of our loved ones, and the true face of those who can't stand us.

With the experience of true meeting, if you are a woman you can respond to the koan "A young man is coming this way," or if you are a man to the koan "A young woman is coming this way," beyond any contrivance. When we first stumble into this, we may still be getting on our feet, but something has shifted, and we will never be the same again.

Encountering the Ancient Mirror: The Theme of Differentiation

Thus far, we've dwelt on the theme of true meeting, in its undifferentiated aspect. Now let us touch on the aspect of differentiation. Dongshan's poem, the "Song of the Precious Mirror Samadhi," gives an account of encountering the ancient or "precious" mirror, which aptly corresponds to the present mode of the Essential within the Contingent.

> As when you face the precious mirror, form and reflection behold each other—you are not him; he is exactly you.

When we encounter the precious mirror we awaken to the fact that those we meet are precisely us, though we are in the same breath distinct from them. When identity is asserted, difference is not being denied. Correspondingly, by dint of engagement with others in the rough and the smooth of it, we come to experience our ever-changing circumstances as awakening. We can't contrive this. However, by remaining open to the challenges posed by natural differences and disagreements, along with their attendant fear, rage, and humiliation, we slowly come to understand that what is hardest to bear can also be, in fact, our true and original face. This is a path for a lifetime.

This is clearly meeting face-to-face—only then is it genuine.

The old woman's experience and ours (if it is genuine) are the same as the Buddha's when he looked up and saw the Morning Star, or as Dongshan's when he awakened upon glimpsing his face reflected in a stream he was crossing. The occasions may differ—catching sight of the Morning Star, glimpsing one's reflection in a stream—but the sense of true encounter is in common. For Dongshan, this is the mark of a genuine experience. In the spirit of genuine meeting, face-to-face, here is a koan for this stage of the journey:

> When the old woman encountered the ancient mirror, what did she realize?

What we have translated from the Chinese earlier as "This is clearly meeting face-to-face—only then is it genuine" can also be translated as, "This is clearly meeting face-to-face—nothing more." In other words, if the encounter is genuine, that's it. No need to think about it, interpret it, or add anything to it. To do so would only ossify the encounter into ideas and stories. And stories and ideas are merely shadows.

Don't lose your head by validating shadows.

As mentioned above, the phrase "don't lose your head" has its origin in the story of the mirror-gazing madman, Yajnadatta of Sravasti, who lost and found his head. After a genuine awakening, I doubt that we can ever quite go back to how we were. Something has changed in our depths, and although none of us are immune from getting it terribly wrong (we're not meant to be proof against that), after awakening we come from a different place to make peace, or to make trouble. Our suffering is held differently, or not even held at all: just that disappointment, just that heartache.

Still, even after the deepest of awakening experiences, habitual ways of thinking and feeling do return. Given the extensive connotations of "shadow" we could drag in the darkness of a lifetime here. But my sense is that Dongshan is specifically concerned with "shadows" such as the all-too-human tendency to mull over an insight, particularly in an attempt to recreate it. If you do that, to use Qinshan's phrase, "You're guarding a stump, waiting for a rabbit." This arresting and very Australian image derives from the old Chinese story of the person who happened to see a rabbit collide with a tree stump and drop down dead. That person then continued to wait by the stump, hoping that it would "catch" another rabbit. Another "shadow" is the attempt to steal someone else's rabbit.[47]

It is also possible to translate this line about losing your head as "Don't lose your head by validating images." Specifically, this focuses the matter of not attaching to an experience of enlightenment. When we do this we reify what is transient and turn it into our story about it. In terms of the path to be traveled, it is important to let go of an experience of emptiness and allow it to do its work in our depths. If it is genuine it effects its changes out of reach of our acquisitive mind. When students would come to Shunryu Suzuki to report "a profound

awakening experience," he would say to them, "You have five minutes." Indeed, our next task is already at hand.

Know Thyself

Catching a glimpse of our true nature is just the beginning. Such experiences can move us in our depths, but if we are going to be able to
embody the Way and convey it to others, we must take the longer
journey of coming to know our selves. I remember my bewilderment
in the face of Socrates' "Know thyself" cut into one of the limestone
portals of the university where I studied as a young man. Without
self-knowledge, at the very least, we run the risk of releasing our own
darkness on others. In the following verse from Lou Reed's song "Caroline Says," the abused girl's words poignantly express this:

> Caroline says,
> as she makes up her eye,
> "You ought to learn more about yourself,
> think more than just I."

Caroline's partner's "thinking 'I'" is, at least in part, his controlling vio-
lent behavior. She's telling him that he needs to learn about himself—in
particular the fear of having his authority challenged that drives his
need to hit her. When we can see through our fear—fear of loss of control, fear of being shamed, fear of the unknown parts of ourselves—we
reduce the need to hang on so tightly to our assumed roles, as well as
the need to control how others relate to them.

    We come away from our encounter with the ancient mirror with the
means to look more deeply into who we are. This means that we get
to know the lesser in the light of the greater. When the boundedness
of who we take ourselves to be recedes, the possibilities for deeper
self-knowledge and acceptance appear. Seen thus, our inward cowering
is our enlightened self-nature and ancient remorse is also our true face,
no less than bells, stars, and the cries of water birds.

    "If cowering and remorse are enlightenment, I don't like the look of that," you might say. And that's our true face, too. When we get to know the lesser in the light of the greater, we are less inclined to put others out of our heart. The deepening silence where friendship is lost, but love remains, is hard to bear. With the changes that flow from an experience of awakening we learn to more readily include much that we would have formerly found unbearable: malicious gossip being spread about us, humiliation, even betrayal.

In the light of the greater we come to see ourselves for who we are, and over time, the matter of me grows less solid. With this, we grow less preoccupied with our issues—our fear of others, and of ourselves—and can meet whatever comes with a measure of equanimity, if not acceptance.

10. The Mysterious Source: Arriving within the Essential

In nothingness there is a road apart from the dust.
If you don't break the taboo on mentioning the Emperor's name
you will surpass the eloquence of the previous dynasty's
worthies, who cut off tongues.

> It speaks in silence; in speech you hear its silence.
> —Yongjia Xuanjue

WHEN WE INVESTIGATED the previous mode of the Essential within the Contingent, we realized that everything before our eyes—the night sky tall with stars, the raining streets—is intimate with us and is our true face. Now we open to emptiness in more thoroughgoing and subtle ways, particularly with regard to the emptiness of words and language. We have seen how silence can reveal the essential. Now we will investigate how speech, no matter how mundane, can manifest it. This is a radical standpoint; so much so that it presents for many students a new barrier on the koan path. Passing through this barrier, we learn to hear and apprehend the world's chatter—mundane or sublime—as the song of the Way.

We discover, as we go deeper into this matter, that dualistic language with its hooks and snares, even when misused to describe or expound ultimate reality, can in fact evoke the unspoken, inexpressible ultimate itself. A word evokes the universe no less than the morning sun lighting the hill. In the course of investigating this subtle matter of words, we find that even chatter about the Dharma can be a radiant expression of the inexpressible.

Dongshan's subtle account of the mystery of words and language must be brought to bear even on the Five Ranks as they unfold, and upon our understanding of them.

In nothingness there is a road apart from the dust.

It is noteworthy that Dongshan opts for the mundane "road," rather than the more evocative and mysterious "Way." But the sense of Tao is surely implicit. "Dust" is a metaphor for phenomena, the stuff of the world as experienced through the senses. The six dusts are sight, sound, smell, taste, touch, and thought, and their domain is the phenomenal world.

The "road apart from the dust" refers to the path of emptiness. In the case of this mode of arriving within the essential, this is the path where words and language—the very means of communicating and elucidating the Way—are empty. Words and language understood in this way are called "pure," or "flavorless"—meaning that while they retain their conventional sense and meaning, they encode the essential realm, without remainder.

The matter of pure words as "a road apart from the dust" is vividly illustrated in the following exchange, in which the old teacher Zhaozhou makes living dharma out of an earnest seeker's dusty concerns.

> Zhaozhou was sweeping the grounds of his temple. A visitor saw this and asked, "How could a single speck of dust invade this holy ground?"
>
> "Here comes another," Zhaozhou replied.[48]

Implicit in the visitor's question is the idea that there isn't a single speck of dust in the essential realm. Since the six dusts are the six senses, and their domain is the phenomenal world, the visitor implies that there is no sense experience, no thought, or phenomena in emptiness. The visitor may have had in mind the Sixth Ancestor's line, "From the beginning there is nothing at all, so where can dust alight?" But there is more than a speck of dust in the visitor's reverent question itself, loaded as it is with ideas about purity and impurity, and the concept of emptiness. We can rest assured that Zhaozhou knew this, and that his reply—any reply that he might make—would create more dust for his visitor to mull over, and to treasure.

Yet Zhaozhou doesn't renege. His delicate, witty "Here comes another" is, as he suggests, more dust, while "Here comes another" instantly disperses all dusty conceptual notions of purity and impurity, being "pure" or "flavorless" words. This means that "Here comes another" conveys the essential, without remainder, even as the words retain their ordinary sense. The essential has no way to appear but in the guise of the contingencies of dualistic words and language, and it is in no way compromised as it sings its song of "Here comes another."

"Here comes another" cuts off tongues, to borrow Dongshan's phrase. This refers to the way a Zen master's words can "take away the life" of students, or in other words, steal their sense of a limited, separate self, leaving them with nowhere to stand and nothing to say. With the same spirit, I hope that Zhaozhou's "Here comes another" robbed his visitor of attachment to purity and impurity, to holy and sacred.

As we venture into the depths after awakening, we gradually learn to include more and more of our lives. As students undertaking the koan path, we don't hang around cherishing our awakening, or whichever tiny corner of our window is clear. Subsequent work with koans widens the aperture of our experience of the Way, and we awaken to other facets of reality. As a means to this we are encouraged to take up the stories of the ancients as koans, and to see into them. We engage these koans with such resolve that the old teachers live in our words and actions. This is a path to deepening insight and maturity.

As Yongjia Xuanjue says in his "Song of Enlightenment," to be mature in Chan is to be mature in expression. That maturity is, at the very least, knowing when to speak and when to be silent; when to give comfort and when to challenge. It is not just saying the right thing, or making the right noises. It is to speak with the universe implicit in our words or silence, and to have forgotten and embodied all such considerations so completely as to be at ease.

If you don't break the taboo on mentioning the Emperor's name you will surpass the eloquence of the previous dynasty's worthies, who cut off tongues.

Words and the Path of Liberation: Finding Freedom

Let's now take up the issue of words that avowedly "name the emperor," that is to say, words and language employed to discuss enlightenment. Within that type of discourse, we discover that the essential finds a home even in chatter about itself—as the unspoken within the spoken. In effect, we avoid breaking the taboo on talking about enlightenment, even in speaking of it, and understand that even an abstruse explanation of the Way is capable of being, at the very least, the bearer of the essential and eternal. The essence of the foregoing is succinctly expressed in the following koan:

> Mihu had one of his monks go to Yangshan and ask, "Do Chan students today have to experience enlightenment, or not?"
>
> Yangshan answered, "It is not that there is no enlightenment, but it is mostly in the second principle."
>
> The monk returned to Mihu and told him about this. Mihu heartily agreed.[49]

To say that a student's enlightenment is "in the second principle" means that it trades on explanation, or even that it is shaped by accounts of the experiences of others. Yangshan's words display the tone and manner of an experienced teacher, who has seen it all. At the same time—and this is of the utmost importance to note—the words "It is not that there is no enlightenment, but it is mostly in the second principle," with all the doubt and hesitation implicit in them, are themselves the radiant expression of the timeless essential realm. They are—in common with Zhaozhou's "Here comes another"—a phrase that encloses the world.

Words that avowedly name the emperor—that discuss enlightenment itself—can themselves be a subtle and low lit means to avoid breaking the taboo on naming the emperor, who by the way is as apparent as this warm autumn day, the doves cooing in the frangipani, or the low hush of distant traffic.

I will now tell the story of my encounter with Bettina, of the aboriginal tribe of the Ngaanyatjarra and what she taught. For me, her words perfectly exemplify the potency of pure speech. Aside from encoding the deepest sense of this chapter, the themes of her story (particularly that of mutual integration) foreshadow the next mode, Approaching from the Contingent. To my ears, her words were (and still are) a confirmation of the Way.

A friend, Thomas Falke, and I were driving up the Great Central Road to the red center of Australia. I say "road," but it was for the most part nothing more than an unsealed limestone and gravel track. In the heat of late afternoon we were deep in the samadhi of the road, oblivious in its long brown gut, when, suddenly, as we crested a hill, two bodies appeared, sprawled across the warm road. Thomas braked sharply and one of the figures, now visible as an aboriginal man in his middle years staggered up just inches from the bumper bar of our four-wheel-drive SUV, waving his arms. A girl lay there in the road for a while, as if dead, then swayed up, hair covering her face—whining, whimpering.

Too dry to speak, he whispered, "Got to get back to Warburton," but with our Mitsubishi Pajero packed to the gills we couldn't fit them in. Suddenly, she was gone from view. Immediately the left rear door was ripped open and Thomas's tools clattered on the road as she tried to claw her way up on top of our suitcases, while her companion dragged her off, howling and whimpering rhythmically from behind the snarled mats of her hair. I felt the guilty weight of being a white Pajero tourist (why not stow our suitcases behind a rock, and retrieve them later?). We gave them Thomas's fresh pure water, and then again, and then again, and again. We asked if we could take a message for them to Warburton. At that moment a white 4WD came over the hill and the driver agreed to take the man to Warburton.

The girl we now know as Bettina squeezes on top of Thomas's gleaming suitcase, and after praising her one and only ever loving father, extolling him as a crusader and a lawyer in a hoarse cracked voice, then damning her mother as nothing but a trouble maker (all this by way of introduction), she's torrential.

Gulping down water, eyes too bright for bearing, she asked us, "You! Where you from? Australia? Well, you okay. I teach you words. Okay?" She points to her lips, and says in Ngaanyatjarra, "*Muni,*" and spells it for me "M-U-N-I." "*Muni,*" I repeat. "*Yuwa!*" (Yes!) she shouts.

Then *kuru* (eye), *pina* (ear), *mulya* (nose), *tjarlinypa* (tongue), *yarangu* (body), *kapi* (water), and *yilkari* (sky). Her eyes huge and wet, she shouts, "*Yuwa!*" each time I get it right.

She gulps down more water. She's unstoppable. She'll teach us all her words before we reach Warburton.

"My dreaming is water-snake, blue water-snake. He lives inside me. He jumped up so happy when I saw your black *toyoda.*

"Stop! Back! Back!" she shouts. She rolls out of her air-conditioned nest, and leads us barefoot over prickles and hot granite to her grandmother's waterhole. She scoops up the shining water, drinks it.

And down the biscuit-colored oblivious track—*mutuka* (car), *yiwarra* (road), *tawumpa* (town).

"*Yuwa! Yuwa! Yuwa!*"

She guides us into Warburton's bare State Housing, the sky like a fresh graze. She stepped into the dusk, shut the left rear door firmly behind her.

"Goodbye," we called after her.

No response. She walked silently toward a big black woman in a floral dress hanging out washing, staring back at her, silent, unrecognizing.

Bettina opened the Way for me with her "Yuwa!" Across the tense lines of racial division something shifted in me, thanks to her great and lively generosity. I feel grateful, but something beyond gratitude too. Partly, this is a sense of an enduring connection with her and her country. I have been back there and feel an irresistible call to return again.

Yamada Koun, commenting on the fourth stage of the Cycle of Merit—Merit in Common—called it "the degree of freely saving others." As for me, in relation to my experience of Bettina's words, it was more like being saved. *Yuwa*: beyond "yes" and beyond "no."

"*Yuwa*!"

When we awaken to the emptiness of words and language (the theme of this mode of Arriving within the Essential), we are released from the restrictive attitudes and from the stories that close us down. In particular, we are released from the stranglehold of literalism. Words mean, but they can also go beyond meaning to encode the universe.

We conventionally regard words and language as bearers of dualistic baggage. Now, however, even that baggage shines. Conceptual talk about the Way is like this, too. When we have seen deeply into the nature of words, statements about the Way, such as the captions of the Five Ranks, are no longer solely scripts that choreograph our changing relationship with the whole but are the dance itself. Formulations such as "Zen is a special transmission outside the sutras, directly pointing to the heart-mind of humanity—no words, no letters" have become a kind of credo among contemporary Zen students. Such credos dissolve as we realize that words and letters may be the heart-mind itself. And the sutras and their commentaries, too, may be the special transmission. Thus, what has been considered an expedient guide to the Way may be nonetheless the Way itself.

When we awaken to this, we transcend learning and the acquisition of knowledge, without devaluing them in the least. When we have awakened to the true nature of words and language, studying the sutras is like coming home to find an old friend waiting. In fact it is even more intimate than that. When we awaken to the purity of words, we find that words themselves can be a path to liberation. Realizing this, we are no longer at the mercy of slander, or even of our own vicious self-talk. We know what it is to be insulted, and how it rankles. If an earworm gives us no rest—that stupid tune returning over and over day and night—the spreading pain of an insult can be a heartworm.

Insight into the profound nature of words delivers us freedom from abuse. This doesn't mean that we won't feel the pain of abuse; rather, what is hurtful is carried differently, if at all. When we open to insult or malicious gossip as *just those words*, we come to experience abusive words as the timeless void of our true nature, without remainder. To practice thus is to walk the path of liberation.

As we deepen in the mystery, our limited preoccupations are put ruthlessly into perspective—as a vanishing point. As we take responsibility for them, our personal dramas seem less solid, and we are less fixated on them. There's less tendency to sweat the small, or to make an enduring saga out of our pain. These represent the fruits of our deepening experience of the empty Way.

Our exploration of this mode has been primarily concerned with the role of words in presenting the essential, or ultimate truth. We examined the importance of silence, and of pure words, in this enterprise. We saw that, on one hand, words are inadequate to convey the ultimate, while on the other, we realized that the ultimate manifests as words and language, no less so than it does as the dark groves of trees reflected in the stream, or the sunlight glancing off its ripples. On this basis, even expedient teachings that set out the Way, such as the Four Noble Truths, can, at the same time, be its radiant presentation.

Finally, we can bring these insights to bear on the enterprise of the Five Ranks generally, and the five modes of the essential and the contingent, in particular. These modes represent a pure presentation of the Way. I believe that this was not merely a default position, whereby any words can purely manifest the Way, but was Dongshan's deliberate strategy. Like this, the timeless essential reveals itself as the dialectic and poetry of the five modes of the essential and the contingent. At the same time the arduous path inferred from them unfolds in time.

11. Lotus in the Midst of Fire: Approaching from the Contingent

No need to dodge when blades are crossed.
The skillful one is like a lotus in the midst of fire.
Seemingly, you yourself possess the aspiration to soar to the
heavens.

> Perhaps we are here in order to say: house, bridge, foun-
> tain, gate, pitcher, fruit-tree, window—at most: column,
> tower. . . . But to say them, you must understand, oh to
> say them more intensely than the Things themselves ever
> dreamed of existing.
> —Rainer Maria Rilke

*A NOTE ON THE VARIANT TITLES FOR THIS MODE

Historically, there have been two competing titles for the fourth mode
of the Cycle of the Essential and the Contingent: "Approaching from
the Contingent" and "Approaching Concurrence." The former stresses
the importance of reentering the realm of differentiation and discrimination after an experience of emptiness. The latter title, "Approaching
Concurrence"—or "Arrival at Mutual Integration" (as Hakuin reput-
edly expressed it)—conveys a more dynamic treatment of this mode.
The "mutual integration" referred to is in relation to the opposites
of light and darkness, which represent the contingent and essential,
respectively.[50]

Both titles have their merits, and opinion is divided as to which should
represent this mode. Early on, I will focus primarily on exploring this

mode from the perspective of Approaching from the Contingent. Later
in this chapter, I will focus on the perspective of the mutual integration
of the essential and the contingent under the rubric of Approaching
Concurrence. More than elsewhere in our investigations of the Cycle of
the Essential and the Contingent, we will be concerned with the themes
of becoming and process: that is to say, traveling the bodhisattva way
of meditating, and awakening ourselves and others in the midst of
passion and suffering.

Approaching from the Contingent

WHEREAS the preceding mode, Arriving within Essential, characterized awakening to emptiness, Approaching from the
Contingent presents enlightenment emerging from particularity. The
following lines from Don Paterson's poem "Phantom" aptly express
this point in our journey:

> We are ourselves the void in contemplation.
> We are its only nerve and hand and eye.[51]

"The void in contemplation" expresses the spirit of the preceding mode
of Arriving within the Essential, while being "its only nerve and hand
and eye" is the theme of the journey undertaken in this mode. These
two positions, though we deal with them independently here and in
the preceding chapter, are in fact mutually dependent. Although we are
presently focused on the contingent, the essential is everywhere and at
all times implicit.

Approaching from the Contingent, the world appears in its uniqueness, beyond our ideas of it. Irises are purple, the tarpaulin bright blue,
and the dishes are encrusted with fat. You and I—short or tall, fat or
thin, with our lopsided features and habits—are uniquely and inimitably who we are. We have always known this, but now we experience
it as the first morning of the world.

MOVING ON FROM AN EXPERIENCE OF THE VOID

We need to move on from an experience of the void, for it can be so compellingly marvelous that we end up clinging to it. We must emerge from the featureless dark. There's no way that we can live there, although I've met earnest seekers who are still regaling anyone who will listen with stories about their experience, twenty years on—hopelessly circling the inexplicable. Even if they are genuine, such experiences coagulate immediately into our ideas about them, so that we can remain unknowingly entrapped in our rehashing of them—unavailable to others, unavailable for life. If we hoard our experience of emptiness, like a miser his gold, what is insubstantial as a dream ossifies into our ideas about it, and we end by living our life at a deep remove.

The following exchange between two old masters is concerned with just this moving on from an experience of emptiness, conveyed as coming out of darkness into daylight:

> Zhaozhou asked Touzi Datong (819–914), "If a person experiences the great death, how will you treat them?"
> Touzi said, "I don't permit wandering about in darkness. Come back in the daylight!"[52]

After we have died to our limited self and its concerns, we must return to life. We must, as Touzi puts it, come back in the daylight. "Daylight" indicates the realm of differentiation and discrimination: the wall is vertical, the floor horizontal; rainwater is fresh, the ocean salty; the sun goes down, the stars come out. After an experience of emptiness, these particulars surface movingly from what feels like a dream.

Although you have realized that you are none other than those you meet (and those you'll never meet), you continue to address your friends by their names and are named in return. What is your name? Where were you born? Who were your parents? These questions elicit your singularity, anybody's singularity. And none of this is at odds with your most intimate experience of the other as you; rather it is a perfect expression of it. Although we are stressing the importance of the daylight realm of particularity, it is important to note that our experience of emptiness continues to inform our activity. We can't turn back to look into the timeless source—it doesn't permit that—yet it animates our standing up, and our lying down, even as it is none other than them.

Beyond our faintest ideas of emptiness, we are sky, bird's wing, rain, and each of them is us too. We are immediately and challengingly those who despise us, and no doubt to their dismay, they are us. Such mutuality recalls Hakuin's caption for this mode, Arrival at Mutual Integration. We can't consciously bring about this integration. It only becomes possible with our continued meditation, and full-hearted engagement with life and its challenges. That is the integrity of the Way.

With deepening experience of Approaching from the Contingent, we acquire or refine discriminating wisdom. As we deepen in this mode we see people increasingly for who and what they are. We recognize ability in them and can respond to it. We aren't threatened by them and can give them the space to come into their own. When our energies aren't so tied up with protecting ourselves, we get interested in understanding people and can respond to their needs more readily, developing the freedom to change in order to help them. Such discriminating wisdom is different from opposing "this" to "that" in order to protect ourselves. When we confront the world and its constituents as separate and unique, this isn't an abject reversion to a deluded factionalism, rather it is the ground of compassion, which gets traction from our being differentiated from others. The fact is that if we are indistinguishable from those we would help, that may be absolute empathy, but it's of no earthly use.

Approaching Concurrence

From this point on we will explore aspects of the alternative title for this mode: Approaching Concurrence. These aspects are concerned with the integration of the essential and the contingent, as conveyed by the imagery of the integration of dark and light. This integration is important for us if we are to become true persons of the Way, which is to say bodhisattvas enlightening ourselves and others amid the fires and confusion of our own suffering, and that of the suffering world.

No need to dodge when blades are crossed.

Crossed swords represent the opposition of darkness and light, which correspond to the essential and the contingent, respectively. Given that advance or retreat are equally impossible, we stay put and open to our life where we are. That is the sense of "not dodging." Staying put, we live mutual integration, not by trying to unite essential and contingent (as if we could do this by force of will), but by engaging circumstances as they present themselves. Thus, we deal with the divorce papers and the terms of endearment. Forgetting emptiness, we face up to hard-nosed particularity and oppositional circumstance, treating them as all there is. Yet, although we avoid taking refuge in emptiness, we nonetheless deepen and mature our experience of emptiness by facing up to the challenges we encounter.

The image of crossed swords is unlikely to have much currency these days, but it transposes readily into the circumstances of our lives and to our relation to reality at large. The central relationships of our lives, for example, are fine sources of conflict and challenge that can be a means to self-understanding. Our authority and pretensions with regard to our children are continually challenged, and there is no time to sulk when our authority and pretensions are subverted, because the next challenge is surely already upon us. In such ways we get swiftly moved on from self-preoccupation. It's hard to ask more from a spiritual path.

The image of the crossed swords may also symbolize a dilemma: we encounter the crumbling edges of our life and practice, where we sense that whatever we've realized can't light up the darkness and grief of estrangement, or magically resolve our inability to forgive. We must respond by allowing this dilemma, filled with painful confusion and uncertainty, to be just what it is. This is the crux of the matter of not dodging when swords are crossed.

When we are at odds with our environment, we don't need to dodge, which is to say that we needn't look elsewhere for awakening. The following exchange between Dongshan and a student conveys this aptly:

> A monk asked Dongshan, "When cold and heat visit us, how do we avoid them?"
>
> Dongshan replied, "Why not go where there is neither cold nor heat?"
>
> "Where is that place where there is neither cold nor heat?" asked the monk.
>
> Dongshan replied, "When it is hot let the heat kill you; when it is cold let the cold kill you."[53]

The conditions at Dongshan's monastery were known to be tough: blazing hot in summer, freezing cold in winter. So we can empathize with the monk's predicament, while acknowledging that his question, in its relation to the crossed swords, is clearly concerned with dodging. Dongshan's reply points the monk precisely to the place where all contraries evaporate. Maybe the monk imagines that place to be spring in some fortunate location, or a monastery without seasonal extremes. However, the deeper sense of his question is, "Show me how to realize emptiness in order that I can find release from suffering and discomfort."

Dongshan sets the monk right. We don't need to go anywhere. We—just as we are, right where we are—should let heat kill off our ideas about it; let there be nothing but heat. Then the entirety of things sweats and complains.

This is not masochistic—don't cultivate feeling cold! When you are cold, pull on a pullover. When you are hot, turn on the fan. But stop tinkering with those conditions in your mind. Stop bothering the heat! Allow it to be. Just heat all through. And depending on your circumstances: grief all through, rage all through, fear all through.

The essential has no other way to be than heat, cold, or sadness. Thus, unknowingly, we integrate our experience of emptiness into our life. We may not notice this happening, but often our family and friends do, for we are less judgmental and more available. We listen better, and where, previously, we might have come down hard, now we leave a space of acceptance where others feel comfortable, and even thrive.

The skillful one is like a lotus in the midst of fire.

The expression "lotus in the midst of fire" refers to the rarity or impossibility of an occurrence. The Vimalakirti Sutra speaks of the rarity of continuing one's meditation, and indeed awakening, in the midst of desires; nevertheless, for the bodhisattva this is possible. The relevant lines from the sutra are:

> Like that thing most rare, a lotus
> Blossoming in a scorching fire,
> He meditates amidst desires,
> Which also is a thing most rare. [54]

The blossoming lotus is a well-known symbol for getting enlightened and enlightening others. Fire is a metaphor for the suffering world at large. The blossoming of a lotus in the midst of fire, therefore, evokes the image of a bodhisattva on his or her path, capable of remaining steady in the face of oppositional circumstances and of awakening themselves and others in the midst of passion and suffering.

The lotus in the midst of fire is also a fine representation of the mutual integration of darkness and light, corresponding to the mutual integration of the essential and the contingent. This process of integration is at the core of Approaching Concurrence. Finally, the image of the lotus in the midst of fire anticipates the culminating image of the I Ching hexagram Li—the illumination hexagram, with its intertwined fire and darkness. We are considering the dynamic process of integrating the essential and the contingent through our engagement with the suffering world, which is to say enlightening others and ourselves on the Way of difficulty.

There is no place where we are safe from the unanswerable pain of the world. It breaks in everywhere. Even if we flee from suffering, barricading ourselves in, we find that we're not high and dry at all, and we suffer needlessly through our avoidance. Holding back is suffering. The place of avoidance is fraught and lonely. But whether we hide, or whether we front up, the suffering world persists. We can never eliminate it. It is better to stay put, for then at least we may be able to contribute through our presence—and actions, if they are intelligent.

The suffering of the world presses so strongly, because at the deepest level it is not just our business, it is also our matter. The face of suffering is also our own face. When we move to ease the pain of another, we lose our self-protection in doing what we can't ignore, and everything and everyone breathes a little deeper.

What is nearest and dearest to us can be the hardest to deal with. Fatigue and disinclination can make the subtleties of communication feel as difficult as saving Tibet. We may be unable to save Tibet, but at least we can listen to our partners' recital of his or her woes of today. We all vary in our capacity to help others, but whether we join Amnesty International or help our neighbor get her DVD player to work, we give hands to our awakening when we make an effort on others' behalf.

We don't deepen our enlightenment by tending emptiness but rather by engaging with our life: testing our experience of the timeless essential through falling in love, pursuing a long conversation in an everchanging home, and through lulls in affection, as well as through grief and joy.

MUTUAL INTEGRATION AND KARMIC TENDENCIES: ENVY

The practice of compassion extends to the way in which we bear with even our own intractable and obnoxious traits. When we learn to include, over time, karmic tendencies that we would dearly love to lose, we allow the possibility that even they can become the agents of our awakening at deeper levels. With this in mind I'd like to explore the mental habit or karmic tendency of envy to show how even it might enable the mutual integration of the essential and the contingent. I feel that it will be particularly helpful to consider envy in this role, because it is so seldom addressed in Zen, probably because it is so deeply nestled in shame.

For our purposes, I imagine the life of Baizhang's head monk Hua Linjue following his losing encounter with Guishan Lingyou (771–853). Coming out second best is a typical scenario for experiencing envy, and we rightly fear its invasion. It can paralyze our life and make us prey to sickening fantasies. In its pathological form we would willingly derail and subvert our own life, if only we could thwart the other's success. Envy makes us feel shameful, absurd, grotesque, and ridiculous.

In an age in which we are constantly measuring ourselves against others, it seems particularly pertinent to examine the way in which even an emotion as poisonous and unrelenting as envy can be worked with to yield profound awakening.

> Baizhang Huaihai (720–814) wanted to choose a founding teacher for a new monastery. He invited all his monks to make a presentation, and told them that the outstanding one would get the job.
>
> When the monks had assembled, Baizhang took a water bottle and set it on the floor, issuing this challenge: "You cannot call it a water bottle. What will you call it?"
>
> Hua Linjue, the Head Monk, said, "It can't be called a wooden clog."
>
> Baizhang then asked the monastery cook, Guishan, his opinion.
>
> Guishan kicked over the water bottle, and walked out.
>
> Baizhang laughed and said, "The Head Monk loses!"
>
> Guishan was made head teacher at the new monastery.[55]

If you were the Head Monk, how would you respond to the teacher's "The Head Monk loses?" Could you clap your hands and call out, "Congratulations!" We might smile bravely, but would your heart be smiling?

I think I'd have had some difficulty with this one, and I suspect Hua may have had too. Let's suppose he felt envious of Guishan and that he took offence at Baizhang's words and laughter. The whole matter set fire to his complacency and seared his heart. His fall into envy, and the resulting shame and humiliation, were made even worse for him because Baizhang had once suggested that Hua might be the founding teacher at Mt. Gui. Now he was feeling abandoned and betrayed, and because he was a sincere student, he felt ashamed at the invasion of such primitive infantile feelings.

As Head Monk, Hua had become attached to the eros of power: to being close to his teacher, and to being looked up to by the other monks. Consequently, he experienced his feelings of envy as a fall from grace. Because he would have rather died than taken the brunt of such envy and self-hatred, he retired to the mountains, far from the solicitations and knowing smiles of the junior monks, and safe from Baizhang's penetrating questions concerning how he felt about Guishan's appointment. Anything but that!

Hua built his hermitage deep in the mountains. The hard physical labor of building in extremes of heat and cold provided a measure of respite from his envy and resentment. But they were not gone. They returned, especially in his meditations, and because he was high-minded, he struggled with them, thinking, "I should be better than this. I should be beyond this." This doubled his agony.

A wandering monk brought him news that Guishan was having trouble establishing the new monastery at Mt. Gui. Even after some years, the only inhabitants there were Guishan and the monkeys. Yet even news of Guishan's difficulties did nothing to ease the envy Hua felt. Even the complete abandonment of the Mt. Gui project wouldn't have done that.

Sitting late one night trying to practice sympathetic joy for Guishan with Baizhang's words circling in his mind, Hua suddenly heard the words "The Head Monk loses" as if for the first time. They were no longer directed at him, circumscribing his life as abject and infantile. They were just "The Head Monk loses," like a wave crashing on the beach, or the clouds silvered by moonlight just visible through the back window of his hermitage.

Hua wept and bowed in the direction of Baizhang's monastery. Then, in the immensity of his relief, he bowed in the direction of Mt. Gui.

Big Void and Little Void

Opening like that in the midst of his struggle deeply transformed Hua's life. Legend has it that he had taken to feeding two abandoned tiger cubs. He would leave meat for them, which they would hungrily seize, then retreat back into the wilderness of rock and pine. Hua hadn't been able to tame them.

Now they came to him readily and took food from his hands, and sitting regally behind his hermitage, they guarded him against other marauding beasts. Hua felt that his companionship with them was somehow linked to his experience that memorable night when he truly experienced Baizhang's words, so he named them Big Void and Little Void. As the years passed, Hua enjoyed his life as a hermit on the trackless secluded mountain. His reputation grew, and many people came to pay respects and to receive his teachings.

Robert Aitken tells a story about Hua and his tigers, to illustrate the hermit's mature style:

> One day a high official called upon Hua and remarked, "It must be very inconvenient to live by yourself in this way without an attendant."
>
> Hua said, "Not at all, for I have two attendants." Turning his head, he called out, "Big Void! Little Void!"
>
> In response to his call, two tigers appeared from the back of the hermitage, roaring fiercely. The high official was frightened out of his wits.
>
> Hua spoke to the tigers saying, "This is an important guest. Be quiet and courteous." The two tigers crouched at his feet and were as gentle as kittens.[56]

Having done the hard work of bearing with what is hardest to bear, we emerge blinking in the sunlight and find that the tigers come at our bidding and enjoy our company. They get all the jokes and know exactly what to do to make a terrified politician feel completely at home.

Each time we touch envy, or its underlying sorrow and barrenness, we encourage release. With release we can weep a while, and breathe a little deeper. In time we grow less preoccupied with ourselves, and our passions—the prevailing moods of the soul—roll through like the seasons.

This is the dawn at the end of a long and arduous journey with difficult emotions, noticing them, opening to them, and including them. It's also the fruit of experiencing emptiness. Such work, whether with envy or any other karmic tendency, enables the mutual integration of darkness and light, understood here as the mutual integration of the essential and the contingent.

Sometimes our hearts are open, and sometimes, with the best will in the world, they remain clenched tightly shut. We are all suffering bodies on the long path to liberation. We see into the vastness of our original nature through the haze of our pain and our love; our pain and our love are the moon by which we see. What is timeless finds its board and lodging in the stumbling speech of our love and suffering. The work of mutual integration continues as long as we live.

Seemingly, you yourself possess the aspiration to soar to the heavens.

We may seem to "possess the aspiration to soar to the heavens," which means to awaken to the essential and eternal. However, as we have seen, the path to awakening lies in our engagement with the mundane world, in our doing the hard yards in terms of work, relationship, and family. We must grow our lives downward into the world—surely that way heaven.

Dongshan is cautious in his estimation of our aspiration and of our ability to awaken in the midst of our own demons and the snares of the world. As noted in our earlier account of this mode, praise can drain away aspiration. In the end, this matter is beyond the encouragement or discouragement of others. The mutual integration of the essential and contingent, the embodiment of our awakening in the midst of the challenges that we face daily, is our own responsibility. It comes down to us. It's us.

12. The Return: Arriving at Concurrence

Who would presume to join their voice with someone
who has surpassed "there is" and "there is not"?
Everyone longs to leave the mundane stream, yet finally you
   return to sit in the charcoal heap.

> Men must endure
> Their going hence, even as their coming hither:
> Ripeness is all.
> —Shakespeare, *King Lear*

WHEN WE ARRIVE at concurrence, all that we have regarded as the essential and the contingent are found to be none other than each other. The polarities of the earlier modes are annulled, and the algebra of the spirit disappears without remainder into our lives lived as the Way. What is this? As the sun sinks below the horizon, stars appear in their ancient ordering. Intricate streams seek the river, goose-bumped with rain. Now we feel fatigue, now uplift; now we draw breath and ease our backs when tired.

Having awakened, having learned the matter of words that are no-words, and having embodied the teachings and our insights, we now have to forget the whole shebang and make our idiosyncratic way through this life of cause and effect. We don't strive to be extraordinary, for that would be to raise a ghost. When we are thoroughly ordinary, or even less than ordinary, we are more available to others. We deal freely and generously with people as they present themselves. We laugh with them, we grieve with them; we enlighten and are enlightened by them. Enlightenment is a two-way street without end. There is an untrammelled quality to it all.

Regarding concurrence, Caoshan gave this formal account in his "Commentary on the Five Positions of Ruler and Minister," which I love:

> The concurrent responds silently to myriad conditions. It does not fall into affirming various existences. It is not stained, not pure, not essential, not contingent.
>
> Therefore, we call it the empty mysterious great way; the genuine teaching of nonattachment. From earliest times, eminent masters have considered this position to be the most mysterious and profound.[57]

After a long struggle with the modes, concurrence feels like grace. It is completely present as we respond to the demands of family and colleagues. The genuine teaching of nonattachment manifests as our love and work. The empty mysterious great Way finds a home in our vulnerability, and brokenness, no less so than it does in our admirable strengths and abilities.

Caoshan keeps his distance, yet his words boil down to our beating hearts and the feeling of our feet on the ground. When he writes that the concurrent "does not fall into affirming various existences," he means that it isn't reducible to any of the Buddhist realms. Neither is it reducible to categories like existence and nonexistence. The concurrent, being "not stained, not pure, not essential, not contingent," is us—beyond being and nonbeing, tying our shoelaces, straightening up, and heading out for our morning appointments.

Arriving at Concurrence evokes an end game with no ending. What looks and sounds like an ending is folded back into the fire of our present experience. What sounds like a culmination has through it all had at its core a need for us to sustain our practice and to engage with life.

Concurrence: The Identity of Essential and Contingent

Arriving at Concurrence, we realize that the essential and contingent are not other than each other, and we embody that matter in even our most ordinary activity. Even so, the concurrence of essential and contingent, without a hair's breadth between them, has been implicit in each step of our journey up to this point.

Although concurrence appears last in Dongshan's series, it is actually fundamental to each of the modes, including itself. While each mode, even as it presents enlightenment, is also an aspect or facet of what we are calling "Concurrence," concurrence can also be understood as "the all-at-onceness of the five modes," for we read in Dongshan's "Song of the Precious Mirror Samadhi":

> In the six lines of the doubled Li hexagram,
> essential and contingent mutually correspond.
> Ranked in pairs they yield three; transformed, they make five.

Dongshan positions Li, the thirtieth hexagram of the I Ching, in all its dark radiance at the heart of his poem, and configures the five modes within it. The Li hexagram's imagery of intertwined fire and darkness suggests the transformational place of concurrence and prefigures the charcoal heap, which we encounter in the verse for this final mode. The Li hexagram can be understood both as the source of the five positions of the essential and the contingent and as the destination at which our journey through them arrives, for Li, or Concurrence, is the final mode. Thus, using the Li hexagram to present the simultaneity of the five modes is a vivid way of evoking concurrence.

So concurrence represents the totality, source, and destination of the five modes of the essential and the contingent. Concurrence is an image for the achieved integration of light and darkness—that is, of the contingent and the essential. Whereas in the previous mode Dongshan presented the mutual integration of the contingent and the essential primarily in terms of process, he now gives us an idealized image of their integration, in which opposites are reconciled and held. Here the five modes of the essential and the contingent are revealed as being concurrent, interdependent, and integrated. This image invokes the awakening of the Buddha, prior to consideration of any of its aspects.

Let's now turn to Dongshan's verse on concurrence, to explore it in detail, line-by-line.

Who would presume to join their voice with someone who has surpassed "there is" and "there is not"?

When we cling to "there is," or what we can provisionally call "existence," we fabricate a controlling self at the center of the labyrinth of our thoughts and feelings, and we spend our lifetime protecting it. We compare ourselves with others and find that we are lacking or superior. This can be a touchy business, and even the lightest criticism can strike home.

When we cling to "there is not," or what we provisionally call "nonexistence," we are trying to assuage our suffering by elevating a momentary insight into a broad lit paradise. Attached to such purity, and immunized against surprise, we miss out on the humorous pitfalls of engagement with tea ladies and cheeky kids. Both "there is" and "there is not," taken alone, are delusory, and we suffer when we attach to either of them exclusively.

The middle way, on the other hand, is not about finding averages or means, or somehow getting the balance of existence and nonexistence right. Instead, Dongshan challenges us to step beyond the polarities of existence and nonexistence—and implicitly beyond the contingent and the essential—to harmonize with the song of the Way. It's good to take Dongshan's question personally. It's good to play.

Everyone longs to leave the mundane stream . . .

In Buddhist teachings, the mundane stream traditionally corresponds with change and impermanence. More precisely, it is the stream of birth and death where, fed by ignorance and craving, we fabricate the self and become entangled in its dramas.

We long to leave the mundane stream because we suffer there. Our longing to escape the stream of birth and death is the deep impulse that underlies our seeking the Way. We want what is changeless and pure—really an indefinite extension of our best moments—rather than the vicissitudes of our lives. We long to experience that still point at the heart of everything changing.

When we enter the Way, we hope to escape sorrow and pain. Although awakening might shift our existential angst, we still experience pain and grief in their full intensity, and our exploration of concurrence must take this into account. In this respect, the story of Satsujo grieving her granddaughter is exemplary:

> Satsujo had been a student of Hakuin's. When she was old her granddaughter died, and Satsujo was distraught with grief. An old man from the neighborhood (most likely a priest) told her off.
>
> "Why are you wailing so much? If people hear this they'll all ask why this old lady, who was once a student of Hakuin's and is supposedly enlightened, is mourning her granddaughter so much."
>
> Satsujo glared at her neighbor and scolded him, "You bald-headed fool, what do you know? My tears and weeping are better for my granddaughter than your incense, flowers, and lamps."[58]

Satsujo's granddaughter is in her heart and tears. That's true mourning. Nothing else is needed; certainly not the tools of priestcraft. Satsujo's pain and tears are the presence of the child she loved.

. . . yet finally you return to sit in the charcoal heap.

The image of the charcoal heap recalls the previous mode's lotus in the midst of fire. We awakened others and ourselves in the blazing midst of the world's (and our own) suffering. There we aspired to ascend the heavens. Here we emerge into our most ordinary lives, surely changed, and—because our journey is embodied and forgotten—with little sense of how we reached this place, or how we came to be thus.

"Returning" carries the sense of coming home, and "coming home" carries the sense of accepting life as we find it. "Returning to sit in the charcoal heap" has many meanings, but one that is certainly not in play is that of "giving up on working for change in the world." Sometimes Buddhist practices of acceptance and equanimity might seem to encourage this, but here "return" surely means that, freed from preoccupation with ourselves, we can now invest our love and energy into encouraging others and into changing our world for the better. Whatever else the charcoal heap may represent, here it definitely represents a place of work, where we ought to be prepared to get dirty.

For me, "returning" or "coming home to the charcoal heap" also means that we allow our woundedness, and thereby minimize unnecessary suffering for others and ourselves; and also that we recognize and allow our darkness, without letting it loose on those around us. We can't sustain luminosity through all this, and if we try to, we're not really in our lives; we end up lacking laughter, and make others uneasy.

Glenn Wallis jokes that the charcoal heap reflects the miraculous mishap that we are carbon-based life forms, as well as the indiscriminate circumstances in which we find ourselves. In that regard, today's cold radiant West Australian midwinter full of bird song is some charcoal heap! "Returning to the charcoal heap" especially means that we continue to practice through it all, enduring setbacks and disappointments without ostentation.

The following lines, which conclude Dongshan's "Song of the Precious Mirror Samadhi," perfectly express for me the spirit of returning to the charcoal heap:

> Conceal your practice, function in secret,
> seem for all the world like a fool or an idiot—
> if you could only continue, it would be called
> the host within the host.

They convey the sense that, even with the realization of concurrence, practice continues indefinitely. With this, we begin to feel that we know less and less, partly because age shows us how little we actually do know, but also because we begin to let go of the naive surety of "self." We don't know the dark abyss before we were born; we don't know the dark immensity after we die. We may have beliefs about these, but we don't know. We don't know what will happen, yet we continue to plan. And it takes courage to imagine and plan for an unimaginable future, to sink pylons for an imaginary bridge in airy nothingness.

Our not-knowing also deepens as we become intimate with the essential and eternal. In a way there is less of us, in terms of a separate self, and so less of us to know. The limit case for this kind of not-knowing can be found in the verse for the corresponding stage of the Cycle of Merit:

> In the vastness of the empty kalpa there is no one
> who knows.

When we grow intimate with those "unknowing" timeless depths, we are acknowledged in our timeless life as "the host within the host," as Dongshan provisionally names that state. We might also refer to this state as "the emptiness of emptiness."

The Emptiness of Emptiness

Concurrence upholds the entwined essential and contingent of the Five Ranks, with their pure words, and the emptiness of their positions. The point here is that even concurrence is empty, and we can understand that the enterprise of the five modes is, in fact, "the emptiness of emptiness."

I asked Ian Sweetman, who coteaches with me in the Zen Group of Western Australia, "What is the emptiness of emptiness?"

"The red flower in the vase," he replied.

Emptiness is itself emptied out, and we are confirmed in our lives of grief and love: evanescent, but mysteriously changed by all that we have undergone. Like that, the emptiness of emptiness finds its true expression and its home. Dogen conveys this sense of home in his lines on the precept of not indulging in anger. In these profound words, which may well have been inspired by the Five Ranks, "empty" corresponds to "the essential" and "real" to "the contingent."

> Not advancing, not retreating, not empty,
> not real; there is an ocean of bright clouds:
> there is an ocean of solemn clouds.[59]

Thus is our passionate life, experienced, seen into, and seen through— all preoccupations and concepts burned away—with eyes of emptiness. That gaze takes in our life with its suffering and delight, without fuss or concern. Whose providence is this long beautiful evening? Whose providence is this year of failed enterprises? Whose providence is this great earth, which rolls through space with its living and its dead, its marriages and burials? We take on the mystery of that. We live out, and die into, the mystery of that.

With Concurrence we return (and have always been returning) to find that the glory is not elsewhere. Each day offers itself, unconcerned that we're so little there for it. Now we open our eyes and find that those parts of our being that we set aside for the quest, and which we have been blind to, are there with us. Perhaps we recognize our neediness, and how much we want to love and be loved. This clinging is no impediment, and it can't be set aside. Thus, our fear and anger, our lust, greed, and generosity can be included.

Now our heart is laid open for the bed and board of the world, which gathers as our friends and opponents, as our children and partners, those we have loved, those we have hurt—all of us limited, tender, and mortal. We realize that this offer of a life with its opportunities for love has been a miracle that we often squander. Yet even our remorse and disappointment can be a light by which we see.

THE CYCLE OF MERIT

13. An Overview of the Cycle of Merit

D ONGSHAN'S TITLE for the second cycle, *Wuwei gongxun*, means "The Five Positions of Merit and Honors." However, because the positions are so clearly progressive, and imply an unfolding over time, in what follows I will refer to them as "stages."

*A NOTE ON THE TERM "MERIT"

Merit suggests "quality," "worthiness," and "excellence" and carries the sense of "the fruit of labor" or "service." It also suggests "ability," "achievement," or "accomplishment." I have settled for "merit," rather than "merit and honors," because it feels to me that "honors" is, at least in some measure, implicit in "merit." Merit also conveys an ethical aspect, as well as a sense of accomplishment. In this regard, it is no accident that "Merit" is the title for the third stage, that of personal awakening.[60]

The five stages of merit, as they are set out in the captions to the verses, are:

1. Orientation
2. Service
3. Merit
4. Merit in Common
5. Merit upon Merit

Each caption marks a stage on our journey to maturity on the bodhisattva path. Importantly, in the Cycle of Merit, each stage—including the first two, which apparently precede awakening—is an expression of enlightened mind, as well as presenting a step toward it. This cycle presents five images of the unfolding Way and suggests a training path on which we practice, deepen, and mature.

As noted above, the stages of the Cycle of Merit, unfolding over time, are cumulative. Each stage represents a level of maturation that serves as a basis for the next one. As long as we continue to practice, the earlier stages are not lost but remain like the growth rings of an ancient tree. From this perspective, there is no shortcut to maturity.

Overture to the Cycle of Merit

In Dongshan's Record, a dialogue between Dongshan and a monk introduces the Cycle of Merit.[61] The main thrust of this introductory dialogue is to show that the Cycle of Merit—the stages of the path of training and maturation, their expedient means, and the accumulated authority conveyed by them—are completely empty. Thus considered, the path of merit is no-path. The very expression of the stages of the Way, as conveyed by the captions and verses, is, in the same breath, to be understood as purely empty. As we shall see, this encourages us to regard the Cycle of Merit not simply as the steps and stages of a path to enlightenment and beyond, such as we might regard the Ox-Herding Cycle. In its nonprogressive aspect, the Cycle of Merit resembles the first cycle of the essential and the contingent, and it is no accident that Dongshan uses the term "positions" to delineate the particular "moments" or "events" in each cycle. In the Cycle of Merit, however, we can say that the progressive aspect can be more readily, and correctly, inferred.

The dialogue below is rather abstract, but it is important for establishing the Cycle of Merit in the dimension of the essential and the eternal. It accomplishes this by employing the emptiness of expression that we term "pure words": that is to say, expression that, while remaining meaningful and understandable, at the same time encodes ultimate and inexpressible truth. Dongshan alerts us to this emptiness of expression by employing a ritualized rather artificial question-and-answer format.

The dialogue itself was provoked by a series of questions Dongshan asked his disciples about stages of the Way: "How is it when you orient

to it? What is it like to be serving it? What is it like to have merit?
What is it like to have merit in common? What is it like to have merit
upon merit?" The dialogue proper begins when a monk steps forward
and queries Dongshan about each question. Dongshan's replies to the
first three questions are questions of his own. The monk's enquiries
seem like "Dorothy Dixers."[62] For this reason the exchanges seem to
be starkly ritualized.

> A monk asked Dongshan, "What is orientation?"
> "When eating a meal, what is it?" replied the Master.
>
> "What is service?" asked the monk.
> "When turning your back to it, what is it?" replied the
> Master.
>
> "What is merit?" asked the monk.
> "When putting down the mattock, what is it?" replied the
> Master.
>
> "What is merit in common?" asked the monk.
> "Not taking form," replied the Master.
>
> "What is merit upon merit?" asked the monk.
> "Nothing shared," replied the Master.[63]

Dongshan places the onus of seeing into the stages of the Way back
onto the questioning student. By responding to the first three questions
with questions of his own, it's as if he is saying to the student, "Look
at your own activity and you'll find the Way right there." The effect
of question in response to question is artificial, even unreal, and this
reinforces the notion that this cryptic exchange is tilted so as to catch
the light of timeless inexpressible truth. In fact, this exchange creates
a ground where both questions and answers are of themselves pure:
comprehensible, yet as beyond meaning as the sound of the waves
breaking on the beach at night. Understood thus, each question, and

each answer, is itself a presentation of the Way beyond its stages. The empty calling and responding in this exchange sets up the theme of the timeless emptiness of the progressive stages of the Way that we will explore below.

Let's take a closer look at this exchange.

> A monk asked, "What is orientation?"
> "When eating a meal, what is it?" replied the Master.

The Chinese term *xiang* (translated here as "orientation") means "to be directed toward," "to face," or "to be oriented toward something." So the sense here is "How do I direct myself toward the Way?" In Nanquan's words, if you try to direct yourself, you deviate. In terms of eating a meal, there is only the brilliant green of the broccoli, the white of the potato soup, subtle tastes, and the warm sunlight streaming through the window. More intimately, Dongshan's "When eating a meal, what is it?" is a meal in itself.

> "What is service?" asked the monk.
> "When turning your back to it, what is it?" replied the Master.

The sense of service (*feng*) at play here is the same as that indicated in the "Song of the Precious Mirror Samadhi" when it says, "The minister serves the ruler, the son accords with the father; it is unfilial not to obey, disloyal not to serve." Regarding these lines, Peter Wong comments:

> This is the sense in which "serving" needs to be understood: It is much more specific than what is being connoted by the English word "service." It is to be understood in the context of propriety: There is no question about the appropriateness of serving—it is the way of a vassal to serve his lord; the way of a son to serve his father.

"Service" also carries the sense of honoring, upholding, and cleaving to the Buddha Way. Dongshan's reply to the question about serving—"When turning your back (*bei*) to it, what is it?"—reflects the first among the questions that elicited the dialogue: "How is it when you orient (*xiang*) to it?" "Turning your back" is ignoring. This is an allusion to the monastic path of turning away from the seductions and distractions of the world to commit to the Buddha Way, to enter the gate of emptiness, and, concomitantly, to secure a favorable rebirth.

"Turning to face" and "turning one's back" are paired terms that characterize our turning toward and our turning away from phenomena. This notion appears elsewhere among Dongshan's lore in an exchange between Dongshan and his successor, Yunju Daoying (d. 902), through whom the Caodong (Soto) line came down to us:

> Dongshan said, "There is a person who, in the midst of a thousand or even ten thousand people, neither turns his back, nor faces a single person. Now you tell me, what face does this person have?"
>
> Yunju came forward and said, "I am going to the Monks' Hall."[64]

In coming forward and saying, "I am going to the Monks' Hall," Yunju, through those ordinary yet ineffable words, conveys his own true face beyond the dualistic pairing of facing and turning one's back. In our current context, his words can be understood to represent the third stage of merit beyond the earlier stages of orientation and service, with their turning toward and turning away from phenomena. In this regard, Yunju's "I am going to the Monks' Hall" resembles Dongshan's stark responses to the student's questions: timelessly empty, and beyond such dualities as turning toward and turning away.

In terms of this cycle, considered as progressive, the stages of Orientation (facing) and Service (turning one's back) precede awakening and prepare the ground for it. At the same time, each of these stages is an expression of our timeless, dimensionless Buddha nature. In this spirit, with the stage of orientation, even the first thought of embarkation gathers the steps and stages of the Way, and the compendious Way finds its expression as our dawning curiosity.

"What is merit?" asked the monk.

"When putting down the mattock, what is it?" replied the
Master.

"Merit" denotes achievement, ability, function, and accomplishment.
In the present context it means seeing into our true nature. So we may
rephrase this exchange in the following way:

"When you've seen into your true nature, what is it like?"

"When putting down the mattock, what is it like?"

This is Dongshan's image for the experience of emptiness. Elsewhere
he characterizes the same matter, saying, "One stops work in order
to sit quietly, and one has leisure in the depth of white clouds."[65] He
conveys the empty realm with images of nonaction. These images
conjure a world of no work, where there is no person, no task, only
the vastness and purity of the empty realm. In that place there is no
turning toward and no turning away; all oppositions vanish into its
immensity. Putting down the mattock may be a convenient image
for this, but clearing away dead roots in order to plant a paddock of
wheat embodies it as aptly.

The monk asked, "What is merit in common?"

"Not taking form," replied the Master.

"Merit in common" means "enlightenment in common." Having personally realized, we now realize that all beings, including ourselves,
share the enlightened nature of the Buddha. Each of us participates
equally in the dimensionless vastness, and this is succinctly conveyed
in Dongshan's "Not taking form"—pure words that resonate with the
timeless immensity of the Way.

What is merit upon merit?" asked the monk.

"Nothing shared," replied the Master.

"Nothing shared" indicates that we must turn our backs on the form-less mutuality of "merit in common," where everything is shared, that we encountered in the previous stage. Now all the preceding stages are completely actualized in us as autonomous individuals, in whom all categories, including those of the five modes of the first cycle and the five stages of the second, are now embodied, transcended, and forgotten. We can't find any trace of the path that led us to this point, and no one can detect any trace of the words of the ancestors in our words. "Nothing shared"—words that are no words—entombs all considerations of progress and no progress, coming and going, birth and death; yet in the empty universe, potentially, our words and actions enlighten others.

After this overture of exchanges, like rain breaking drought, Dong-shan offers the verses of the Five Stages.

The Verses of the Five Stages

> Sage rulers have always modeled themselves on Emperor Yao.
> Treating others with propriety, you bend your dragon waist.
> At times, passing through the thick of the bustling market,
> you find it civilized throughout and the august dynasty
>   celebrated.

In the stage of Orientation, we discover the Way and realize that it is for us. We embark into it and begin to see the world and ourselves through the eyes of the teachings. Intimations gather; we are allured and drawn in. The qualities necessary for walking the Way at this stage are integrity, which means that we are consistent and just in our dealings with others, while at the same time showing grace, courtesy, and generosity toward them. On the one hand we learn to hold the line, and cleave to principle; on the other we give others a better than even break. In orientation, we turn toward the Way, and that is the Way in its turning.

For whom have you washed off your splendid makeup?
The cuckoo's call urges you to return.
The hundred flowers have fallen, yet the call is unending,
moving deeper and still deeper into jumbled peaks.

In the stage of Service, we deepen our commitment to the Way and make the sacrifices necessary to place it at the center of our lives. We find that service and commitment are not solely ethical considerations, as important as those are, but are also service and commitment to essential nature.

Even though our delusions fall away, the call of the cuckoo—the voice of our essential nature—draws us deeper and deeper into the jumbled peaks of passion and suffering, where we learn to commit to the Way by helping and attending to others, and by doing the hard yards of coming to really know ourselves. In the more detailed account of this stage below, we see how this training may be experienced in a practice community. Even as this stage shows us, from the perspective of emptiness, the Buddha nature of all beings in service to the Way, in the same breath it indicates the need for us to turn from distractions and commit to practice and to the precepts to prepare the vessel of awakening.

A withered tree blossoms in timeless spring.
You ride a jade elephant backward, chasing the unicorn.
Now, as you dwell hidden high among the thousand distant
    peaks—
a white moon, a cool breeze, an auspicious day.

Merit, or achievement, acknowledges our awakening, which in this cycle appears as an outcome or reward for our cleaving to and wholeheartedly serving the Way. In this stage, we explore the theme of awakening from the perspective of timelessness, as conveyed through the image of the withered tree blossoming in timeless spring. This stage focuses the themes of time and eternity that are at the core of the Five Ranks enterprise.

Dongshan beautifully captures the spirit of awakening in the two closing lines of this verse. However, personal awakening is not the end of our journey. Indeed, in one sense, our journey only begins with it.

The many beings and buddhas do not intrude on each other.
Mountains are high of themselves; waters are deep of themselves.
What do the myriad differences and distinctions clarify?
Where the partridge calls, the hundred flowers bloom afresh.

In the fourth stage of Merit in Common, we realize that when we awaken we share that awakening with all beings. That insight was implicit in the Buddha's exclamation upon awakening to the Morning Star: "Now I see that all beings are tathagata—are just this person," or as another account has it, "Tonight all beings and I have attained the Way." Dongshan's "not taking form" is how he expresses enlightenment in common. These words convey, and indeed are, the empty realm where one's enlightenment is the enlightenment of all, just as one moon reflects in the many waters of the world.

However, we live this shared awakening fully by turning from the emptiness of all phenomena and events toward a world appearing in its uniqueness, beyond our ideas about it. From this perspective, each thing—even as it conveys the whole—stands alone. This is similar to the fourth mode of the first cycle, understood in terms of the title "Approaching from the Contingent." There, in the spirit of Approaching from the Contingent, we turn to the world—conceived in terms of difference and distinction—and treat it as all there is. This means that we meet it fully and see people, things, and events as they truly are. With this we are turned about and opened up. We may awaken others, even as we strive to realize more deeply ourselves; that dance is unending.

This current stage of Merit in Common is a subtle poetic evocation of difference and distinction opening to timeless immensity, but the imagery of the crossed swords and the lotus in the midst of fire from the corresponding mode of the first cycle speak more eloquently of the bodhisattva path where we slowly embody and deepen our realization in the midst of difficulties and oppositional circumstances, and cultivate compassion and saving grace.

As if to reinforce the importance of the association between the stage of Merit in Common and the mode of Approaching from the Contingent, the opening lines of the former, "The many beings and buddhas do not intrude on each other. Mountains are high of themselves; waters are deep of themselves," are a most apt illustration of the latter.

As we consider the stage of Merit in Common it is good to keep in mind the training of the bodhisattva as it is conveyed through the imagery of the fourth and corresponding mode of the first cycle.

> **If horns sprout on your head, that's unbearable;**
> **If you rouse your mind to seek Buddha, that's shameful.**
> **In the vastness of the empty kalpa there is no one who knows—**
> **Why go to the South to interview the fifty-three sages?**

In the fifth and final stage, Merit upon Merit, Dongshan admonishes us not to regress or to cling to earlier stages, and not to renege on our responsibility to walk on after our awakening. There is finally no need to seek Buddha, and yet our practice continues endlessly, as our ordinary life with its joy and its grief. In the end, even the forgetting of awakening is to be forgotten. All that we think we might have gathered—everything we might be tempted to think we know—are let go.

It is of interest to note that, in contrast with the tenth and concluding stage of the Ox-Herding Cycle, there is no mention here in the concluding verse of the Cycle of Merit of saving or enlightening others. If anything this is rather implied in the preceding stage's counterpart mode in the Cycle of the Essential and the Contingent, Approaching from the Contingent (and most especially under the rubric of its alternative title, Approaching Concurrence), with its imagery of the lotus in the midst of fire and its suggestion that when we practice in the midst of the passions and suffering of the world we are bodhisattvas enlightening ourselves and potentially others. We will discuss this further below, when we examine the Cycle of Merit in relation to the Ox-Herding Cycle.

Key Themes in the Five Stages of Merit

In each and every one of the aforementioned five stages we are shown the Buddha nature of all beings. It manifests in our seeking Buddhahood, and in our serving it. Thus, even the first two stages, Orientation and Service, which apparently precede realization, are expressive of the awakened mind which is inherently ours. In time, we see into our true nature, following which we realize that our insight is the birthright of all beings. Finally, we embody awakening, and in time forget it, as we vest the Way in our most ordinary activity.

When we understand that the stages of the Cycle of Merit show the Buddha nature of all beings, we likewise understand that the stages of Merit, like those of the Cycle of the Essential and the Contingent, are completely empty. This means that Orientation includes all subsequent stages, as does Service, and so on. Thus, with orientation—with our first hesitant step—the entire journey is already complete; likewise with Service, and so on. However, although each step is enlightenment complete itself, we still walk a path of training that unfolds over time, and over time, we are transformed. We still have to sweat the Way in order to clarify what has been clear since before time.

Now we will explore the Cycle of Merit as a path of training. As we work through the five stages, we will maintain awareness of the essential core of the expedient means that informs each stage. This makes for a richer and more comprehensive approach, and one that is made inspiring by the profundity and beauty of Dongshan's verses.

14. Orientation

Sage rulers have always modeled themselves on Emperor Yao.
Treating others with propriety, you bend your dragon waist.
At times, passing through the thick of the bustling market,
you find it civilized throughout and the august dynasty
  celebrated.

THIS IS THE first step on our journey. Everything lies in front of us. We hear about the Way and recognize that it is for us. Then, perhaps even years later, we embark and begin to find our home there. As we orient ourselves, we begin to see our life through the eyes of the teachings, and to identify with them. We sense a mystery that resists explanation, and we turn toward it. Like the discoverer of the tracks of the ox in the second of the ten pictures from the Ox-Herding Cycle, we haven't yet entered the gate, but we've discerned the path. As we cultivate inquiry and learn to meditate, we begin to travel it in reverence and awe.

The etymological meaning of the English word *orientation* is "turning eastward," implying turning toward the rising sun—an auspicious image that evokes the dawn mood of setting out. When we make a commitment to travel the Way, circumstances most often gather to support us. It is a time of intimations and significant meetings. Sometimes it is hard to tell them apart!

I remember when I flew from Perth to Sydney for my first *sesshin*—my first intensive Zen meditation retreat. I met Robert Aitken in one of the personal interviews he so generously gave to new students before sesshin. We sat up on the balcony of the zendo and looked out over the treetops. Neither of us spoke, and I sensed that he was shy.

After a long time, and still looking straight ahead, he cleared his throat, then said, "When Kumarajiva translated the sutras into Chinese, he found that there wasn't a word for the Sanskrit *sunyata* (emptiness), so he used *ku*, the Chinese character for sky."

His words linked my naïve and azure intuitions with the Zen tradition. He then suggested that I work on the koan *Mu*, and he told me the story of Zhaozhou's dog. That very moment a dog burst onto the veranda and scampered joyously around us, barking excitedly. We both burst out laughing. I felt that I was meeting my life, although I didn't have the words for it.

With regard to true meeting, I love the story of Zhaozhou's meeting with his teacher Nanquan. The story relates one of those encounters in which both teacher and student know that nothing will ever be the same again for either of them.

> Zhaozhou was young at the time, probably in his late teens. When Zhaozhou entered the teacher's quarters, Nanquan was lying down resting.
>
> Nanquan asked him, "Where have you come from?"
>
> "I've come from Ruixiang," Zhaozhou responded [Ruixiang means "auspicious image," which was also the name of Nanquan's temple].
>
> Playing along, Nanquan asked him, "Have you seen the auspicious image?" [In other words, "Have you awakened?"]
>
> Zhaozhou responded, "No, but I've seen a reclining Buddha."
>
> That was enough to shake Nanquan out of his lethargy.
>
> "Do you have a teacher or not?" he asked.
>
> Zhaozhou replied, "I have a teacher."
>
> Nanquan then asked him, "Who is your teacher?"
>
> The question was redundant. Zhaozhou stepped in front of Nanquan and bowed, saying, "In the middle of winter the weather becomes bitterly cold. I wish all blessings on you, Master."[66]

Zhaozhou's gracious words convey his heartfelt connection to his teacher, as well as the extent of "Master," which includes the freezing cold of midwinter. Given that Zhaozhou was actually standing in Ruixang Temple, his response to "Where are you from?" is a play on the notion that this very place is my true home. Zhaozhou stayed and had his awakening with Nanquan, remaining with him as his disciple for forty years.

In the stage of Orientation, reverence is where it's at for the student. For the teacher, who has to bear with all that naïve identification and admiration, benevolence is the thing. Later, if the training is effective, the relation between teacher and student becomes more robust and provisionally equal.

If this Way is for you, seek out a teacher who is worth her or his salt: one who will thoroughly test anything you may think you have realized and who won't approve you readily. Such a teacher will encourage you during the arduous stretches of training. If you decide to commit to a teacher, stay with that teacher until you have at least passed the first barrier. Under the influence of a good teacher we make changes for the better in our life and may awaken to our true nature. We may also, in turn, become helpful to others, and this brings us to the virtue and wisdom of Emperor Yao.

Sage rulers have always modeled themselves on Emperor Yao. Treating others with propriety, you bend your dragon waist.

The legendary Emperor Yao (2357—2257 BCE) was the first emperor of China's first dynasty, the Xia. This Emperor is remembered for having redirected the flow of the Yellow River, thereby preventing floods that threatened his subjects who lived along its banks. This redirection of the Yellow River is what Dongshan is referring to when he writes that "you bend your dragon waist." It's said that Yao's light encompassed the extremities of the empire and extended from heaven to earth—an image that hints at his awakened nature. Rather than killing off opposition, Yao seems to have been able to bear complaints and to incorporate objections into his rule. Being modest, he preferred to parley rather than to overpower. Yao can therefore also be understood as an exemplary figure who represents the wisdom and compassion of the Buddha.

"Treating others with propriety" suggests maintaining proper form and being consistent and just in our dealings. In short, it suggests behaving with integrity. "Bending the dragon waist" can also be understood as courtesy, grace under pressure, even forgiveness and mercy. On one hand we hold the line, and cleave to principle; on the other we give others a better-than-even break.

The qualities that we associate with propriety and "bending the dragon waist" may appear to be opposed. However, they accord readily in the conduct of a true person of the Way. "Bending your dragon waist" means that you are available to talk to a friend who rings late at night to discuss what's troubling him, and "treating others with propriety" means not ringing others late at night to discuss your problems. Instead we hunker down, meditate, and examine our own hearts. For me this comes down to friendship in another's trouble; courage in one's own.

Here "propriety" and "bending the dragon" resemble the dialectical relationship between the essential (*zheng*) and the contingent (*pian*), in the first cycle. Propriety resembles "the upright," one way in which zheng can be translated. "Bending the dragon waist" resembles "the inclined," one of the ways in which pian can be translated. Thus, propriety corresponds to emptiness, while bending the dragon waist suggests its compassionate expression in daily affairs. Additionally, these qualities of integrity and grace—of "holding on" (to principle), and "letting go"—likewise reflect the essential and the contingent, respectively. In these ways the stages of the Cycle of Merit parallel, at points, the modes of the Cycle of the Essential and the Contingent.

Propriety also has a personal dimension, especially as it relates to practice. When we cultivate a daily regimen of zazen, and commit to stick with the particular form of practice that we've taken up, that's the integrity of the Way. Sitting thus, we sit the universe—people and stars, cats and kings. And it sits us, with our unrepeatable quirks and quiddities. It was in this spirit that the old teacher Linji said, "Just make yourself master of every situation, and wherever you stand is the true place."

Mastery of every situation isn't about imposing oneself on others. We're not being invited to fulfill our fantasies of power and control like some autocratic three-year-old. Rather, wherever we stand, the glimmering waters of the world are right there as us. Linji continued, "No effort is necessary. You only have to be ordinary, with nothing to do—defecating, urinating, putting on clothes, eating food, lying down when tired." You are noble right where you are, just as you are. The night sky flares on your out-breath; the night ocean circulates within you. No need to be arrogant though. A newborn baby is like this, as is a blade of grass, or a stone.

"Treating others with propriety" and "bending the dragon waist" may also be understood as learning to take form and learning to let go, respectively. Sitting with others we learn the guidelines, and we observe them out of respect for our companions and for ourselves. We hold the form so that others learn to trust it and be deepened and nourished by it. This is "governing with propriety." We wouldn't drink water during a round of zazen, but the woman sitting next to us is pregnant and sips water when she needs to, and we're at ease with her doing that. Learning the form is one thing, but you must also be able to respond compassionately, forgetting the rules when the occasion demands.

All that propriety and pliancy: how majestically they go together! When we practice wholeheartedly, and engage with our lives, we unknowingly touch others. We shift the field and bring ease and release to situations that were formerly difficult. In this regard, a student whose practice has begun to mature told me how she brings "big mind" to her fights with her partner: "Where I would have come down hard in the past, now I leave a space, an opening. Then I notice that instead of coming back at me, he's also silent. And I see that there are tears in his eyes. And then I can say something quite different . . . actually encouraging. And then after a while he says . . ." Opening a space in this way allows tenderness and compassionate warmth.

At times, passing through the thick of the bustling market, you find it civilized throughout and the august dynasty celebrated.

I like it that Dongshan begins our journey in the marketplace: the place to where we return at the end of our journey, according to the Ox-Herding Cycle. To say that we find the marketplace "civilized throughout" is to express the sense that it is our own true nature in its unfolding. The brightly colored, noisy stalls steal our sense of separation. We are allured and joyous, and we can't fathom why. Simply walking down the street feels large and alive. A sudden wind lifts the shining leaves and we are gusted away.

We discover the ancient teachings, and they shake up the kaleidoscope of our presuppositions. It's like being in love: we see our beloved everywhere—in changing light, in a mountain, in a flight of birds, and in our own smile. We see things through his or her eyes too: "That's how my beloved would see it." We know this unerringly, and like Shakespeare's Juliet, we wish but for the thing we have. When we get to know the stories and sayings of the old teachers in this spirit, their words open a path for us. The story of how widow Fazhen came to awakening back in twelfth-century China is exemplary in this regard.

Chan Master Dahui Zonggao (1089–1163) sent a monk to call on the widow Fazhen's son. The monk stayed for a time and talked to the son about Chan.

Although the teachings were not intended for her, Fazhen was fascinated by what she heard, and she took the opportunity to ask the visitor about Dahui's methods. He told her his teacher required that students investigate the koan of Zaozhou's Mu with every atom of their being, and that he didn't allow them to comment on it, or think about it.

Fazhen was inspired by the adept's words. She did the housework during the day, and sat with Mu at night.

One day her mind became clear and she could respond unhesitatingly to the monk's questions. He approved her realization, and Fazhen gave him a letter to take back to Dahui in which she wrote some verses. The final verse read:

> All day long reading the words of the sutras,
> It's like meeting an old acquaintance.
> Don't say doubts arise again and again—
> Each time it is brought up, each time it's new.

When Dahui received the widow's verses he was delighted that she had accorded with his own words, "When you've seen into your deepest nature, reading the old stories is like going outside and running into an old friend." Or like coming home and finding an old friend waiting.[67]

This is the freshness of the Dharma. Each encounter is the first. Even doubts about our grasp of it are part of its richness. The old stories illuminate us, and we shyly illuminate them. We find glimmering intimations of this everywhere. The widow's story shows us how, even with meager opportunities, we can awaken.

We are always orienting. We seem, at any stage of the Way, to lose contact and then regain it. The process is a bit like air traffic control bringing a plane in to land. Now we are on-beam, now off, but always correcting. Whether we are a beginner or an old-timer, each stage of the way, including Orientation, is expressive of our inherent Buddha nature.

In the stage of Orientation, intimations gather, and we are allured and drawn in. We encounter the teachings and see the world with changed eyes; we learn to meditate and set it at the center of our lives. We may seek out a teacher. In orientation, we turn toward the Way, and that is the Way in its turning. In the subsequent stage, Service, we commit ourselves to practice in earnest, and further prepare the ground of awakening.

15. Service

For whom have you washed off your splendid makeup?
The cuckoo's call urges you to return.
The hundred flowers have fallen, yet the call is unending,
moving deeper and still deeper into jumbled peaks.

AT THE STAGE of Service we deepen our commitment to the Way and make the sacrifices necessary to place it at the center of our lives. Here "service" and "commitment" mean not only ethical considerations but also service and commitment to essential nature. When we open our eyes in the morning and roll out of bed, feeling the cold floor with our toes, that's service to the essential. In this regard, even our dreams serve, though they resist being pressed into service!

The Chinese term that we translate here as "service" is *feng*, which also carries the meanings of "holding something devoutly" or "being obedient to a teaching." In addition to these, feng can also mean "to honor," "to pay homage to," "to esteem," and "to offer." All of these senses of feng are variously at play in this chapter.

I asked an old friend of mine who doesn't practice Zen formally, "What should I do when I feel depressed?"

"Do something for someone else," was his reply.

We find relief from self-preoccupation when we make efforts on behalf of others. With luck, the other person will have been helped and given a lift too. When a student asked Soen Nakagawa, "What can I do when I feel discouraged?" he famously responded, "Encourage others!" His words are a timeless spring of service and commitment, and are an inspiration for this chapter.

In Latin, *attendare*, from which the English word "attention" is derived, means "to lean toward," or "to serve." We serve others when we open an attentive silence in which they can express their joy and suffering. In order to accomplish this we need to let go of rehearsing our eager story as they tell theirs. Whatever else enlightened activity is, it surely includes this. One of the finest acknowledgments one human can give another is to say of that person, "He was there for me," or "She was there for me." Idealistic and self-congratulatory notions of service disappear in such moments—we simply help the child with her homework, or push the neighbor's car when its battery is dead. Enlightenment is as enlightenment does.

For a ninth-century Chan monk or nun, service was unquestioningly vested in fulfilling one's obligations to the Buddha and to one's teacher. In order to be undivided in his commitment to the Buddha Way, and to secure a favorable rebirth, Dongshan would have taken up some 250 precepts and committed himself to a life of unremitting meditation. Such a lifestyle was much more rigorous than anything we could, or probably would, undertake as lay people.

In the light of the towering past, modern lay Zen practice can look like a long shot. If we do commit to practice as laypeople, chances are that for most of us it will be within the context of family, relationships, and work, where it takes ingenuity to carve out time to meditate. However it's often more possible than we allow ourselves to imagine. If we can be open to opportunities as they present themselves, we will find that gaps appear in even the busiest schedule.

A story circulates within Hasidic Jewish communities of a man who, caught up in the pressure of the day's business, suddenly realized that he would be unable to make it to the synagogue for his daily worship. During a brief moment of quiet between tasks, he prayed a hurried prayer of contrition, and then hastened to his next appointment. It is said that God blessed him threefold. I don't know about the triple blessing, but momentarily returning to my breath refreshes a torrid hour in the recording studio.

It is difficult to sustain zazen in a life that is too ramified, with too many counter pulls. I wrote "ramified," but when I read it back it looked like "rarefied"—and truly, a life that is too simplified and pure can also be problematic. The practice of zazen thrives in busy lives, where it creates its own joy and feeds commitment. Sitting alone makes us strong; sitting with others opens us up. It's good to do a lot of both.

Taking up the bodhisattva precepts[68] is also an expression of our commitment to the Way and should help us to reduce the harm we do to others and ourselves. We come to know ourselves through the challenge of trying to keep the precepts, because they make us more conscious of our motives and help us to know our own hearts. Regardless of our commitment to keep the precepts, we can still hurt others and cause harm. We aren't proof against that. To live is to hurt and to be hurt, and making apology, forgiving, and being forgiven remain at the core of our relationships with others.

As regards that core, it is important that we know our own hearts. Our loves and our fears are also our true nature in its unfolding. We serve the essential when we allow the presence of those feelings. Otherwise we run the risk of divorcing what we mistakenly take to be the purity of the essential from the messiness of our lives.

In Dongshan's verse the voice of the cuckoo calls us into greater depth, and we enter the jumbled peaks of passion and suffering to find that they too are expressions of awakened mind and heart.

For whom have you washed off your splendid makeup?

The reference to removing makeup conjures the image of a woman, well versed in the ways of the world, who decides to wash off her makeup and commit to the one she loves. This is Dongshan's image for renouncing worldliness to commit to the Buddha Way. Most of us are not in a position to renounce our worldliness, so to bring the verse into closer accord with contemporary lay experience, I will reframe Dongshan's question as Robert Aitken does: "For whom do you bathe and make yourself presentable?"[69]

This is a koan of daily custom. In it, the "for whom"—or more aptly the "who"—disappears into the fact of our showering, of our drying our hair, and of our dabbing on deodorant. There is nothing ulterior here, nothing hidden. Our being born is like this. Our dying too. This long day here—the sun that rises, the cat that glides through the long grass, the figure that stands at the sink making coffee, the dark purple, almost indigo, morning glories twined on the fence opposite—is clearly that, and clean as a whistle. All ages and limitless space disappear into the least of these.

The cuckoo's call urges you to return.

Here in Australia it is the crow's "caaaark!" that calls me home, and which surely is home. "To return" is the integrity of practice, and we do this undeterred by any awakening experience we may have had. In this spirit, Yamada Koun, after his great awakening, practiced every day for the rest of his life with what some might regard as a beginner's koan: "Who is hearing that sound?"

The wind on our faces—our ever-faithful breath—calls to us, as us. As we move into accord with this, our half-lives become a life. With repeated returning, over time, the genuine person emerges. We emerge in our true colors.

The hundred flowers have fallen, yet the call is unending, moving deeper and still deeper into jumbled peaks.

Even though our delusions fall away, still the call continues to draw us into greater depth. Our heart yearns for its release, and that too is the call. The heart's yearning is its release. With the confidence that comes from our surrender to the softest of invitations—a long-ringing bell, a flickering star—we embark on a journey into the jumbled peaks of our suffering, and of the suffering world.

Regarding our suffering, and our journey with it, it is important to get to know our propensities and our demons, and to learn to work with them. This process usually entails fear: of the journey itself, and of what we might discover. When I touch on the topic of fear when giving a Dharma talk, I feel the atmosphere in the zendo change, and I have the sense that everyone's on board for this bit. Fear seems so fundamental to how many of us feel much of the time.

We are often more afraid of life than death. This isn't reasoned or even reasonable. We fear shame, in particular. And shame surely can feel like a death. My mother used to say, "I could have died!" or "I felt as big as sixpence!"[70] Contrariwise, we often need signs of respect from others in order to behave tolerably toward ourselves, even to feel that we are alive in a way that's worth the living.

When we learn to acknowledge our fear, we also learn a lot about the sources of our aggression, manifested both as lashing out and as being uncooperative. We see how painful it is when we allow fear to shape our lives, as when we constantly contort ourselves trying to avoid others. If we could see the tracks of our avoidance from above, what a confusing maze of scuffmarks that would be!

By attending to our fear and anger, over time we are changed. This is not least because with attention to our fear and anger we are more in touch with our sorrow and vulnerability. We can then connect with the world from a much more settled, open place. When we speak, our words have much more heart and body in them, and our compassion feels less entangled with our codependent need to please others.

Even a moment free from attachment to our isolated self can release helpful energies and abundant love that many can share in, without quite knowing what draws and holds them. Groups form and benefit from this. Over time, as we settle into such communities, our less appealing traits get unerringly reflected back to us (our more appealing traits having mostly shown up earlier). For this reason, being in community can be rough. As Subhana Barzaghi, a fellow teacher, says, "It's in the communal vegetable garden that words are said, and tears are shed."

When we begin to cultivate the Way we're often naïve and blind sighted to our heart's darkness, which is perhaps just as well. Later, when we encounter our own ill-will and cruelty, and that of others, we may feel daunted. But in a maturing community such experiences are part and parcel of our journey together. The old master Wumen Huikai wrote:

> If you want to support the gate and sustain the house,
> you must climb a mountain of swords with bare feet.[71]

Huikai is saying that if we wish to teach and to cultivate a practice community, we must bear the difficulties involved. Dealing with the trickiness of Sangha relations, as well as with our own deviousness and self-deception, can be confronting. The first four letters of Sangha are *sang*, the French word for blood. The ties that connect us in Sangha are blood ties: the shared pain and joy of a second, third, or fourth go at family.

As we learn to open and allow more of the world in, we hear the sorrow that lies beneath the anger in the voice that criticizes us. We feel our own shame, nearly to the point of incapacitation, in that moment. We begin to open to truths embedded in our interactions with others, and we slowly come to see our own part in the conflict.

We lean in, we serve, by giving our awareness to each painful situation. We allow whatever is there to be there. Every subtle movement of feeling is just what it is. This is the voice that calls us home. This is home. No one asks us to do this work, and for the most part we didn't come to the Way for it. But we do it nonetheless, cultivating a path of opening to and seeing into our karmic inheritance, as we struggle to come to terms with what is most obdurate in us.

When we take this on, we undertake to practice with devotion to the end of our lives. This means accepting disappointment without giving up, and enduring in the face of discouragement. All of this requires courage, understood here as that quality that carries us beyond petty resistance and self-pity. Having made the commitment, it's good to keep going. There's still so much (who knows how much?) to be discovered. It's as though we've found our way into a dark cave. We grope our way forward. We glimpse a stalactite and see what looks like water glimmering in the dark. Is it a lake? How far back does it go?

By undertaking service to the essential, we learn to distinguish stream from lake, stalactite from stalagmite, and we begin to emerge from the shadows. Even with our ordinary activity—bathing, cleaning our teeth, squinting in the steamy mirror to comb our hair—we make the subterranean caverns eloquent, no less than the night of turning stars.

Exploring the stage of Service in its compassionate and essential aspects, we see that service expresses itself as commitment to the Way.

We practice commitment to the Way by helping and attending to others, and by doing the hard yards of coming to really know ourselves. Implicit in the conduct aspect of service is a commitment to practice as a means to awaken to our true nature. Fortuitously—for awakening has its own time and season—it is to the season of awakening that Dongshan next turns.

16. Merit

A withered tree blossoms in timeless spring.
You ride a jade elephant backward, chasing the unicorn.
Now, as you dwell hidden high among the thousand distant
  peaks—
a white moon, a cool breeze, an auspicious day.

AT THIS STAGE, we first encounter the "merit" that gives its name to this cycle. As noted above, the Chinese word *gongxun* can be translated as "merit," "ability," "achievement," or "accomplishment." These terms pay tribute to our awakening, which, after many privations, feels like the first morning of the world.

In this Cycle of Merit, awakening appears as an outcome, or even as a reward for our cleaving to the Way, and serving it wholeheartedly. Elsewhere, Dongshan conveys this reward as ease after effort: laying down the hoe, or resting among the white clouds.[72] However, in the much looser weave of reality at large, we awaken as awakening determines and in our own unique ways. There is no royal road to realization, the five modes and five stages notwithstanding. The path is crooked, and we walk it at night under our own stars.

Dongshan's verse expresses awakening, which is as fresh as this moment, yet ancient and elemental. This experience is an important step on the path to maturity, and with it comes a measure of freedom from constricting attitudes and stories. In time, we develop a sense that the lights are dimming on our self-preoccupation, and the teeming world feels less like a painted backdrop to our fantasies of power and control.

Still, we can't know in advance how we will realize, any more than we can know how we will die. Each of us will die; not all of us will realize. Even if we do realize, it may not be as it is extravagantly described in books like *The Three Pillars of Zen*, or indeed, in Dongshan's flamboyant verse for this stage, where we "ride a jade elephant backward, chasing the unicorn." Realization may arrive more like the dawn sun lighting a dark hill: picking out first a rock, then a tree, until, after much devoted practice, the entire slope is in the light. However it is for you, personal awakening is not the end of our journey. There is so much more to discover and to live, as will be shown in the later stages of this cycle.

The outcomes of awakening tend to be as various as the ways taken to them. I've known people who, with a mere glimpse, have devoted their lives to serving others in the Sangha. These were people who thought of themselves as no more than foot soldiers of the Way, but who turned out to be generals. Others, having had apparently profound experiences, just drift away.

Like the verses of the first cycle, this verse is a poem of true meeting, of intimacy with Buddha mind—one that marks and celebrates our encounter with our timeless nature. Although the experience of awakening to emptiness has been presented in the first three modes of the first Cycle of the Essential and the Contingent, here Dongshan's choice of expression is strikingly different, which bears testament to how individual awakening really is, as well as to the richness and variety of poetic responses that it can inspire.

A withered tree blossoms in timeless spring.

The image of the withered tree is a Chan image for emptiness. It also extends the imagery of falling flowers used in the previous verse for the stage of Service. There, with the dying off of our delusions, we responded to the voice of our essential nature inviting us to realize, and then more deeply. By the stage of Merit we've journeyed so far in that there is no turning back, and we've lost track of what brought us here in the first place. Perhaps we wanted peerless enlightenment, but that urge has receded, and we find that we are becalmed in a place where we can neither advance nor retreat.

Our enterprise feels pointless, yet we persevere in that stuck place, not knowing what else to do. We experience humiliation and shame at our incapacity to resolve the koan. It is as if we have been given a "sky burial" and are being pecked clean by the vultures of our own doubt and negativity.

We may have experiences of emptiness, but they don't penetrate deeply and are not enough to release us. If after such experiences our hearts are not at rest, we should honor that, endure our disappointment, and not settle for less. Like this, we undergo a withering away of our hopes and expectations, and are unknowingly open to the possibility of genuine experience. All the while we continue to build the vessel of the Way with our struggles and efforts to resolve the koan. The following exchange reflects this season of practice and points a way for us:

A monk asked old master Yunmen Wenyan (864–949), "How is it when the tree withers and the leaves fall?" Yunmen replied, "Golden Wind is manifesting herself."[73]

We might rephrase the monk's question as "Even though I have meditated sincerely for years, and seen off my cherished delusions, why can't I awaken?" "Golden Wind" is the deity of autumn. Here she manifests herself as the monk's bare state. The reply, "Golden Wind is manifesting herself," points to the monk's condition. There is no need for the monk to look elsewhere, for his condition is the Way unfolding at ease.

The states and conditions that permeate our lives convey the timeless empty realm, no less than fundamental actions such as walking, sitting, or lying down. At the deepest level, they are none other than us. It's also heartening to consider that our joys and pleasures also convey our source and origin, no less than our negative moods and feelings.

Implicit in the monk's question, "How is it when the tree withers and the leaves fall?" is the matter of moving on to the next stage: "Everything is empty, sure. And then?" Yet it's important not to get a step ahead of ourselves. There is no royal road to awakening, and we can't contrive one. Nor can we preempt awakening. Our unsteady course in the dark, with our longing, questioning, and even our anticipation of awakening, is itself the manifestation of what we seek.

Don't mistake a withered tree for a lifeless one! We may doubt that we'll ever get enlightened, but enlightenment is not deterred by our doubts.

> In this one instant, infinite numbers of kalpas are
> realized.
> —Avatamsaka Sutra

Spring opens the flowers with a single puff. In such blossoming, all ages gather as our least breath. We are vast beyond reckoning, but we dance, laugh, cry, and feel such gratitude. After years of paying dues—propitiating beggars and gypsies as we wait for our blind date—we are met and spoken for. Looking back, we cannot see how we traveled here. The years of effort are as nothing. In the ordinary course of things, none of this is possible, but it is possible for us.

Timeless spring is true timeless meeting; it isn't about endless time. Duration and sequence have no purchase here. Does that mean we still have breakfast before lunch? When there is breakfast, there is only breakfast; when lunch, only lunch. At this stage, we are focused on the timeless, but the temporal is its expression. The timekeeper leans in and strikes the bell to end the twenty-five-minute round of zazen. Everything that we regard as before and after gathers in that bell strike. Any moment is up for this; any moment is thus privileged.

Zen is precise about time, so much so that in the beginning years of practice, I thought that only those with good time management would get to experience eternity.

When my first teacher, Robert Aitken, came to Western Australia, I took him sightseeing. We were running late to pick up the senior student from Sydney, who was helping organize our first sesshin with a teacher.

As we took in the view of the city, which, given my illustrious company, felt quite intimate, I asked him, "How do I show my family this splendor?"

"Be punctual," he replied.

You ride a jade elephant backward, chasing the unicorn.

Beyond clock time and our concerns about it, there's the mythological *qilin*—part dragon, part deer. In medieval China the qilin was identified with the giraffe and the unicorn, and we have chosen to translate *qilin* as "unicorn." Legend has it that devas—creatures of the airy realms—rode about on qilins. Dongshan exploits this spectacle to express awakening in all its joyous absurdity. This is the Way at play; the timeless Dharmakaya playing catch with itself.

Heraclitus wrote that "time is like a child playing chess, a kingly game." Self and other, subject and object, are our playthings: now we set them up, now we demolish them. The old order is overturned. Shoushan Xingnian (926–993) conveys this sweetly in the following exchange:

> A monk asked Shoushan, "What is Buddha?"
> Shoushan replied, "The new wife rides the donkey; the mother-in-law leads it by the bridle."[74]

Shoushan's reply reverses the customary Confucian roles, in which the mother-in-law would have ridden the donkey, and the bride would have led it by the bridle, no doubt enquiring persistently about her new mother's comfort.

When we awaken, we ride like a bride into our new lives. The moment of our standing at the stove to throw a handful of onions into the sizzling pan swims up from unimaginable depths, as does the mauve of the jacarandas and the dark blue harbor. Our ordinary struggles and joys are the stumbling speech of the earth.

With awakening, we are invited to live more fully: to see through and to go beyond the dull, cramping attitudes and stories that close us down. Except at the deepest, most unhelpful level, we are not our stories. With awakening, we are invited to embark, to risk everything, and to find, like Shakespeare's Juliet, that

> My bounty is as boundless as the sea,
> My love as deep: the more I give to thee
> The more I have: for both are infinite.[75]

With deep experience, our hearts are opened, and energy and compassion are there for the asking. The more I give, the more I have to give. It wells, inexhaustible, even in the midst of exhaustion.

**Now, as you dwell hidden high among the thousand
distant peaks—
a white moon, a cool breeze, an auspicious day.**

Hidden among the snowy peaks, the crevasses, and the chasms, you are vast and completely indistinguishable from them. You also dwell, completely hidden as the throng of early morning cyclists and joggers with their subtle scent trail of talcum and sweat, and as the liquid sun that wobbles up over the horizon.

With such an experience, we may feel that we are high and dry beyond worldly troubles. However, we must come to include the suffering of others, and our own. This will be an important theme in the following stage of this cycle, Merit in Common. For now, there is only the coolness and ease of dawn after an unimaginable struggle in the darkness. Our hearts are easy. Our eyes are sluiced clear. And truly, the years of struggle and frustration are forgotten as though they never were.

17. Merit in Common

The many beings and buddhas do not intrude on each other.
Mountains are high of themselves; waters are deep of themselves.
What do the myriad differences and distinctions clarify?
Where the partridge calls, the hundred flowers bloom afresh.

W E HAVE TRAVELED through the stages of orienting to the Way, of serving it, and of the personal awakening that ensued from those efforts. We might regard the path as ending there in some private ecstasy beyond the jumble and confusion of human suffering. Dongshan, however, urges us on to realize the stage of Merit in Common (enlightenment in common). Our core sense of this is "Our own enlightenment is exactly the enlightenment of all beings." This sense is implicit in the words of the Buddha when he awakened upon seeing the Morning Star, "Now I see that all beings are tathagata—are just this person."

The spirit of Merit in Common is beautifully conveyed by the koan "Each branch of coral holds up the moon."[76] If we regard each branch as a family, then humanity is a branch, the various cats are a branch, angels, dragons, unicorns, and basilisks are the imaginary beings branch, and so on, through the various families, each of which is lit by the moon of enlightenment. This evokes our interdependence and our enlightenment in common.

We're all in this together. In relation to this koan of the coral and the moon, John Tarrant said that when you hurt your thumb, your whole hand hurts. Correspondingly, what we do to the Earth and its creatures matters. With increasing damage it is harder for the Earth to come back. Relationships, too, are corrupted by denigration and sarcasm, let alone physical violence. The failure of a marriage can spell the end of many of the individual friendships that were nourished by it.

The following story is emblematic of enlightenment in common:

> Xuefeng Yicun and Yantou Quanhou were trying to reach the village of Chinshan, but they got caught in a blizzard and had to take refuge in an inn on Tortoise Mountain. There they were snowed in.
>
> While Yantou slept, Xuefeng meditated ceaselessly.
>
> Finally, Yantou shouted, "Why are you meditating all the time? Get some sleep!"
>
> Xuefeng, pointing to his breast, said, "My heart isn't yet at peace. I don't dare to deceive myseslf."
>
> Yantou asked Xuefeng to recount the various experiences he had had, so that he could check them. Xuefeng obliged, and Yantou dismissed each of them in turn.
>
> Finally he shouted at Xuefeng, "Haven't you heard that what comes through the gate is not the family jewels?"
>
> At a loss, and utterly vulnerable, Xuefeng asked, "Then, what should I do?"
>
> Yantou said, "In the future, if you want to propagate the great teaching, let each point flow out from your own breast, to come out and cover heaven and earth for me."
>
> Upon hearing this, Xuefeng had a great awakening. He bowed, crying out again and again, "Tonight Tortoise Mountain is enlightened! Tonight Tortoise Mountain is enlightened!"[77]

Yantou had the gift and great capacity for the Way, and had come to awakening with relative ease. He was what musicians call "a natural." Xuefeng, on the other hand, had struggled to awaken over many years, to no avail. So Xuefeng felt that he could not afford to sleep while this matter remained unresolved for him. In being faithful to his own doubt, he was true to himself.

Yantou's rebuke, "Haven't you heard that what comes through the gate is not the family jewels?" removed the last intellectual supports for Xuefeng's position. And Yantou's magisterial follow up, "In the future, if you want to propagate the great teaching, let each point flow out from your own breast, to come out and cover heaven and earth for me," was the heave that tipped Xuefeng over. What is closest—our beating heart, our fear, our exaltation—encompasses, and indeed *is,* the timeless empty universe.

When I worked on this koan with Robert Aitken, I naïvely asked him, "What happens to the little villages at the base of Tortoise Mountain?"

"Well, they get to dance too," he responded.

When you awaken and dance your joy, the tiger lilies dance, as do the ploughed paddocks, and the icy stars. What you might have regarded as yours is equally the mountain's and the ocean's. That's a lot of enlightenment in common! We actualize enlightenment in common by not resting in the realm of personal awakening, but by practicing with others. Like this, we make what is implicit real, and out of our awakening, others awaken, too.

As noted above, in some places Dongshan represents the experience of emptiness as laying down the hoe, or resting among the clouds. Here, in a world seen fresh from awakening, we take up the hoe—or more likely these days the i-Pad and the mobile phone—and work on behalf of others according to their needs. This is the broad country of the human heart, where not only family and friends but even sworn enemies can find a home.

In his verse for the stage of Merit in Common, Dongshan explores the theme of enlightenment in common—the notion that our own awakening is exactly the awakening of all beings—touching initially on aspects of difference and singularity, before surprising us with a heart opening image of accord.

The many beings and buddhas do not intrude on each other.
Mountains are high of themselves; waters are deep of themselves.

In terms of the unfolding of the Way, these two lines provide the necessary antidote to "dwelling hidden high among the thousand distant peaks"—which is to say "dwelling in emptiness"—expressed in the preceding stage. Now we turn from emptiness toward that which is unique and singular, and we treat that as all that there is. From this perspective, each thing stands alone even as it configures the whole. It's the nature of mountains to be high; it's the nature of oceans to be deep. Buddhas are complete, in and of themselves, lacking nothing. Just as each of us—drunk, sober, miserable, enraged, exultant—emerge, moment by moment, from vastness into lone, inimitable life. Each such appearance is the face of timeless immensity. The spirit of these lines is the mystery of things as they are, or rather, the mystery of things that they are, in all their precipitous uniqueness.

In the brilliant and clarifying light of "Mountains are high of themselves; waters are deep of themselves," even if we fail to live up to others' and our own expectations, or fail to come into our own, we are still irrevocably unique. Dongshan's point cuts deeper than our shallow attempts to stand out from the crowd—a position aptly encapsulated in the slogan "Let me be different, like everybody else!" In truth, each particular thing unstintingly pours out its song: the cicada sings itself to death as the cicada. The chair, the butterfly, and the parrot eating berries are fathomlessly and inimitably themselves. Regarding inimitability, I am reminded of my composer friend Michal Murin's great aunt in Lengow, Slovakia.

When I met her, she was frail, almost blind. Michal talked family with her in Slovak, while she responded in Ruthenian. I listened in English.

Meanwhile she plied me with Polish vodka—"If you can't understand, at least you can drink!"

Michal asked me to explain Zen to her.

I said, "Ask her if the birds are singing in her heart!"

Maybe he did, but she just poured me another vodka.

As she labored to get a log on the fire, Michal told me that it took her an hour and a half to get to church. I asked how far it was, because the village was tiny. It turned out to be about a hundred meters.

"Is it because she is blind; because she can barely walk?"

"Yes. But mostly because she keeps stopping to enjoy what she can make out of the shadows and light. She picks up rocks and pebbles so she can feel them, talks to the dogs and cats, and to anyone she meets. It's a long journey."

Blind or sighted, it's important to engage, like Michal's great aunt, with what is close at hand. Then, even the most customary acts—washing our hands, cleaning our teeth (often felt to be boring by people in a rush)—when we engage with them fully, are never boring. Boredom disappears into the runneling of cold water over the backs of our hands and the glittering spray.

However, it's challenging to be present, and we avoid discomfort by anticipating what's to come. This is like when we turn on the light in a room that we are approaching, wanting to be with what's to be, rather than where we are in the shadowy hall, tired and longing for bed.

Shunryu Suzuki (1905–1971) said that there is nothing mystical, apart from ordinary things. This isn't to say that there is nothing mystical— that is, nothing essential or empty. It's just that without the small, the momentary, and the limited, the mystical has no way to appear; has no means to express itself. Rocks and pebbles, and heartbeats and breath, are its means.

There is a Zen saying, "The elbow does not bend outward." "The elbow" is our humanity expressed as limitation and vulnerability. It is the elbow's nature not to bend outward; it is our nature to be fragile and fleeting, even as we embody vastness. Yet we don't dwell on that connection; we don't seek to dwell in vastness. Instead, we invest that immensity in our connection with world, and in how we treat others.

How do we do this? When a child comes to us, we open to her as a child and deal with her as a child; when a wise person comes, we open to her wisdom and honor the gifts that she brings. We deal appropriately with each particular being by meeting her fully, and acknowledging her completely.

The saying "When dew enters the willow it becomes green; when it enters the flower it becomes red" beautifully expresses such true meeting. When we meet each person fully, we lose (and find) ourselves over and over, enlightening others and becoming enlightened ourselves in an unending dance. I assume the guise of a scary monster for the delight of my daughter; I become the parent that urges her to bed; I act as her coconspirator, planning her mother's birthday. Now she guides me, helping me to choose a suit in a labyrinthine menswear shop. Each of our roles flashes from darkness; each is the face of that darkness.

What do the myriad differences and distinctions clarify?
Where the partridge calls, the hundred flowers bloom afresh.

Dongshan's question here conveys the essential realm, and is itself a response to its own query. We shouldn't be unduly fascinated with this, though. We can easily spin our wheels in the mud, going nowhere fast. Dongshan responds to his question-that-is-itself-an-answer with a profound and mysterious line. His reply invites us to see the bright kingdom of the unique and contingent as mysterious all over again. He urges us to live our realization more fully, and to succumb at deeper levels.

This isn't simply about realizing wholeness or uniqueness—and their inseparability—but stepping beyond all that, to express and embody the Way in our least activity. The willingness to "step beyond" is born of the love and compassion that flow from a lifetime of walking the Way. It is difficult to put this into words, but the following brief exchange captures its spirit:

> Tongan Guanzhi (n.d.) came to the teacher Tongan Daopi (n.d), and said, "The ancients said, 'I do not love what worldly people love.' I wonder, what does your Reverence love?"
> Tongan Daopi replied, "I have already become like this."
> When Guanzhi heard this he had an awakening.[78]

The student, Guanzhi, was consumed with love for the Way. Such love pulls us into depth, drawing us deeper into our relationship with the Way. Living expressions of this love appear when we struggle with our practice and go to bed feeling discouraged, yet in the morning everything feels fresh and alive. How can that be? We fight with her, but she doesn't quit on us. Embarking into the Way we're like teenage lovers plucking petals from a flower: "She loves me, she loves me not . . ." As we venture deeper and deeper in, it's just: "She loves me, she loves me, she loves me . . ."

So the student asks his teacher, "What does your Reverence love?" He's asking, "Are you worldly? Are you attached? After such long training and practice, how do you stand in relation to love?" And his teacher comes out with this mysterious response, "I have already become like this." Become like what? In great teachers there is a center, a core that wells. Their activity comes from nourishing it, and being nourished by it. Mystery resonates in their words and actions. They walk the Way; they sleep the Way. A student comes to hear her teacher teach, but more importantly, to see how he or she loves.

In old China, it was said that the partridge was by nature fond of going south and uninterested in flying north. Whenever southerners hear the call of the partridge, it reminds them of their homeland. The call not only reminds us of home, it is home. Where the magpie sings, where the train crashes through, where the airplane roars over opening up my heart, nothing obstructs, and I die over and again into it: into meetings and partings, and sleepless inchoate journeys.

I meet my son as he came off the plane to start his new life in Sydney, loaded up with his bike and synthesizer, on a drenching autumn afternoon. Then, as I am about to fly home to Perth, we stand together in a lighter rain, hugging as we say our goodbyes, neither of us wanting our time together to end—an embrace of meeting and parting in which bridge, tower, and harbor gather. Wind blows over the water, and what is unfathomable—unsayable—starts up as the stumbling, articulate speech of love.

18. Merit upon Merit

If horns sprout on your head, that's unbearable;
If you rouse your mind to seek Buddha, that's shameful.
In the vastness of the empty kalpa there is no one who knows—
Why go to the South to interview the fifty-three sages?

THE RATHER GRAND title, Merit upon Merit, and Dongshan's accompanying low-lit verse have always struck me as being in strange conjunction. The verse's assertion of the primacy of not-knowing points to the end of the journey through the Cycle of Merit resting in a place where the stages along the way, and even emptiness itself, are empty. In Dongshan's cycle we find no enlivening and memorable return to the marketplace to enlighten publicans and prostitutes, such as we find in the Ox-Herding Cycle. Dongshan's concern is that we not put something where there is nothing at all.

To arrive at the stage of Merit upon Merit is to be enlightened beyond enlightenment. There are no medallions struck to indicate such attainment, and hopefully, if we try to apply this personally, it is not us. Whatever Merit upon Merit may be, it includes our delusions about the world and ourselves. Our deepest misunderstandings of the Way—not to mention our faults and our foolishness—are lit by the moon.

Merit upon Merit, or Enlightenment beyond Enlightenment, as I like to call it, entails that the Way becomes a lived matter, and is none other than our unique life in its unfolding. Our experience of emptiness is now so embodied in our ordinary activity that it is forgotten. The stages of our journey—Orientation, Service, Merit (personal awakening), Merit in Common (enlightenment in common)—are subsumed within the least of our activities. The world and we ourselves have passed into each other, and we live the realized life in accord with our circumstances. I say "the realized life," but here "life" is more than enough. In the grown-up world this can only be taken up fully at the price of including our pain and fear, and that of others.

In a way, there is less and less to say, because the timeless spring of awakening is now so invested in our lives that it has become time out of mind. James Joyce's comment about his marriage with Nora is reminiscent of this lived, embodied Way: "After thirty years of marriage, what is there to talk about?"

In the concluding line of his verse, Dongshan refers to the Avatamsaka Sutra, alluding to the journey of the pilgrim Sudhana, who engaged fifty-three teachers of the Way. At the end of our own journey through orientation, commitment, personal awakening, and enlightenment in common, the cycle concludes with just the quiet question, "Why go to the South to interview the fifty-three sages?"

It's good that our journey ends with such a question. It opens us to the unknown all over again. In this spirit, we can explore Dongshan's verse in detail.

If horns sprout on your head, that's unbearable;
If you rouse your mind to seek Buddha, that's shameful.

Dongshan's opening lines for this verse echo the following exchange between Nanquan Puyuan (748–835) and Daowu Yuanzhi (769–835):

> Nanquan asked Daowu, "What can you say about the place where knowledge doesn't reach?"
>
> Daowu replied, "One should absolutely avoid talking about that."
>
> Nanquan said, "Truly, as soon as one explains, horns sprout on one's head, and one becomes a beast."[79]

When we attempt to describe the place where knowledge doesn't reach, we "descend in the social scale," to use the language of Dongshan's time. When we give an explanation of enlightenment beyond enlightenment, or set out the stages of the Way in a series of obscure and dazzling verses, we end up with "suspicious bulges on our forehead," as Robert Aitken suggests.[80] That said, I reckon beasts do a better job of manifesting the Dharma than humans do of explaining it.

In a way, rousing our mind to seek Buddha can be a commendable urge to go deeper, for inevitably we feel that whatever we've realized isn't enough. But continuing to ask, "What is Buddha?" after we've realized can also be a way of refusing to cross the bridge to fully enter our lives. If we find ourselves dazzled by the ancient koan, and if its allure makes our life seem shabby in comparison, we need to take care.

Rousing our minds to seek Buddha can also be a way of showing off our striving, to ourselves, at least. It can become an addiction and a pose. It's disingenuous to say, "I've become a beginning student all over again," when that apparent humility is subtly infected by our knowingness, or by the pride we take in our humility.

Often we don't notice the build up of pride, which grows out of commendable self-confidence, but then climbs unnoticed until we find that we are stiffly defending our position and our patch. An old Hasidic teacher compared the unnoticed inflation of pride to taking a journey by carriage. We look out of the window and swear that the countryside is level. Only when we begin the sharp descent do we realize the preceding slow climb of our pride.

Again, we might believe that it is wrong to give up our efforts after enlightenment, and consequently rouse our minds to seek Buddha as a way of confirming that each thought is Buddha, and that our very questioning is Buddha. By doing so we unwittingly reintroduce subject and object all over again.

Now, finally, there is no need to seek Buddha. With no separation between our lives and our practice, we are hopefully at ease. Hopefully too, not even the wisest can detect any residue of realization in our words or actions; nor find the tracks of the ancestors in our footprints.

In the vastness of the empty kalpa there is no one who knows—

The Sanskrit term *kalpa* means "a world age," an endlessly long period of time. Imagine a block of stone a cubic mile in volume. Every century a swallow flies over the stone, brushing against it with the tip of its wing. When the block has been worn away by these caresses, not even one kalpa will have elapsed!

So that everything can breathe again, Dongshan consigns the Cycle of Merit to this timeless vastness. "In the vastness of the empty kalpa there is no one who knows." This line empties out time, knowing, and the stages of the Way. However, this doesn't mean "abandon all hope." It's just that, having walked the darkling path into not-knowing, we are so sunk in emptiness that we are it, and have forgotten even that. Who do we think we are, and what do we think we know in a place without a single thought? Ole Nydahl says, "If your practice is making you stupid, stop." I'd say, "Keep right on." I'm not advocating some know-nothing piety, though. This isn't an argument for abandoning knowledge, but rather for seeing it for what it is and not clinging to it.

You can't think without thinking a thought, and any thought thus thunk is empty, and so are its contents concerning the world and ourselves. In this spirit, it is important not to attach to the five stages of the Cycle of Merit (or the Five Ranks overall) as modes of knowledge. This is the main thrust of Dongshan's final verse. If you attach to the stages as knowledge, you cash out the spirit of the Way.

Having climbed the ladder, we kick it away. We step beyond knowing and not-knowing, and even beyond forgetting. Emptiness and all its modes of expression are empty. The final verse encodes its own release, and ours. Even as their beauty and profundity entrance us, we learn the modes and stages, realize them, embody them, and finally forget them. In the light of this, if there is no one who knows, why would we go to the South to interview the fifty-three sages?

Why go to the South to interview the fifty-three sages?

It is fitting that Dongshan invokes the Avatamsaka Sutra to conclude his Cycle of Merit, and the Five Ranks as a whole. By doing so he honors the Five Ranks' grand precursor and reminds us of its subtle background presence in the Five Ranks, courtesy of the Huayan masters. The final chapter of the Avatamsaka Sutra is entitled "Entry into the Realm of Reality" and relates the journey of the pilgrim Sudhana to visit fifty-three bodhisattva teachers, including women and men, laypeople and priests, beggars and kings and queens. It's good to get such a diverse training!

Toward the end of his pilgrimage, a richly blessed and grateful Sudhana arrives at the bodhisattva Maitreya's place. He enters the inconceivably vast tower, which represents the universe experienced as profound and all-encompassing enlightenment. Words can't do justice to the vision.

When the door shut: He saw the tower immensely vast and wide, hundreds of thousands of leagues wide, as measureless as the sky, as vast as all of space, adorned with countless attributes; countless canopies, banners, pennants, jewels, garlands of pearls and gems, moons and half moons ... sweetly ringing bells and nets of chimes, flowers showering, celestial garlands and streamers, censers giving off fragrant fumes, showers of gold dust, networks of upper chambers, round windows, arches, turrets, jewel figurines of women ... Also, inside the great tower he saw hundreds of thousands of other towers similarly arrayed; he saw those towers as infinitely vast as space, evenly arrayed in all directions, yet these towers were not mixed up with each other, being each mutually distinct, while appearing in each and every object of all the other towers.[81]

Maitreya's tower represents the apotheosis of Sudhana's pilgrimage: all these universes within universes, each reflecting the others to infinity. This is Indra's Jewel Net, where each unique jewel in the infinite net perfectly reflects all the others. The image of Maitreya's tower presages the dialectic of inclusion and separation that informed Shitou's Accord and Dongshan's Five Ranks after that.

After the long pilgrimage from orientation to commitment,

from commitment to personal awakening, from personal awakening to enlightenment in common, and from enlightenment in common to supreme awakening, the conclusion of the final stage is very quiet—"Why go to the South to interview the fifty-three sages?"—wordlessly conveying the Way beyond questions and answers.

19. Reflecting on the Stages of Merit

The Five Stages of Merit and Maturity on the Way

Having examined the Cycle of Merit, stage by stage, we see how Dongshan has laid the cycle out for us as a step-by-step path. And yet the entire journey is also implicit in our dawning curiosity and our first hesitant step. Our study of the five stages of the Cycle of Merit has focused on cultivation of the Way. Cultivation takes place and deepens over time, yet the theme of timelessness is itself present and casts its spell within the process as it unfolds. This is particularly true with regard to the imagery of timeless spring in the middle stage, Merit or personal awakening, and the imagery of the vastness of the empty kalpa in the final stage, Merit upon Merit or awakening upon awakening.

Our study of the steps to awakening encompassed what we must do if we are going to embody that awakening and convey it to others, and what the rewards of such dedication are: ever deepening insight and maturity on the path. Dongshan doesn't explicitly mention the matter of maturity, but it is implicit in the long training in the Way suggested by the Cycle of Merit, and so it feels appropriate to mention it here.

How we deal with suffering is one gauge of maturity in the Way. The suffering of the world is not just our business; at the deepest level, it is also our matter. As the years of training mount, we find that there is less of a pull to seek our own comfort and to close our attention off from the pain of others. When we realize intimacy, when we awaken to the world as our own nature, we recognize that there is no place where we are safe from the unutterable pain of the world.

If we flee from that pain, or try to inoculate ourselves against it, we won't be high and dry at all, but will suffer needlessly because of our evasion. Standing fast, we may be able to help even with our mere presence. When we move to ease the pain of others, we let go of our own self-concern as we engage with them. The development of compassion, and its close relative, moral imagination—that ability to put our self in another's place and to empathize with the other—rest in the kind of wisdom and insight that our journey with Dongshan's Cycle of Merit can provide.

For me, the development of a sense of humor is another gauge of maturity on the Way. We are all error-prone, and our wrong-footedness and its resulting shame and embarrassment seem to intensify, if anything, as we deepen in the Way. Over time we learn that we shouldn't take ourselves too seriously and that we be able to tolerate and laugh at our own foolishness. This is an antidote to the spiritual pride that can easily grow with perceived attainments on the path, especially those signaled by titles such as "Merit" and "Merit upon Merit."

With the development of a perspective on our place in things, comes, hopefully, a gift for not sweating the small. So much angst is typically expended on slights and insults—assumed or actual. In this regard, it can be helpful to ask, "What does this mean in the light of my death?" Usually not much.

With maturity in the Way, we get a clearer perspective on what is important. Shido Bunan's famous line "Those who seek the Dharma in the depths are those who leave it behind in the shallows," is rich in implications. Whatever else it implies, it surely points to the fact that if we are overwhelmingly focused on awakening to emptiness, we may miss the richness of our lives that lies so close at hand in love and work. The quest for enlightenment may mean that we put these on hold. The long journey after awakening should surely include restoring those values in our lives and becoming increasingly available to others.

Lastly, as a gauge of maturity on the Way, I would include grace under pressure: that ability to deal lightly and freely with what is difficult. My father, while not a Zen practitioner in the formal sense, exemplifies this most aptly for me. When he was in his eighties, he was knocked down by a delivery van. In hospital they put him in "treatment," prior to admitting him as a patient. I broke regulations to be with him. Although no one could find time to get him a bottle to piss in, four staff members came round with their clipboards during the three hours he waited there, to ask him his age. He generously gave each of them a fresh response—"twenty-one," "ninety-eight," "forty-seven," and finally, "two-hundred"! I would say (modestly) that his tongue had no bone in it. Always playful, he found the freedom and the grace to play, even in his pain and distress.

The Cycle of Merit and the Ox-Herding Cycle

The Cycle of Merit may have been a forerunner to the Ox-Herding Cycle of pictures and their commentaries, created by the twelfth-century master Kuoan Shiyuan (fl. 1150).[82] The Ox-Herding Cycle conveys the stages of a practitioner's journey to personal enlightenment and then on to enlighten others.[83] This striking sequence of images and verses shows the aspirant's yearning, searching, and struggle to attain the Way as symbolized by the ox herder tracking, finding, and taming an ox. The aspirant's awakening, and his maturing of that awakening, is expressed by the herder's seeing, catching, taming, and riding the ox home. Finally, with his awakening so completely embodied that it is forgotten, the enlightened herder returns to the marketplace, where he compassionately awakens others.

Both the Ox-Herding Cycle and the Cycle of Merit are archetypal accounts of the Zen Way, as it unfolds in time. Both cycles address our need to see the Zen path as a set of recognizable stages, and each cycle provides us with a map of those stages from which we can draw inspiration and encouragement as we deepen our maturity in the Way.

In terms of the stages of training, the Ox-Herding Cycle is more differentiated than the Cycle of Merit, and not only because it has ten steps rather than five. The Cycle of Merit takes the details of training for granted, and its verses are more abstruse than those of the Ox-Herding Cycle. Importantly, the Cycle of Merit presents us with a return to emptiness at its end, and it is framed as empty in each of its stages. Partly this is to encourage us not to cling to the idea of progress on the Way, particularly to milestone experiences. We are also enjoined to let go of trying to locate ourselves on a map of the Way, such as the one that the Ox-Herding Cycle so memorably provides. Ultimately, the Cycle of Merit is best understood as a step-by-step path to enlightenment in which each of the five steps is timelessly empty.

At least in terms of its progressive aspect, we can compare the merit cycle with the Ox-Herding Cycle. The first two ox-herding verses and their corresponding pictures—Seeking the Ox, and Finding the Tracks—coincide broadly with the stages of Orientation and Service, respectively, in the Cycle of Merit. Regarding the stage of Service, the image of the cuckoo's call that draws us ever deeper into the jumbled peaks is reminiscent of the Ox-Herding Cycle's stage of Seeking the Ox, where the herder discovers the ox's footprints deep amid the remote mountains, among impenetrable ravines.

The third stage of the Cycle of Merit, called Merit (personal awakening), corresponds to the third image in the Ox-Herding Cycle, Seeing the Ox (awakening to one's true nature).

There is no clear singular correspondence between any image from the Ox-Herding Cycle and Dongshan's fourth stage in the Cycle of Merit, Merit in Common. However, the sense of one's kinship with all beings—of refining our realization amid oppositional circumstances as a path to embody our realization—can be related to the Ox-Herding Cycle's stages of catching, taming, and riding the ox home. The allied theme of working on behalf of others, touched on in our exploration of the theme of Merit in Common, may be understood to prefigure Entering the Marketplace with Helping Hands—the concluding image of the Ox-Herding Cycle.

After we have seen the ox, tamed it, and ridden it home, we must transcend and finally forget our realization. These steps are symbolized by the three penultimate images of the Ox-Herding Cycle: Transcending the Ox, Transcending the Ox and the Self, and Returning to the Source. We can understand these three as encompassed by the concluding stage in the Cycle of Merit: Merit beyond Merit (enlightenment beyond enlightenment).

The chart below very broadly correlates Kuoan's Ox-Herding sequence with Dongshan's Cycle of Merit:

CYCLE OF MERIT	OX-HERDING CYCLE
1. Orientation	1. Seeking the Ox
2. Service	2. Finding the Tracks
3. Merit (personal awakening)	3. Seeing the Ox (awakening to one's true nature)
4. Merit in Common (enlightenment in common)— and implicitly the fourth and corresponding mode of Dongshan's first cycle: Approaching Concurrence.	4. Catching the Ox 5. Taming the Ox 6. Riding the Ox Home 10. Entering the Marketplace with Helping Hands
5. Merit upon Merit (enlightenment beyond enlightenment)	7. Transcending the Ox 8. Transcending the Ox and the Self 9. Returning to the Source

In terms of correspondences between the two cycles, the Cycle of Merit amusingly begins in the marketplace, which is the goal and destination of the Ox-Herding Cycle. In the concluding verse of the Cycle of Merit, we encounter the line "If horns sprout on your head, that's unbearable; if you rouse your mind to seek Buddha, that's shameful." This statement seems to suggest an unwelcome return of the ox, after it has been seen, caught, embodied, and then properly forgotten.

The stages of the Cycle of Merit are not solely teachings, or straightforward descriptions of the unfolding Way in practice and training. They embody, rather, five states of enlightenment: five enlightened perspectives on the Way. Dongshan's treatment of these enlightened states is subtle and profound, and there is a kind of "all empty, all at once" quality, even as he creates, in the same breath, a clear and credible sequence to the Way considered as progressive stages. Seen thus, the spirit of the Cycle of Merit is quite different from Kuoan's Ox-Herding

Cycle, which is more literally conceived as a progressive account of the
Way, unfolding straightforwardly over time.

A Comparison of Dongshan's Two Cycles

Dongshan presents the Way by means of two distinct cycles. In the first,
the Cycle of the Essential and the Contingent, by means of the intimate
dialectic of the essential and the contingent, he reveals five paradigms
of awakening. In the second cycle, the Cycle of Merit, we are shown
the how of the Way: how we are to prepare the ground of awakening,
and, having awakened, how we are to mature that awakening. The
first cycle is geared toward wisdom and insight; the second has a more
ethical and practical impulse, being concerned, at least in its earlier
stages, with training, commitment, and service. Broadly speaking, the
first cycle lends us wings; the second gives us feet with which to walk
the Way until it is embodied and forgotten.

The Cycle of the Essential and the Contingent and the Cycle of Merit
complement each other: the first is nothing but dark formalism and
abstraction if it leaves our lives untouched; the second is at best wishful
thinking if it is devoid of the light of genuine insight. The study of the
Cycle of the Essential and the Contingent must be supported by the
stages of actual practice, so that the two cycles function together like
left foot and right foot walking. In this regard, it's good not to favor a
leg, or to cultivate an uneven gait.

The positions of the first cycle aren't inherently progressive, but
those of the second cycle clearly are. In this way, the two cycles should
be understood as complementary. I sense that this was Dongshan's
intent. He created one cycle to set out five exemplary paradigms of
enlightenment (the Cycle of the Essential and the Contingent) and a
complementary cycle to set out five stages whereby one might awaken
to the positions of the first cycle (the Cycle of Merit).

The first cycle is non-progressive, with each of its positions opening to eternity. The second cycle primarily unfolds the stages of the
Way over time, even as we can properly regard each stage within it as
timeless. So the first cycle may be understood to convey five modes of

sudden realization, and the second, five stages on a gradual path to maturity.

Both cycles are informed by Huayan's enlightened all-at-once vision of reality. In the Cycle of Merit, in particular, what appear to be sequential steps and stages actually are *that*, and in that capacity they convey a sense of "successive causation." At the same time they should be understood as aspects of the awakened mind of the Buddha, where—all sequence gone—"everything is simultaneously, and interdependently established through total mutual interfusion."[84] In that latter capacity, the five stages of merit, like the five positions of the first cycle, are reflective of a "simultaneous causation," where past, present, and future—the various steps and stages of the Way—are "all-at-once" in their radiant interfusion. In the words of Yongjia's "Song of Enlightenment": One level contains all levels.

The Literary Heritage
of the Five Ranks

20. Shitou Xiqian's "Accord on Investigating Diversity and Wholeness"

ACCORD ON INVESTIGATING DIVERSITY AND WHOLENESS

The heart-mind of the great Indian immortal
is intimately transmitted east and west.
While people may be sharp or dull-witted,
the Way has no northern or southern ancestors.

The profound source is clear and unstained,
flowing darkly through tributaries and branches.

To cling to events is to lose your way;
yet according with principle isn't enlightenment either.

Gates upon gates, all the fields of experience
interpenetrate, yet are separate.
Interacting, they permeate each other,
while each keeps its own place.

Form is originally different from substance and image;
sounds differ as pleasing or harsh.
In the dark, profound and ordinary speech are the same,
while in the bright, lucid and muddled words are clearly distinct.

The four elements return to their nature, like a child to
    its mother;
fire heats, wind shakes, water wets, the earth supports;

the eye sees color, the ear hears sounds, the nose smells odors,
the tongue tastes salt and sour.

With each and every Dharma, according to the root,
the leaves spread out; yet fundamental and peripheral
must rejoin the source, and noble and menial each have
their appropriate speech.

There is dark within the bright, but do not meet it as dark.
Within the dark there is bright, but do not view it as bright.
Bright and dark mutually correspond, like front and back foot
    walking.

Each of the myriad things has merit,
expressed in terms of its place and use.
Events affirm principle like a lid fitting a box;
while principle corresponds to events, like arrow points meeting.

To receive the teachings,
you must encounter the ancestors.
Do not set up your own compass and square.

If you try to see the Way, you can't discern it;
although you travel the path, you do not know it.
Advancing, you are neither near nor far,
but when you are lost and separated, the realm is secure.

I respectfully say to you who would investigate the mystery,
do not spend your time in vain.

A CENTRAL PRECURSOR THAT must be considered in any exploration of the historical and literary context of the Five Ranks is the "Accord on Investigating Diversity and Wholeness," a celebrated poem by Shitou Xiqian (700–790). Admirable in its own right, the Accord anticipated and functioned as a shaping influence on the first cycle of the Five Ranks, the Cycle of the Essential and the Contingent. The poem also drew on the Huayan dialectic of principle and phenomena discussed above, and it is thus a bridge between Huayan thought and the Five Ranks. Dongshan's "Song of the Precious Mirror Samadhi," the likely inspirational source poem for the Five Ranks, seems also to have been heavily influenced by the Accord.

The Caodong (Soto) School, which has its genesis with Dongshan and his disciple Caoshan, alone among the Five Houses, has its own prehistory in which Shitou is accorded the role of founding teacher. The status of founder was accorded him, at least in part, because of the shaping influence of his "Accord on Investigating Diversity and Wholeness" on Dongshan's "Song of the Precious Mirror Samadhi," and the Five Ranks, which were embedded within it.

From the outset, we should make note of the influence of Taoist thought, and of the I Ching in particular, on Shitou's "Accord on Investigating Diversity and Wholeness." To begin with, Shitou appropriated the title of a Taoist text, called *Zhouyi cantongqi*, to name his work— *Zhouyi* being a name given to the I Ching to reflect its connection to King Wen of the Zhou Dynasty, its reputed author. We find other I Ching associations in the body of the poem as well. Shitou's use of the I Ching and employment of the imagery of bright and dark, in turn influenced Dongshan's composition of his Five Ranks. For instance, Dongshan placed the Li hexagram at the core of his "Song of the Precious Mirror Samadhi," a work that served as a womb for the Five Ranks. As a result of this, it is possible to read the Five Ranks as similarly configured by the Li hexagram, and to consider the overall dialectic of the work in the light of the I Ching. Such is the interwoven net of influence that connects these three great poems of the Way.

The terms "diversity" and "wholeness" used in Shitou's title are suggestive of the Huayan terms "phenomena" and "principle," and indeed prior translators of the Accord have relied on these familiar Huayan terms in their work. More immediate to our own concerns, "diversity" and "wholeness" evoke the "contingent" and "essential" of the first cycle of the Five Ranks. And in fact, both the Accord and the Five Ranks may be fairly described as investigations into the nature of the relationship between diversity and wholeness, or between contingent and essential.

In order to highlight the correlations between Shitou's "Accord on Investigating Diversity and Wholeness" and Dongshan's Five Ranks, particularly the Cycle of the Essential and the Contingent, we will explore some of the key passages from the Accord that seem to have most influenced Dongshan's work. While our study of the poem will be limited in nature, the whole of this influential poem is worthy of close attention.

Transmitting the Heart-Mind of the Buddha

The source and spring of the Accord is the heart-mind of the Buddha, and its transmission. Shitou, like Dongshan with his "Song of the Precious Mirror Samadhi," grounds his poem in the Buddha's awakening and its transmission. The poem is dialectical in nature from its opening lines:

> **The heart-mind of the great Indian immortal**
> **is intimately transmitted east and west.**
> **While people may be sharp or dull-witted,**
> **the Way has no northern or southern ancestors.**

The heart-mind of the Buddha has already been transmitted and is not far to find—a cold autumn morning here; I turn up the heater. Historically, Chan has had a northern line of ancestors, as well as a southern line, to which Shitou belonged. Yet in the heart-mind there is no east or west, or north or south. Nonetheless, as Shitou seems to mischievously suggest, we can distinguish differences in acuity between teachers of the northern and southern schools.

Thus, Shitou sets up the seesaw of his dialectic: what cannot be transmitted at all "is intimately transmitted east and west." While in the vastness of the Way of the Buddha there is no teacher, we know a good deal about the lineages of the northern and southern schools of Chan.

The Dialectic of Dark and Bright

The profound source is clear and unstained,
flowing darkly through tributaries and branches.

We can understand "the profound source" as the heart-mind of the Buddha—what Dongshan calls "the essential." "Tributaries and branches" express what is partial, limited, and changeable, and correspond to what Dongshan calls "the contingent." Taken as a whole, this line creates an image that is expressive of the essential and the contingent in their shifting relationship to one another. We can also understand it as a metaphor for the Buddha's awakening and its transmission through various sects and lineages.

To cling to events is to lose your way;
yet according with principle isn't enlightenment either.

This line warns us against one-sided practice. If we cling to events, that is, to contingency, we will be immersed in karma and at the mercy of our circumstances. On the other hand, we can't cling to principle—to be understood here as "the essential"—either. If we do, our lives languish, and we become useless to others and ourselves.

As mentioned above, the Huayan system of the Three Discernments, the Accord, and the Five Ranks all teach the Middle Way and the need to engage it via a dialectic of principle and phenomena, or of essential and contingent.

Gates upon gates, all the fields of experience
interpenetrate, yet are separate.

"Gates upon gates" may be a reference to the Ten Mysterious Gates of the Unitary Vehicle of the Huayan, a work by the second patriarch of Huayan, Zhiyan (602–668), but it refers more broadly to the limitless opportunities that our lives provide for entering the Way. The same notion is captured in the third bodhisattva vow:

Though Dharma gates are numberless, I vow to enter them.

That profusion of opportunity is not to be missed. "Gates upon gates" is our unfolding life, expressed as the realm of sense, the realm of understanding, the realm of affection, and myriad others, all completely involved with one another, yet recognizably unique. "All the realms of experience . . . interpenetrate, yet are separate." This verse anticipates and conveys the spirit expressed in the first two positions of Dongshan's dialectic: the Contingent within the Essential and the Essential within the Contingent. Shitou's verse and Dongshan's first two positions both show the essential and the contingent as mutually pervasive, even as they remain distinct.

**Interacting, they permeate each other,
while each keeps its own place.**

Shitou reiterates the point of the prior line. These lines, again, anticipate Dongshan's first two positions. The realms of our experience interact, and that interaction is mutual, just as the interaction of essential and contingent is mutual. The Chinese word for "place" (*wei*) in "while each keeps to its own place" is the same term we have translated as "position" in Dongshan's first cycle, with its five positions of the essential and the contingent. Shitou employs the term precisely as Dongshan uses it in his presentation of the five positions of the essential and the contingent. Aside from revealing a harmony between the dialectical spirit of the Accord and that of the Five Ranks, the mutuality and exclusivity invoked here are also richly suggestive of how we might live in relationship with others: mutually intimate, yet independent.

In the dark, profound and ordinary speech are the same,
while in the bright, lucid and muddled words are clearly distinct.

Here, Shitou reasserts the dialectic of principle and phenomena, but now in terms of an investigation of words. "In the dark" is evocative of emptiness. The implication of "in the dark, profound and ordinary speech is the same" is that words and language are empty. As we have indicated above, this very theme of the purity of words and language is at the heart of the Five Ranks enterprise, especially, and literally, in the third mode of the first cycle: Arriving within the Essential.

However Shitou avoids stranding us in the emptiness of pure words by immediately reasserting the dialectical tension with his next line, "while lucid and muddled words are clearly distinct in the bright." "Bright" is suggestive of the contingent, the dawn mode where things are revealed as clearly unique. Indeed, we encounter no problem at all in distinguishing the amped up, pressured gibberish of "gotcha" advertisements on commercial radio, from the clarity of a child asking for a raise in their allowance.

Shitou's "Profound and ordinary speech is the same in the dark" anticipates Dongshan's third mode, Arriving within the Essential, and "while lucid and muddled words are clearly distinct in the bright" prefigures the fourth mode, Approaching from the Contingent.

There is dark within the bright, but do not meet it as dark.
Within the dark there is bright, but do not view it as bright.
Bright and dark mutually correspond, like front and back foot
walking.

In these lines we find the clearest parallel between the dialectics at the core of the Accord and at the core of the five positions. As mentioned above, bright and dark correspond to Dongshan's contingent and essential, respectively. With this in mind it is possible to lay out Shitou's dialectic and Dongshan's as mirror images of each other:

THE CYCLE OF THE ESSENTIAL AND THE CONTINGENT	SHITOU'S DIALECTIC IN THE ACCORD
1. The Contingent within the Essential	The Bright within the Dark
2. The Essential within the Contingent	The Dark within the Bright
3. Arriving within the Essential	Just the Dark
4. Approaching from the Contingent	Just the Bright
5. Arriving at Concurrence	The Dark as the Bright

Shitou's provisos in the verse, "but do not meet it as dark" and "do not meet it as bright," caution us against getting entangled with the extremes of "dark only" (emptiness in isolation) or light only (contingency in isolation). Like this, he asserts the Middle Way, where having awakened to, embodied, and finally forgotten emptiness, we let go of considerations such as contingency and emptiness and experience the Way beyond all categories as our ordinary, yet inexpressibly unique, lives of love and work. These admonitions are echoed in the third and fourth positions of the Five Ranks, where we are encouraged to see the Way exclusively from the perspective of essential, and then exclusively from the perspective of contingent, respectively, without forgetting that the opposite polarity is implicit at each point.

Finally, Shitou conveys the essence of Dongshan's fifth position, Arriving at Concurrence, with his image of bright and dark being "like front and back foot walking." When walking, we don't distinguish left foot from right; there is no need to, and only marching demands it. The implication here is that the deep cooperation of the contingent and the essential finds unhindered expression in and as our most ordinary activities. Walking, lying down at night, and opening our eyes at first light convey this utterly. This is precisely what "arriving at concurrence" means.

In effect, Shitou's lines contain within them an embryo of the first cycle of the Five Ranks. It is also likely that these lines inspired Dongshan when he composed his work.

Each of the myriad things has merit,
expressed in terms of its place and use.
Events affirm principle like a lid fitting a box;
while principle corresponds to events, like arrow points meeting.

All objects and events in the contingent realm contain the seed of the essential, which finds expression through "place and use." Thus, we express our essential nature by hammering in nails or cutting lunch for the children. There is no other way for the essential to appear. This is the sense of Shunryu Suzuki's "There is nothing mystical, apart from ordinary things." It is not to say that there is nothing mystical—"mystical" being an expression of the essential—but that what we call "mystical" can only appear through, or more precisely, *as* ordinary things and events.

"Events affirm principle," without remainder, "like a lid fitting a box," and principle affirms events "like arrow points meeting" in midair. "Events" in this context correspond to "phenomena." As the image of arrow points meeting recurs in "Song of the Precious Mirror Samadhi," it seems worthwhile to recount the story associated with this simile.

In ancient China there lived a famous archer who trained a gifted young student. The student, who was ruthless and ambitious, reckoned that if he killed his teacher there would be no one to rival him.

He tried to kill his teacher, but unknowingly failed.

When later the two met by chance on a small country road, the student immediately drew and fired an arrow at his teacher, aiming to get him this time. At the very same instant, the teacher drew and fired his own arrow. The two arrows met in midflight and fell harmlessly to the ground.

Arrow points meeting in midair and a lid fitting a box symbolize the meeting of principle and phenomena, or in Dongshan's terms, the harmonious accord of the essential and the contingent. These are both similes for Arriving at Concurrence, where the essential and the contingent occupy the same place at the same time; where the dialectic is annulled, and we step beyond its oppositions to embody the Way as our ordinary lives.

In this chapter we have seen that Shitou's "Accord on Investigating Diversity and Wholeness" prefigures Dongshan's Five Ranks in important ways. Aside from its influence on the Five Ranks, the dialectic of Shitou's Accord may have been an influence in Dongshan's structuring of his Stream Gatha, and was clearly an influence on his "Song of the Precious Mirror Samadhi," two poems to which we will now turn.

21. Dongshan's Stream Gatha

JUST PRIOR to leaving his master, Yunyan, Dongshan approached him and asked, "If, after many years, someone should ask if I am able to portray your likeness, how should I respond?"

Having remained quiet for a while, Yunyan said, "Just this person."

Dongshan was lost in thought.

Yunyan said, "Jie Acharya,[85] having assumed the burden of this Great Matter, you must be very cautious."

Dongshan remained dubious about what Yunyan had said. Later, as he was crossing a river, Dongshan glimpsed his own reflection in the water below and experienced a great awakening as to the meaning of the previous exchange.[86] Dongshan immediately composed the following gatha:

DONGSHAN'S STREAM GATHA

Taking heed not to seek it elsewhere,
as if it were distant from myself,
I now go on alone,
yet I meet him everywhere.
He is now exactly me,
but I am not now him.
You should meet in this way,
for only then can you realize thus.

These are the words of a teacher who has begun to teach.

The Five Modes in the Stream Gatha

Let's explore this poem of true meeting. Although it is brief, it is full of entry points into the Way. Additionally, and in this it resembles the "Song of the Precious Mirror Samadhi," it intimates Dongshan's first cycle of the Five Ranks: the five modes of the essential and the contingent.

> **Taking heed not to seek it elsewhere,**
> **as if it were distant from myself,**
> **I now go on alone,**
> **yet I meet him everywhere.**

If we seek awakening "out there," one oasis after another dries up at our approach. With "I now go on alone," everything and everyone dies into the sound of Dongshan's footsteps. The weave of things gathers as him: lone, inalienable. In the instant of seeing his own reflection, Dongshan met his old teacher at last. "Him," in this context, refers to his old teacher, Yunyan, who is, in the same breath, the timeless dimensionless nature of Buddha mind manifesting as Dongshan's reflected face, the cry of the water birds, and the dark groves lining the banks.

> **He is now exactly me,**
> **but I am not now him.**

Each arising thing is Dongshan, but, to honor his subtle distinction, he is not it. On the one hand there's Dongshan, awed and joyful, splashing his way across the stream; while on the other, there is his old teacher's body mouldering in his memorial stupa. We need to honor these natural differences, yet if we think that this is two, that's a problem.

> **You should meet in this way,**
> **for only then can you realize thus.**

The experience of true meeting is exemplary, and in that moment of meeting and recognition, our surname is written as stars. And our Christian name? Well don't we answer when someone calls us? For Dongshan, with true meeting the contraries of "I now go on alone, yet I meet him everywhere" and "He is now exactly me, but I am not now him" are held and reconciled. He's saying that for our awakening experience to be genuine we need to meet reality just as intimately, and just as comprehensively. That's true meeting; that is meeting thus. "Thus" suggests the Buddha's experience of tathata, or "just this (person)." These three words were also Yunyan's parting words to Dongshan, and they may have constituted the koan that he mulled over and finally resolved when he saw his face reflected in the stream.

The Stream Gatha corresponds closely to the five positions of the essential and the contingent, right down to their order. The following table illustrates their correspondence:

THE CYCLE OF THE ESSENTIAL AND THE CONTINGENT	DONGSHAN'S STREAM GATHA
1. The Contingent within the Essential	I now go on alone,
2. The Essential within the Contingent	yet I meet him everywhere.
3. Arriving within the Essential	He is now exactly me,
4. Approaching from the Contingent	but I am not now him.
5. Arriving at Concurrence	You should meet in this way, for only then can you realize thus.

To meet truly is to experience concurrence, which is to encounter the empty mysterious great Way where contraries are resolved and past, present, and future breathe as this person. Just as the Stream Gatha configures the five modes of the essential and the contingent, so does the poem, "Song of the Precious Mirror Samadhi." The implication with both of these poems is that—when we genuinely encounter the ancient mirror—all five modes are immediately present as dark and brilliant facets of that experience. This theme, in particular, is at the core of the "Song of the Precious Mirror Samadhi," and it is to that profound and subtle poem that we now turn.

22. Dongshan's "Song of the Precious Mirror Samadhi"

SONG OF THE PRECIOUS MIRROR SAMADHI

The dharma of *just this* is passed down from the Buddha in
  confidence;
today it's yours: take good care of it.
A silver bowl filled with snow, the bright moon concealing
  egrets—
categorized, they are not the same: inchoate, the place is known.
The meaning does not reside in the words, but a pivotal moment
  brings it forth.

Move, and you are mired; hesitate, and you fall into
  doubt and vacillation.
Neither ignore nor confront what is like a great conflagration;
attempting to give it shape, refinement or color
  immediately defiles you.
Fully illuminated at midnight, hidden at daybreak, it is an
  exemplar for all beings, used to liberate them from suffering.

Although it does not act, it is not without words.
As when you face the precious mirror, form and reflection
  behold each other—
you are not him; he is exactly you.
Like an infant endowed with the five features:
not going, not coming, not arising, not abiding, *ba ba wa wa*,

speaking without speaking. In the end there is nothing said,
as the words aren't properly formed.

In the six lines of the doubled Li hexagram,
essential and contingent mutually correspond.
Ranked in pairs they yield three; transformed, they make five.
Like the five tastes of the schizandra berry, and the five-pronged
    diamond vajra,
in the profound inclusiveness of the essential, drumming and
    singing are upheld.

Penetrate the source, explore the muddy paths,
include the concurrent and the dusty road.
Treading carefully is propitious;
You would do well to respect this; do not depart from it.

Naturally genuine and profoundly subtle,
it does not belong to delusion or enlightenment.
In the time and season of cause and effect, it quietly illuminates.
It is so minute, no gap is too small for it to enter; so vast, it is
    without boundaries.
Miss this by a hair's breadth and you are off key and out of tune.

With the arising of sudden and gradual, traditions and paths
    are established.
With the distinguishing of traditions and paths come
    the compass and the square.
Plumb the tradition and walk the path into its depths;
then the genuine and abiding flows without restraint.

Externally calm, inwardly shaking, like a tethered horse
    or a cowering rat—
the former sages took pity on such people and made a gift
    of the teachings.

People's upside-down views lead them to mistake black for white,
but when inverted thinking ceases, the affirming mind
   naturally accords.
To conform to the ancient tracks please emulate the ancestors.
On the verge of realizing the Buddha Way, you have been
   contemplating a tree for ten kalpas and are like a tiger with a
   tattered ear or a horse that is hobbled.
For the lowly and inferior, there is a jeweled foot-rest and the
   discarding of adornments and sumptuous robes;
 for those capable of surprise and wonder, a wildcat or white ox.

Yi, with his skill and prowess, hit the target at one hundred paces;
Yet when two arrow points meet in midair, what has this to
   do with skill?
When the wooden man starts to sing, the stone woman rises
   to dance;
this is not arrived at through thought and feeling, so why
   reflect on it?

The minister serves the ruler, the son accords with the father;
It is unfilial not to obey, disloyal not to serve.
Conceal your practice, function in secret,
seem for all the world like a fool or an idiot—
if you could only continue, it would be called
the host within the host.

Reading the Five Modes of Essential and Contingent in the "Song of the Precious Mirror Samadhi" (for Glenn Wallis)[87]

THE "SONG of the Precious Mirror Samadhi" is intimately related to Dongshan's Five Ranks, for the five modes of the first cycle of the essential and the contingent can be discerned, enfolded and in sequence, within the Song. Thus, a study of the Song will give us the opportunity to explore the Five Ranks in a fresh context. The Song is also worthy of exploration in its own right, for it is rich in insights beyond its associations with the Five Ranks. Here, however, we will limit ourselves to exploring the correspondences between the Song and the Five Ranks.

Discovering the modes of the essential and the contingent unfolding within the Song is like focusing a telescope on the moon and watching its topography appear through ever-shifting light and darkness; it is enlivening and inspiring.

Hakuin observed that after Yunyan, Dongshan's teacher, had transmitted the Song to him, Dongshan "made clear the gradations of the Five Ranks within it, and composed a verse for each rank, in order to bring out the main principle of Buddhism."[88] Now we will reveal the topography of the Five Ranks within the Song by observing the shifting shadows and light of the modes within it.

As we shall see, the Song conveys the gift of the Buddha's awakening, while the five modes of essential and contingent present five brilliant facets of that gift. The Song also substantially preserves the five modes according to Dongshan's sequence. Moreover, the Song notably encapsulates, in microcosm, the five modes in the thirtieth hexagram from the I Ching (*Yijing*), Li, "The Clinging/Fire." The rest of the poem—including the stretches that precede the lines on the Li hexagram—encapsulates the five modes in a wide-ranging way. Lastly, toward the end of the Song, the Cycle of Merit is invoked.

Because the "Song of the Precious Mirror Samadhi" is so rich, and not just in terms of its Five Ranks references, it really is worthy of a book in its own right. However, given that the current work is focused solely on the Song as it relates to the Five Ranks, we will only draw on those key images from the poem—often but a single image out of many possible ones—that convey the relevant modes or stages of the Five Ranks. Sadly, this means that much that is worthy of investigation in the Song will be left out.

In Chinese, the "Song of the Precious Mirror Samadhi" consists of ninety-four lines of four characters each, making 376 characters in all, arranged into forty-seven couplets. Its rhythmic and tonal qualities make the Song easy to memorize and chant. The Song is traditionally coupled with Shitou Xiqian's "Accord on Investigating

Diversity and Wholeness" as morning and evening chants in Caodong (Soto) temples.

As discussed above, some of the themes in the Song are anticipated by the Accord, which was written at least a century and a half before it. The earlier poem draws on the Huayan dialectics of principle and phenomena, presenting them in vivid, memorable imagery. Shitou's Accord also anticipates the Song in its use of imagery from the I Ching. In his Song, Dongshan draws on and responds to the Accord in a way that sometimes seems to be clearly calculated. Whatever the case may be, the two poems share core imagery, with the Accord intimating some of the ideas expressed in the Song.

Although there has been much conjecture concerning its authorship, we don't definitively know who wrote the "Song of the Precious Mirror Samadhi." Following convention, I attribute it to Dongshan. It is possible that the Song was composed much later, during the Song dynasty, as an encapsulation of the core teachings of the Caodong School and to celebrate its prehistory back to Shitou Xiquian, and indeed to the Buddha.

It is said that Yunyan, Dongshan's teacher, having received it down the line of descent from Shitou to Yaoshan, and from Yaoshan to himself, secretly entrusted the Song to Dongshan, "thoroughly conveying its essence" when Dongshan stayed at Yunyan's place as his disciple.[89] The "essence" referred to is surely the five modes of essential and contingent, which are configured within the Song. In turn, the legend goes, Dongshan passed on the Song, with the Five Ranks encoded within it, to Caoshan in a secret midnight ceremony of transmission.

Caoshan went on to make the five modes of the essential and the contingent, if not explicitly the Song, an important basis for his own teaching, creating his own verses, prose comments, and elucidations of them. We will encounter several of those below.

The Song is a song of praise that celebrates the gift passed down by successive generations of teachers from the time of the Buddha. That being said, it is worth remembering that talk of "passing down," while true in its way, is also misleading. It is far too compendious to be passed down. No matter how we dress it up in abstruse formulations, it remains as apparent as "I feel tired this morning."

That's the gift passed down. Who gives it? Who receives it?

*A NOTE ON THE TERMS "PRECIOUS MIRROR" AND "SAMADHI"

The correspondences between the Song and the Five Ranks begin with the image of the "precious mirror," a metaphor for our intimacy with the cosmos, and its intimacy with us. The image of the precious mirror represents the Buddha's awakening and the mutuality of cosmos and person. At the same time the mirror motif conveys distinction, difference, and uniqueness: a person is not his or her reflection; the Buddha and the cosmos are clearly distinct.

A precious mirror that simultaneously reflects both mutual inclusiveness and difference immediately calls to mind the dialectic of the essential and the contingent of the first cycle of the Five Ranks. There the image of an ancient mirror is used as an expression of essential nature, and we can understand the precious mirror used here as an image similarly evocative of our essential nature.

"Samadhi," considered from the perspective of practice, is that state of absorption where the meditator unites with the object of meditation, whether it be the breath, the body, or the environment, or all of them together. In the context of the Song, "Samadhi" is expressive of the Buddha's primordial awakening, where the world and its creatures took up lodgings where they already had long-term tenancy as his intimate nature.

The dharma of *just this* is passed down from the Buddhain confidence;
today it's yours: take good care of it.

As Buddha awakened upon seeing the Morning Star, he is said to have exclaimed, "Now I see that all beings are tathagata—are just this person." The intimacy between cosmos and person that Buddha expressed upon awakening is what Dongshan here calls "the dharma of just this." Dongshan conveyed the gift of "just this" to his disciple, Caoshan, and to all of us, by means of the image of the five facets of the precious mirror as they appear in the remainder of the Song: all mutually reflective, and all corresponding with the five modes of the essential and contingent.

The Dharma "is passed down in confidence" can be understood to refer to the transmission of the Way from master to disciple, but it also carries a much broader and more generous sense than this. The universe is always transmitting. While our awakening to that transmission is personal and incommunicable, it is immediately open to all. Indeed, right now, children are playing on brightly colored swings, and dogs splash in the river. It is good to take the matter of "just this"—so brilliantly elaborated in this profound and subtle poem—as very personal, intimate, and local.

The Contingent within the Essential

A silver bowl filled with snow, the bright moon concealing egrets— categorized, they are not the same: inchoate, the place is known.

The silver bowl is an image of the essential, and snow, of the contingent. In this realm everything seems indistinguishable in its purity. This is brought home by the similarity between the bowl's silver and the bright snow. This quality of "sameness" corresponds to the essential. We are nestled in that brilliance, yet we can make distinctions and detect differences within it—between the silver bowl and the snow, between the egrets and the bright moon. This quality of difference corresponds to the contingent, and the resulting "difference within sameness" accords with Dongshan's first mode, the Contingent within the Essential.

When we classify, we understand that the bowl isn't the snow and that the egrets aren't the bright moon. Yet "inchoate, the place is known." "Inchoate" means "unclassifiable," "primordial," and "unformed" and is thus suggestive of the essential. "Known"—and this must be understood with some delicacy—gives the nod to what is beyond the reach of conceptual understanding, even as it allows for the classifying, comparing mind. So this verse intimates the presence of what is classifiable within the inchoate, and thus it corresponds to the Contingent within the Essential.

The Essential within the Contingent

As when you face the precious mirror, form and reflection behold each other—
you are not him; he is exactly you.

These lines recall the second of Dongshan's five modes of the essential and the contingent, where an old woman encounters the ancient mirror, in particular the lines:

> Having overslept, an old woman encounters the ancient mirror.
> This is clearly meeting face-to-face—only then is it genuine.

In such a face-to-face meeting, the universe is none other than our true nature. As I write this, it's three in the morning. I look up and through darkness see my neighbor's kitchen lit up like a chandelier. On his table there is a white cereal bowl on a green striped mat, and a red peppershaker. Experiencing thus is meeting the ancient mirror, where form and reflection behold each other. In this encounter I recognize my true face.

Although in the foregoing I have emphasized the intimate, essential aspect of the experience, I do not deny difference. A person is not their reflection. Each one of us is distinguishable from our environment. This mutuality of sameness and difference is neatly summed up as "You are not him; he is exactly you."

"Him" (or "her" or "it") refers to timeless, dimensionless reality. However, in the face of what is being invoked, no words cut it. Caught up in the ingeniousness of dialectical formulations and their ready transpositions, it is easy to forget how incomprehensible the universe is and how unavailing our expressions are in the face of it. In this regard, "him" (or "her" or "it") is not a word. "You are not him" points to difference. We are not our reflections, which is to say that we are not the universe. Yet the universe is intimately us: "he is exactly you." There's not a hair's breadth between these positions.

"You are not him; he is exactly you"—or alternatively, "You are not her; she is exactly you"—provides a memorable dialectical formulation, a subtle koan, to carry into our lives, perhaps especially into their relational aspects.

One might ask if it would make a difference if we reversed this formulation, so that it reads, "He is not you; you are exactly him." It's a subtle point, but the preeminent direction here is universe to person. We may take as an answer Dogen's statement, "That the myriad things advance and confirm the self is enlightenment. That the self advances and confirms the myriad things is called delusion." The two statements, being differently "directed," aren't quite symmetrical, their logic notwithstanding.

"You are not him; he is exactly you" aptly captures the spirit of the second mode: the Essential within the Contingent. Whatever we encounter is our true nature, and yet we, and those we meet, are, at the same time, singular, unique, and entirely distinguishable.

Arriving within the Essential

Like an infant endowed with the five features:
not going, not coming, not arising, not abiding, *ba ba wa wa*,
speaking without speaking. In the end there is nothing said,
as the words aren't properly formed.

These lines evoke the Tathagata as intimate and coextensive with the whole of reality, such that, short of a miracle, the Tathagata can't enter the world of coming and going and is incapable of uttering a single word. Taking all these incapacities together, the Tathagata is as helpless as a newborn baby. The unintelligible baby talk of that baby is an image for "speaking without speaking."

"Speaking without speaking" announces the third mode, Arriving within the Essential, where we encounter the theme of pure words, which is to say mundane words and language that represent the essential, without losing their sense and meaning. To recall Dongshan's expression of the third mode in his Cycle of the Essential and the Contingent:

> In nothingness there is a road apart from the dust.
> If you don't break the taboo on mentioning the Emperor's name
>   you will surpass the eloquence of the previous dynasty's
>   worthies, who cut off tongues.

"Not breaking the taboo on mentioning the Emperor's name," in terms of the path of training, means letting our silence concerning the matter of enlightenment deepen through meditation on koans, until we mature the articulate speech of the Way. Such speech—well exemplified by our simplest "Good morning! How are you doing?"—is completely pure. That is to say, our words are the words of the Tathagata, as the Song implies. More directly, the image of a baby eloquently conveys the tathagata, the ultimate, the essential, and all, through its baby talk—*ah wa wa wa, dada, dada* . . .

The correspondence between these lines from the Song and the third mode of the essential and the contingent thus rests on a subtle appreciation of the emptiness of words. Because of the emptiness of words and language the elegant distinctions conveyed in the first two modes of the essential and the contingent by a phrase such as "You are not him; he is exactly you" are likewise beyond distinction, transcending sameness and difference. Like this, the third, and middle, mode of emptiness—in particular the emptiness of words and language—casts its spell over the preceding and succeeding modes, as well as itself. The center, the middle realm, is expressive of emptiness. It affects the whole sequence and each mode within it.

All Five Modes Condensed in the Li Hexagram

In the six lines of the doubled Li hexagram,
essential and contingent mutually correspond.
Ranked in pairs they yield three; transformed, they make five.

These lines on the Li hexagram mark a turning point within the "Song of the Precious Mirror Samadhi." We are still within the frame of the third mode, Arriving within the Essential—that pure empty realm where each particular thing, word, or event encloses the universe. Being in that realm "enables" Dongshan to configure the five positions of essential and contingent within the radiance and darkness of the Li hexagram.[90] Dongshan employs the Li hexagram to expose the pattern of our journey—entire—just as if the dark landscape through which we have been traveling, and through which we will continue to travel, were to be illuminated by a single flash of lightning.

Having presented the first three modes in sequence, he now presents all five modes concurrently by means of the Li hexagram. This deft use of the Li hexagram comprises the thematic center of the poem, and this corresponds to, and is indicative of, the profound inclusiveness of the empty realm. The use of I Ching imagery to convey the five modes is subtle and detailed. Let's examine how the Li hexagram can configure the five modes of the essential and the contingent. Consider the Li hexagram itself:

Li 離

Li is the thirtieth hexagram in the I Ching. Being associated with the element fire, it is closely tied to the idea of light and illumination. Indeed, the Li hexagram is sometimes referred to as "the illumination hexagram." According to the I Ching commentary on it, "Li stands for nature in its radiance."[91] The hexagram consists of two identical three-line elements called trigrams, each consisting of two solid (yang) lines enclosing a broken (*yin*) line. This pattern evokes the imagery of light enclosing dark. These trigrams are placed one on top of the other to create the hexagram.

The I Ching's commentary on the Li hexagram further reads, "What is dark clings to what is light and so enhances the brightness of the latter."[92] This comment strongly suggests the interdependence of dark and light, and is evocative of the relationship between the essential and the contingent as choreographed in the first cycle of the Five Ranks. We recall that light is an image for the contingent, and dark, for the essential. Let's look more deeply at this theme of the interdependence of darkness and light, and their correspondence with the essential and the contingent. Consider the Li trigram:

☲

The central line is the ruler (*zhengwei*) of this trigram. This yin line is not so much a broken line as a line with an obscured middle, and as such is suggestive of darkness and, by extension, the timeless, dimensionless realm of the essential. The bright yang lines that enclose the yin line suggest the differentiated realm of phenomena—of birth and death in their endless flux—that we are calling the contingent.

In a striking simile, Peter Wong suggests that the yin line with the obscured middle resembles the Australian Aboriginal constellation of "The Emu in the Sky," which is delineated, or rather suggested, by dark nebulae visible against the background of the Milky Way. The Emu's head is the dark Coal Sack Nebula next to the Southern Cross. The body and the legs are other dark clouds trailing out along the Milky Way to Scorpius. This is darkness emerging from darkness, like the Tao Te Ching's "darkness upon darkness, the gateway to all mysteries."

Regarding that gateway, the obscured middle suggests the void beyond knowing and ignorance, the darkness within darkness, the empty within the empty—and all of these evoke, in turn, the emptiness of words, language, and imagery. This theme of the emptiness of all expressive means pervades the Song. Elsewhere, Dongshan urges us "to darken the darkling, then darken again"—which is to say that we should enter the gate of mystery, realize emptiness, then realize that even the most exquisite means of conveying the experience of emptiness are themselves empty. This same profound inclusiveness "allows" the five hexagrams within the single Li hexagram, and their five corresponding modes of the essential and the contingent.

HEXAGRAMS CORRESPONDING TO THE FIVE MODES OF THE ESSENTIAL AND THE CONTINGENT

Dongshan did not specify which hexagrams were to be associated with which modes of the essential and the contingent. Different paradigms have been advanced since the time of Caoshan.[93] In what follows, we will explore one such paradigm, which for me aptly captures the spirit of the individual modes of essential and contingent. That paradigm is shown in the chart below:

THE CYCLE OF THE ESSENTIAL AND THE CONTINGENT	HEXAGRAMS OF THE I CHING
1. The Contingent within the Essential	57. Xun The Gentle; Penetrating; Wind
2. The Essential within the Contingent	58. Dui The Joyous; Lake
3. Arriving within the Essential	28. Daguo Preponderance of the Great
4. Approaching from the Contingent	61. Zhongfu Inner Truth

5. Arriving at Concurrence	 30. Li The Clinging; Fire

Dongshan alludes to this expansion of the Li hexagram with the formulaic statement, "Ranked in pairs they yield three; transformed, they make five." Let's unpack Dongshan's statement. In what follows, the terms "pairs" and "pairings" refer to the identical trigrams in a hexagram. The first pairing is the source hexagram Li itself, with its two identical trigrams. The second pairing occurs when we extract the second, third, and fourth lines of the Li hexagram to derive the Xun trigram, which when doubled yields the Xun hexagram (The Gentle; Penetrating Wind). The third pairing occurs when we extract the third, fourth, and fifth lines of the Li hexagram to derive the Dui trigram, which when doubled yields the Dui hexagram (The Joyous; Lake). This is the meaning of Dongshan's "Ranked in pairs they yield three."

"Transformed, they make five" refers to two further maneuvers. Initially we position the Dui trigram on top of the Xun trigram to form the hexagram Daguo (Preponderance of the Great), and finally we position the Xun trigram on top of the Dui trigram to form the Zhongfu (Inner Truth) hexagram. These last two maneuvers bring the tally to five, and the process of deciphering Dongshan's cryptic formula—"ranked in pairs they yield three; transformed, they make five"—is complete.[94]

However, we note that these five maneuvers are abstract and devoid of transformative power. To grasp that power hinted at here, we must grasp the living matter of "transformed they make five." This is best conveyed in the form of a story, and the one that follows has considerable charm, showing that even the relatively abstruse material we have been discussing can elicit sparkling Dharma.

Shoju was transmitting the secrets of the Five Ranks to Hakuin. When he reached the passage in the "Song of the Precious Mirror Samadhi": "In the six lines of the doubled Li hexagram, essential and contingent mutually correspond. Ranked in pairs they yield three . . ." Shoju abruptly stopped.

Hakuin begged Shoju to continue, to impart to him the secret of "transformed they make five."

"You can't expect to get it all in just one visit," Shoju replied. "Take a look at Dongshan's verses on the Five Ranks. Don't read anything else. Pay no attention to the comments or theories others have made about them, for if you do, you'll find yourself down inside the same old hole as the other polecats."

Hakuin asked a favor of his fellow student, Sokaku, saying, "Shoju is advanced in years. It may not be possible for me to see him again. Brother Kaku, I'd like you to get him to teach you the secret of the phrase 'transformed they make five' from the "Song of the Precious Mirror Samadhi," so that you can pass it on to me."

Sokaku agreed, and the two men set out on their separate ways.

Just as he had promised, Sokaku arrived from Shoju-an during the lecture meeting. Hakuin asked him for the secret of the "transformed" passage from the Song. "It's not easy," said Sokaku.

"Sokaku," said the master, "Would it make it any easier if we enlisted the aid of some liquid wisdom (sake)?"

The master's fellow monks went and tracked down a flask of sake. Sokaku's cup was filled. But as he raised it to his lips the master caught his hand.

"Have your drink after you give me the secret," he said.

"No," Sokaku said, "let go of my hand."

"After you drink all that sake," explained the master, "you won't be in any shape to explain it to me."

Unable to come up with any reason to refuse, Sokaku finally began to explain the passage. He had done no more than utter the words "transformed they make five," when the master suddenly realized its meaning.

"Stop! I've got it now! I understand it!" he cried.

The others were indignant. "Don't stop him!" they said. "We don't understand it yet."

"You can learn it from me," replied the master.

Sokaku had by then finished off several cups of sake and they all had a good laugh.

The following day, when the master found time to be alone with Sokaku, he set forth for him the understanding he had grasped. Not a word he spoke was inconsistent with the teaching Shoju had entrusted to Sokaku.[95]

"Transformed they make five" roars out of darkness, as that darkness. What Hakuin apprehended in Sokaku's account of Shoju's words was the core of the Song, and of the five modes of the essential and the contingent hidden within it. Intimate with the purity of "transformed they make five," we are transformed, and our words, and indeed our lives, are "transformed they make five." This is the secret sense of "transformed they make five."

We expect illumination from what we read and ponder, but we ourselves also illuminate the old texts: they require our participation. This is a profound aspect of koan practice, in particular, and in this we include the five modes in their containing Song, as well as the Song itself. We illuminate these poems, including their nest of koans, with our lives, even as they illuminate us.

SUPPORTING IMAGES FOR THE FIVE-IN-ONENESS OF LI

Having provided a formula for extrapolating the five modes from the Li hexagram, Dongshan then provides a cluster of supporting images for the hexagram, with the five modes configured in it. His images take us from the abstract imagery of the hexagrams into the world of color, taste, shape, and sound, and vividly evoke the five modes of the essential and the contingent.

> **Like the five tastes of the schizandra berry, and the five-pronged diamond vajra . . .**

Schizandra is a creeping woody vine and the berries that it produces have an unusual taste. It's rather sweet and salty, slightly bitter with a hot sour tang. Significantly, the schizandra berry is actually termed "five taste fruit" (*wu wei zi*). Eating it apparently improves concentration, coordination, and mental clarity. The berry has strong medicinal and curative properties, and it is valued as sexually restorative for both men and women. The schizandra is native to China and Japan.

The five flavors of the schizandra symbolize the five hexagrams configured in the Li hexagram and, correspondingly, the five modes of the essential and the contingent.

The vajra was originally a mythical Indian weapon of war wielded by the god Indra, but it was later adopted within Buddhism as a symbol of the all-conquering power of the Buddha. The quality of the vajra evokes the ultimate strength and brilliance of Buddhist enlightenment. Buddhist ritual vajras are commonly composed of one central prong and four prongs arranged in branching pairs at each end, making five prongs in total. In this way, the five-pronged vajra can be seen to symbolize the five modes: the central axis representing the third mode of emptiness, and the two pairs of outer prongs representing the first and second modes, and the fourth and fifth modes, respectively.

The five-flavored taste of the berry and the five-pronged shape of the vajra reflect the configuration of the five modes within the Li hexagram at the core of the Song. These are metaphors that engage the senses and evoke the passionate core of the Way. In this they memorably lift the empty center of the Song out of abstraction and make it vitally expressive.

THE WAY OF THE CENTER

Inherent within our investigation of the Li hexagram is the notion of the Way of the Center. When we invoke it we extend the inclusiveness of our investigation from the sensuous imagery of the foregoing account of the schizandra and vajra to the realms of feeling and emotion. We also find that the Way of the Center is a means of expressing the concurrent, which as we have seen above is evoked by the Li hexagram itself with the five modes of the essential and the contingent configured within it.

To present the Way of the Center I will introduce a commentary on the Li hexagram from the I Ching (or Zhouyi), a text with which Dongshan would have been familiar. In the I Ching's account of the Li hexagram, key notions like *zheng*—"the proper" (what we are calling "the essential")—and the Way of the Center emerge, and we find that their sense resonates with the themes of the five modes.[96] Below are the Judgment and the Image for the hexagram Li from the I Ching:

Li 離[97]

To cast Li is auspicious. Success. Raising cows is propitious.

The Judgment
Li means to cleave to something. The sun and moon cleave to the heavens. The various grains, grasses, and trees cleave to the earth. Like the double radiance (*ming* 明) that cleaves to the proper (*zheng* 正), one therefore transforms and brings the world to completion. Because the yielding cleaves to the center (*zhong* 中) and to the proper (*zheng*), therefore success; and therefore raising cows is propitious.

Nine in the first line: Treading with care; respecting it, no blame.

Six in the second line: Yellow Li. Supremely propitious.

Nine in the third line: Cleaving to the declining sun. If you don't strike the earthen pot and sing, then there'll be regretful sighs when you are seventy. Harmful.

Nine in the fourth line: In the manner of arriving abruptly—like a blaze, like death, like being abandoned.

Six in the fifth line: Like someone in tears, sighing sorrowfully. Propitious.

Nine in the top line: The king leads the military campaign. There is merit: Killing the leaders (of the enemies), capturing accomplices and followers. No blame.

The Image

[Nine in the first line]: Having respect for treading with care is how blame is avoided.

[Six in the second line]: Yellow Li. Supremely propitious. This is because one has attained the way of the center.

[Nine in the third line:]: Declining sun. How could it endure?

[Nine in the fourth line]: In the manner of arriving suddenly; one can find no refuge.

[Six in the fifth line]: The Six in the fifth is propitious because one cleaves to the noble.

[Nine in the top line]: The king leads the military campaign in order to bring proper order to the State.

In the judgment, we note that the double radiance cleaves to "the proper," which is none other than what we have been calling the essential (*zheng*). This is the pattern of the trigram where the outside radiant lines cling to the obscured middle, with its suggestion of the void. This cleaving of light to darkness (of yang to yin) has the power to transform us, as well as enabling us to "bring the world to completion." I understand "bringing the world to completion" to mean coming into accord with nature in its unfolding and finding intimacy with all beings through profound awakening. This auspicious image of cleaving to the center, and to the essential, provides a rich set of associations for the five modes, and it shows once again how effective the Li hexagram is as a means of conveying the dark core in which the five modes are configured.

Within the Image, we find a commentary on the second line of the Li hexagram, and hence one of its rulers. In particular, we notice a reference to attaining the Way of the Center. The Way of the Center is described in the ancient text of Zisi's *Focusing the Familiar* (*Zhongyong*) as follows:

The moment at which joy and anger, grief and pleasure, have yet to arise is called the nascent equilibrium (*zhong*); once the emotions have arisen, that they are all brought into proper focus (*zhong*) is called harmony (*he*). This notion of

equilibrium and focus is the great root of the world; harmony
then is the advancing of the proper way (*dadao*) in the world.[98]

The sense of zhong as nascent equilibrium is suggestive of the essential
(understood here as emptiness), while "proper focus" corresponds to
the contingent. Taken together, nascent equilibrium and proper focus
are "the great root of the world," which is no less than the Way, and,
in particular, the Way of the Center.

When we are there for others, and open a space of listening in which
they can express themselves, we live the Way of the Center, the way of
heart and mind. Our grief, where everything is gathered in as our pain
of loss, as our weeping eyes and constricted heart, is also expressive
of the Way of the Center. To live "the great root of the world"—our
embodied insight into the essential and the contingent—as the challenging circumstances of daily life is surely our "advancing of the proper
way in the world." In doing so, we are there for what comes and deal
open-heartedly with others.

Thus Li, and implicitly the five modes, are intimately bound up
with the Way of the Center. We note that both nascent equilibrium
and proper focus can be represented by *zhong*, which means "within,"
"centered in," and "at the place of." It can also be translated as "heart-
and-mind." Zhong, in the sense that it includes the concepts of equilibrium and focus, is, as Zisi puts it, "the great root of the world." This
expression of the Way is entirely intimate to us and is indeed none other
than each of us in our struggles, dilemmas, and joys.

The advancing of the proper way (*dadao*) in the world also corresponds to bringing our awakening into the world through our return
to the charcoal heap, where we continue the practice of the Way and
are not afraid to get dirty helping others. This too, as we have seen, is
the fifth mode, Concurrence, as it is symbolized by the entwined fire
and darkness of the Li hexagram.

> . . . in the profound inclusiveness of the essential, drumming and
> singing are upheld.

The "inclusiveness of the essential" upholds our breathing in and our breathing out, our eyes opening and our eyes closing, as well as our joys and our disappointments, being inseparable from them. Nothing and nobody is left out. All dichotomies find a home in the profound inclusiveness of the essential, including the dialectic of the five modes of the essential and the contingent.

"Drumming" and "singing" stand for the contingent and the essential, respectively, and the implication here is that those contraries are themselves empty. This is to say that the very dialectical means employed within the Five Ranks are themselves empty.

I asked the Zen teacher Glenn Wallis about the profound inclusiveness of the essential. He said, "Profound inclusiveness is the entry price for drumming and singing, for covering the mouth when sneezing. This morning my eyes are tired and watery." Glenn's words convey the Way beyond drumming and singing, and their associated dialectic of the five modes of essential and contingent. His response points to our lives lived as the Way, which is the spirit of Concurrence. I am grateful for his words.

In terms of our journey through the Song, having presented the first three modes in sequence, Dongshan then presents the five modes all at once using the imagery of the Li hexagram, subsequently expanding its implications with the supporting imagery of the five-flavored schizandra berry, the five-pronged vajra, and the profound inclusiveness of the essential.

The image of the Li hexagram, with the five modes of the essential and the contingent configured in it by means of its constituent hexagrams, corresponds to the fifth and final mode of concurrence, which empties out even emptiness itself, and thereby includes each and all of the five modes of the essential and the contingent, even as they configure it. When we realize the emptiness of the Five Ranks and all its strategies, we step beyond existence and nonexistence, the karmic and the essential, to live the Way as our life of love and work on this good earth with its starry skies rolling back forever.

Penetrate the source, explore the muddy paths,
include the concurrent and the dusty road.

The dusty road seems like a tongue-in-cheek reference to his line, "In nothingness there is a road apart from the dust," which appeared in the third mode of the essential and the contingent, Arriving within the Essential. What is being implied is that even after awakening, study of the Way is important, and that this includes coming to terms with conceptual accounts of it. As we have seen, even chatter about enlightenment can be its radiant expression. Everything is included within concurrence.

Commenting on this line, Glenn Wallis says, "Deal with what is already bright and apparent, whether it be the bright, the dusty, the dark, or the luminous—all are the unmitigated life of profound inclusiveness." When we live the unmitigated life of profound inclusiveness, every circumstance, no matter how miserably limited, is not only radiant with the eternal, it is none other than the eternal as it grieves, lusts, and dies. The eternal is not only in love with the productions of time, as Blake has it, it is none other than those productions.

Treading carefully is propitious;
You would do well to respect this; do not depart from it.

Dongshan continues to draw on the I Ching for our guidance and inspiration, for these lines have as their source the I Ching's imagery for the Li hexagram as we have explored it above.

"Treading carefully" is an image for beginning—perhaps a little hesitantly—the enterprises of the day. In the preceding lines, Dongshan urges us to realize our essential nature and to widen the aperture of whatever we realize through study and practice in the multifarious circumstances of our lives. He also recommends implicitly that we study and practice the five modes of the essential and the contingent. In the dawn mood of the current lines concerning treading carefully, everything is still fresh, and we are finding our way. Thus, we approach the practice and study of the Way with an open, inquiring mind—what Shunryu Suzuki called "beginner's mind." In that spirit, each moment, each phase of the day, and indeed each phase of our life is fresh and ripe with potential. Dongshan encourages us to respect our tentativeness, even our confusion, as we embark into the study, practice, and embodiment of the Way in our lives.

Approaching from the Contingent

Dongshan now shifts the focus away from the radiant mirror of the Buddha's awakening toward the ways and means of conveying that experience to others. The one becomes many; the path branches into various schools, particularly into the Northern and Southern schools. We begin to use "the compass and the square" to distinguish and evaluate paths and traditions. More generally, we move from the indivisible to the partial, from the timeless into the stream of the mundane. This movement is akin to the Buddha's descent from the heights after his awakening, to teach the Way to thousands on the dusty back roads of India for forty years or more.

What Dongshan is laying out for Caoshan, and for us, is the bodhisattva path with its many challenges. Accordingly, from here on the tone of the poem is generally more admonitory, and practical aspects of teaching the Dharma rise to the surface. Given that the "Song of the Precious Mirror Samadhi" was conferred as a token of transmission, the following lines sound like practical advice being passed down from a senior teacher to his junior, for our benefit. This portion of the poem is concerned with the how of the Way: how to navigate in a divided or even broken world. It is also involved with the conduct and propagation of the Way. As such, these lines resonate with the second cycle of the Five Ranks, the Cycle of Merit, which is concerned, in part, with the conduct of the Way and how we live the essential in our daily lives.

This region of the poem also evokes the spirit of the fourth mode of the first cycle of the contingent and the essential, capturing the spirit of both its titles. Firstly, it accords with Approaching from the Contingent, with its focus on differentiation and multiplicity. It is also evocative of Approaching Concurrence, with its senses of struggle, resistance, and difficulty that arise from trying to realize the Way and convey it to others in a suffering world. The image of the lotus in the midst of fire (intimated here by the fire and darkness of the Li hexagram) is itself suggestive of the transformation we undergo at this stage of our training.

> **With the arising of sudden and gradual, traditions and paths are established.**
> **With the distinguishing of traditions and paths come the compass and the square.**

Dongshan conjures the hoary debate that pitted sudden enlightenment against gradual cultivation. Sudden enlightenment is associated with the Southern School and gradual cultivation with the Northern School. We might recall the lesson within the story of Deshan, related above, who was an expert on the Diamond Sutra. In order to exterminate the "sudden" devils, he made a long journey to the south, where he got enlightened for his comeuppance.

When we compare one path with another, and weigh up what we take to be their virtues and drawbacks, we are faced with a problem of choice, because so many spiritual paths are on offer. It's good to commit to stay with that path you have chosen, and with a teacher that you can trust. Otherwise you run the risk of nothing happening.

"The compass and the square" represent measurement, guidelines, rules, and demarcations. In his Accord, Shitou writes, "To receive the teachings, you must encounter the ancestors. Do not set up your own compass and square." It is tempting to set up our own rules and procedures, but "knowing best" can block our light.

> **Plumb the tradition and walk the path into its depths;**
> **then the genuine and abiding flows without restraint.**

This surely means to meditate and to realize deeply; that's a given. But it also means to exhaust the inexhaustible teachings through study and meditation, treasuring them as they come down in their many forms from the Buddha. When we do that, in Dongshan's beautiful image, "the genuine and abiding flows without restraint." When we study and awaken like this, the waters of eternity flow as our lives in all their precious and challenging uniqueness.

Teaching the Way in a Broken World: Varieties of Student

As the "Song of the Precious Mirror Samadhi" unfolds, it moves from the ineffable and indivisible toward limitation, comparison, and myriad distinctions; toward the temporal rather than the eternal. This is the broken world with its many paths and confused students, where we take up the bodhisattva path and cultivate compassion for our fellow beings. Awakening and teaching in such challenging circumstances is akin to being a lotus in the midst of fire: Dongshan's metaphor for a person attaining enlightenment and enlightening others in the midst of the suffering world.

To aid Caoshan in that task, Dongshan outlines the various types of student, or more loosely, the types of people drawn to the Way, that he will encounter as a teacher.

> **Externally calm, inwardly shaking, like a tethered horse**
> **or a cowering rat—**
> **the former sages took pity on such people and made a gift**
> **of the teachings.**
> **People's upside-down views lead them to mistake black for white,**
> **but when inverted thinking ceases, the affirming mind naturally**
> **accords.**

The first type of student can adapt to the form of the practice and sit steadily in meditation, but inside they are a mass of contrary impulses. We are all like this in varying degrees. Dongshan urges the new teacher to be like the compassionate sages of old, who freely offered the teachings and guided such people to realization.

Others harbor "upside-down views": thinking that reifies the self and places it like a little emperor at the center of our experience. "Black" stands for the undifferentiated darkness of the essential, and "white" for the contingent realm. To mistake black for white is to stumble past nirvana, innocently disguised as our footsteps in the hall as we head out to do the shopping. A genuine awakening experience is an antidote to such inverted thinking.

For the lowly and inferior, there is a jeweled foot-rest and the discarding of adornments and sumptuous robes;

The teacher makes himself, or herself, into countless shapes for the benefit of all beings, including for the lowly and humble. When it is appropriate, the teacher appears in full regalia, and the teaching is conveyed through splendid ceremonies. This is the dharma in "Ottoman mode" as it were. Other times, she steps out of her sumptuous clothes and appears in jeans. Regardless of attire, the teacher always appears in his, or her, blemished humanity.

The point that Dongshan is making for his successor is that he should teach in accord with the circumstances in which he finds himself. For us to do so, we must understand and be able to respond to whoever appears before us. In my experience the teacher is sometimes called on to deal with people who are broken, and who, at least initially, may be better served by psychotherapy than by Zen. It is a mark of honesty to recommend to such people that working with a good psychologist or counselor may be more helpful than Zen training. By the same token, it is also helpful if the teacher has some psychological understanding, if not training, though this isn't to suggest that Zen should be thought of as psychology, or that teachers should psychologize the Dharma. It is a matter of practicality to know something about the discipline of psychology, in order to better serve those we are likely to encounter.

The images of a "jeweled footrest" and "sumptuous robes" are drawn from the Lotus Sutra.[99] There we find the story of the prodigal son, who upon returning home and seeing his estranged father dressed in brocade robes with his feet resting on a jeweled footrest, fails to recognize him. The father makes efforts to reconnect with his son, even changing out of his finery in order to avoid frightening him. He employs his son doing menial tasks, for which the son is grateful, never suspecting the true wealth to which he is heir. As the father lies dying, the secret is finally revealed to his son.

The father waiting patiently for his prodigal son to come home and claim his inheritance reflects the generosity and patience of Buddha, not so much the historical Buddha, but our own essential nature. Failing to recognize what is essential and eternal in us, and settling for less, we are, in Hakuin's terms, like the child of a wealthy home wandering among the poor. The precious mirror of awakening now reflects a place where others must be accommodated, in order that they might not settle for less. We are in the territory of embattled compassion, the province of all teachers of the Way, as they strive to find fresh means to express the Buddha Way and encourage their students to awaken to it.

. . . for those capable of surprise and wonder, a wildcat or white ox.

The Song began with egrets concealed in bright moonlight, the tattered-eared tiger, the cowering rat, and the hobbled horse make their appearance, and now we encounter the wildcat and the white ox. The precious mirror has its own bestiary!

Here Dongshan refers to Nanquan's words "Buddhas and ancestors do not know reality. Wildcats and white oxen do."[100] Knowing or not knowing reality is a human problem, just as enlightenment is a human problem. Wildcats and oxen live lives of grace in accord with their circumstances. In that regard, they leave buddhas and ancestors in their wake. Guishan Da'an (793–883) speaks of the transformation wrought by years of attending to the ox—to bringing our attention back to the matter at hand—and by continuing to do so, even during the worst of times:

> Now he has changed into the white ox on bare ground, and always stays in front of my face. Even if I chase him, he doesn't go away![101]

The white ox? Even in sleep, even in death, it never reneges. The white ox on bare ground is nothing less than the all of it, which is none other than yourself. As Glenn Wallis put it, "Good luck with chasing it away!"

A startling metaphor can turn a student around. The risk is that those who are receptive will treasure such expressions and fail to take responsibility for their own journey and its expression. Such people end by dining out on the words of others. I reckon that this is a risk worth taking though, and that without creativity—poetry in particular—the expression of the Dharma quickly petrifies.

Arriving at Concurrence

Images multiply in the precious mirror, but all must be traceable to you in your place. You must sheet it home. You must secure it. Each mode is enlightenment itself. Yet, having realized one mode, it is important not to rest on our laurels but to push on. Which brings us to the fifth and final mode configured in the Song, Arriving at Concurrence.

Here, as it was in Shitou's "Accord on Investigating Diversity and Wholeness," concurrence is conveyed by means of the image of arrow points meeting in midair. However, in the following lines the metaphorical correspondence is even greater between the Song and the five positions of ruler and minister.

The minister serves the ruler, the son accords with the father;
It is unfilial not to obey, disloyal not to serve.

Here the imagery of minister and ruler is identical to that of the title "Gatha of the Five Positions of Ruler and Minister," which Dongshan employs for his first cycle. As we have seen, "ruler" corresponds to the essential, and "minister" to the contingent. In this particular verse, the father represents the essential, which implies emptiness, and by extension wisdom, while the son represents the contingent, and by extension form and compassion. The reference to service and accord suggests the merging of the ways of ruler and minister, and hence concurrence.

Glenn Wallis has said of "it is unfilial not to obey, disloyal not to serve" that it is an expression of concurrence:

> In a way there is little choice here. As minister and ruler correspond to the apparent and absolute; eyes open the way they open. There is no space for unfilial behavior or disloyalty. Arrow points meet, and that is that.

The term *feng* (a Chinese character translated as service, honor, and obedience), which Dongshan employs here, is the same feng with which he titles the second stage of the Cycle of Merit, Service. As we have noted, there is a gathering sense of the presence of the second cycle of the Five Ranks within the Song as we near its end:

**Conceal your practice, function in secret,
seem for all the world like a fool or an idiot—
if you could only continue, it would be called
the host within the host.**

The poem is brought home with an admonition about continuing the practice. These lines are meant to address the new teacher and all of us. There is no place to finally put down our pack. We shouldn't draw attention to our efforts, though. Even if we succeed in impressing others, it's as if we have our reward already, and some things are better unrewarded. When we function in secret, we seal the vessel of our practice. We immediately plough under whatever we realize, letting go of knowing and attainment at deeper and deeper levels. We may look idiotic to others, yet what others think of us need be of no concern. Mainly we just continue to practice, and unwittingly we may even become helpful to them.

Dongshan is saying to his successor and to all of us, "If you could only continue, it would be called the host within the host." This is the ironic style of a man who organized a delusion banquet for students who were lamenting his imminent demise. "If you could only continue" points to our resistance to going deep. Having experienced a little, we want to boil off the process and get value there and then. But Dongshan encourages us onward: "If you could only continue, it would be called the host within the host."

This image of the host within the host is derived from that of host and guest. "Host" corresponds to the essential and "guest" to the contingent. When we occupy the host position, we speak from the ground of the essential. To take the role of guest is to speak from the ground of the contingent. As with the essential and the contingent in the five modes, these roles are not permanently associated with particular people or situations, but rather they are determined according to context. There are no forms of expression exclusive to host (conventional shouts of "katsu!" notwithstanding). and, correspondingly, there are no forms of expression exclusive to guest, either.

In the current context, "the host within the host" is suggestive of "the essential within the essential," or of "the emptiness of emptiness," which, as noted above, is a key theme of the final mode in the Cycle of the Essential and the Contingent. This is Concurrence, which corresponds to the profound enlightenment of the Buddha, and is thus prior to position, number, division, and sequence. In concurrence we invest this timeless vastness in negotiating the crowded aisles of the supermarket looking for sultanas, or a special doll for a grandchild.

The metaphor of the host within the host is also related to the line from the final stage of the Cycle of Merit: "In the vastness of the empty kalpa there is no one who knows." This line empties out time, knowing, and the stages of the Way. Then, with the journey forgotten, we make our way in the mysterious realm of ordinary life as we find it, with its win and lose, its heartbreak and joy. We understand both cycles as arrays of positions that are, in the end, transcended. Such transcendence can be likewise understood as "the host within the host": a manifestation of life as continuing practice and exploration, without ostentation, and without trying to impress others, even as we remain available to them.

It is important not to attach to the Five Ranks and "Song of the Precious Mirror Samadhi" as modes of knowledge. We learn them, embody them, and in the end forget them. This notion is perfectly summed up by a line of the Zhuangzi:

> Nets exist for catching fish: once a fish is caught, the net
>   is forgotten. . . .
> Words exist for expressing ideas: once the ideas are
>   expressed, the words are forgotten.[102]

Thus bereft of words, we might seem for all the world like fools or idiots. The ability to continue in this way places us in line with the mob of old worthies, who absurdly keep on filling up a well with snow. Such activity, corresponding to the noble absurdity of passing on the Dharma, is ceaseless. With regard to passing on the Dharma, the following anecdote is apt.

Recently I was in dialogue via email with my first teacher, Robert Aitken. Our exchange concerned this last line of the Song. I had sent to him a copy of the translation of the poem by Peter Wong and myself.

He said that he liked it, and sent his own translation, which he said he also liked. The last line about the host within the host was missing in his translation.

I asked him—it was irresistible—"So what is the host within the host, Roshi?"

"I'll get back to you on that," he emailed back.

Shortly after, I heard that he had died.

He was ninety-three at the time, and even after a number of strokes had remained active, turning up for Sunday zazen at Palolo Zen Center, continuing to write, and encouraging us all. This despite the fact that he was down to two fingers. The other eight kept sliding off the keys. "I'll get back to you on that" was a perfect reply, even without the obliterating follow-up.

In this chapter we have looked at the correspondences between the two cycles of the Five Ranks and the "Song of the Precious Mirror Samadhi." The first cycle unfolds within the Song, broadly in sequence, and the second makes its appearance toward its end. Although we have been focused principally on viewing the Song through the lens of the Five Ranks, I hope that the reader has been able to grasp some sense of the magnificence of the Song itself.

III.

Coda to the Five Ranks

23. The Five Modes of Time and Timelessness

Time that is moved by little fidget wheels
Is not my Time, the flood that does not flow.
Between the double and the single bell
Of a ship's hour, between a round of bells
From the dark warship riding there below,
I have lived many lives . . .
—Kenneth Slessor, "Five Bells"

THROUGHOUT THIS BOOK we have seen that Dongshan again and again returns to themes of time and timelessness, and their mutuality, in his Five Ranks. Here, we will draw out these themes and examine the timeless and the temporal as a dialectic, imagined broadly in parallel with the form of Dongshan's dialectic in his Cycle of the Essential and the Contingent. We will then briefly explore the implications of such a dialectic and its particular applicability in an era when we are perhaps most anxious about time and driven by it.

Our first step toward imagining the dialectic is to note that the timeless and the fleeting are mutually contingent. Neither can exist alone. Here we recall Nagarjuna's question, "What can be ephemeral, without eternity?" Implicit within Nagarjuna's succinct formulation is its opposite: What can be eternal, without ephemerality? "Ephemerality" entails measurable time: a progression from past, to present, and on into the future. Timelessness has no other means by which to express itself other than through tense and the grid of clock time. Our time-bound lives, just as they are, with their steady parade of birthdays, weddings, and funerals, are the intimate expression of timelessness.

Our experience of time is one of trying to live wholly in the present, while being haunted by our past, and anxious about our future. Through all this, we may be experiencing timelessness, but it doesn't feel like it. Everything has to be done by yesterday, and, because the subdivisions of time seem to increasingly matter, we end up by trying to do more and more in less and less time. We become like the harassed and over worked woman in Robert Frost's poem "A Servant to Servants," who resigns herself to the toil: "I sha'n't catch up in this world, anyway."

Yet, between breaths, lifetimes pass, all of them gathered into this puckering of time we call "now." Surely we know about this. In love, at the extremities of pain and pleasure, in meditation, and in the samadhi of music our separation vanishes, and with it our sense of fleeting time. Engrossment is next to happiness; sometimes it is happiness; and occasionally something more, as borne out by this story told to me by Milan Adamciak, the father of experimental music in Slovakia:

> When I was twenty-one I strapped my cello to my back and climbed a couple of thousand feet up onto a ridge in the high Tatras. It was just dawn. I unstrapped my cello, sat on a rock and played my lowest C—soft and long. And the birds stopped their song, utterly. You could have heard a leaf move. When I found the courage to play on at last, the birds shyly joined in, so that after a time—I couldn't say how long—I was a bird.

Adamciak's "not knowing how long" evokes what is timeless within his experience of intimacy. Travel far enough into time's sequence and number and we find that it is, in that same moment, timeless. When we count our breaths—our first practice, our lifelong practice—we enter the breath count "one," fully. Then "two." Then "three." At each instant, nothing but that breath count—home to all that is timelessly vast. "One!"

Let's recall the five modes of Dongshan's Cycle of the Essential and the Contingent:

1. The Contingent within the Essential
2. The Essential within the Contingent
3. Arriving within the Essential
4. Approaching from the Contingent
5. Arriving at Concurrence

We note right away that the third, fourth, and fifth modes have titles that imply time. Expressions such as "arriving" and "approaching" conjure a journey unfolding over time, as well as moments in that journey. "Concurrence," particularly in the sense of "simultaneity," evokes an all-at-onceness of past and present. By extending the implicit temporal dimension in Dongshan's first cycle of the Five Ranks, we arrive at a complementary dialectic of time and timelessness, which can be expressed as follows:

1. Time within the Timeless
2. The Timeless within Time
3. Arriving within the Timeless
4. Approaching from Time
5. Arriving at the Concurrence of Time and the Timeless

These five modes of time and timelessness constitute five koans, especially significant in these times, when time itself is such a preoccupation.

THE FIRST MODE: TIME WITHIN THE TIMELESS

In this mode, we awaken to the fact that our time-bound activity is not solely in hours and minutes, and in past, present, future. Rather, a moment configures the timeless and the eternal. We experience, even within our overscheduled lives, timeless life: as when someone taps a teaspoon on a cup, and that sweet ring of china opens us beyond inside and outside, beyond now and then. With this experience, we are set free from measured, divided time.

When we live this mode of the temporal within the timeless, each moment of our life is the middle moment. There is no point of change-over from middle moment to middle moment, either, for each is timeless and dimensionless: the middle moment of setting sun, the middle moment of chill.

THE SECOND MODE: THE TIMELESS WITHIN TIME

We may rephrase the title of this mode as "eternity in the now." The timeless expresses itself as our intimate lives with all beings. This is eternity in action—eating breakfast, walking in the park, having an afternoon nap. Eternity has no other means to appear than these. Or as Valentine's Day—shy, tender, silly:

> You're my funny valentine, sweet comic valentine;
> you make me smile with my heart.

Our lives, with our falling in love and falling out of love, are eternity's opportunity, and its song. Although the music unfolds in time, immersed, we lose our sense of time's passage. In music in particular, time is permeable, and we are permeable. My old piano teacher, Alice Carrard ("Madame" as we called her), was perhaps the finest classical pianist who ever lived in my home city of Perth, Western Australia. Once I eavesdropped on her as she rehearsed Beethoven's Sonata no. 30, op. 109. I wrote these lines for that occasion:

> I arrive for my lesson to find you muttering
> as you rehearse that late Beethoven sonata, dizzying
> the summer morning, angling trills at heaven,
> making the fugue an iron cliff that rings each time
> you strike.

> Nearly one hundred, you live on a sliver
> of chicken and a spoonful of broccoli a day.
> Arthritic eagle hunched over the blue gorge,
> an unfiltered Gauloise stuck to your lower lip, smoke
> pours up into your itching eyes over your wet cheeks.
> You forget your way, circle back.

> At nineteen you played this sonata for your Budapest debut.
> Now, no bigger than a child, you groan as your hands struggle
> against their own tightening, as a starry sky twists and sings.
> Blind sighted a moment you just miss old Ludwig, drunk and
> beaming as he ambles into the dazzled gap—the intact swift-
> ness of your mottled hands swallow diving into ivory.

This is true meeting in its timeless aspect. In experiences such as these,
we meet our true contemporaries.

THE THIRD MODE: ARRIVING WITHIN THE TIMELESS

We recall Dongshan's line from his verse on awakening in the Cycle
of Merit: A withered tree blossoms in timeless spring. We cannot find
the track that led us to such an awakening, nor know where it leads.
It feels ancient, yet it's not as though we have returned upstream on
the supposed waters of time, either. All that we regard as before and
after are gathered, and our relation to the past, or the future, is like a
single mirror reflecting itself. Any moment is up for this; any moment
is thus privileged.

What does this mean in the light of our death: a moment as privileged, or unprivileged, as any other? Though its ramifications involve
those we love, and those who love us—finally, regardless of our attitudes to our death, there is only the sluice of that moment. How can
we awaken there?

Doushuai Congyue (n.d.), in the third of his Three Barriers, states,
"When you are free of birth and death, you know where to go. When
your four elements—earth, water, fire, air—scatter, where do you
go?"[103] In other words, where do you go after you die? To put a human
face to this:

> Ram Das was performing as a clown for children who were
> dying of cancer (surely the most heartbreaking and challeng-
> ing of artistic vocations).
> One child asked him, "Where do I go after I die?"

He responded, "When the light goes left, go left. When the light goes right, go right."

His words were compassionate, and entirely appropriate for the child, as well as for the occasion. However, when we see into Doushuai's koan about where we go after we die, we find that there is actually no need to project a journey in some imagined time after our death. Whatever occurs after we die finds its expression most intimately as our present activity. To enter that activity completely is to accord with it as timeless, even beyond death itself.

I wasn't with my father in his last moments. After having suffered what we thought was a heart attack and been admitted to hospital, he seemed to make a startling recovery. I visited him with my son and daughter, and he sat up in bed cracking jokes and entertaining us with his stories. We'd never seen him better. The next morning at 4.00 a.m. he quietly slipped away. He was too much of a gentleman to impose his dying on us. I'm sure that he would have found it distasteful to have his weeping family around him when he went. I offer this conversation that I had with my father shortly before he died. For me, it was as eloquent as any deathbed moment could be.

My father was quite deaf, and as we were conversing I was cleaning one of his wax-encrusted hearing aids, and trying to fit it into his ear.

I asked him what he felt about dying.

"What's the alternative?"

"Do you worry about dying?"

"I try not to think about it."

"Would you want to be awake when you went?"

"I'd rather be asleep."

"I'd like to die when I am awake. Wouldn't want to miss it. I'm curious."

"I'm curious too," he says, "but …" There was a long pause. The hearing aid was feeding back again. It sounded like Percy Grainger's free electric music.

My dad cupped my left hand over his ear making the pitch of the feedback go down. He released my hand and it rose again.

He went on, "They say there's a corridor."

This took me by surprise. "Yeah, I've heard that. They say there's a light."

He looked puzzled.

"Light!" I tried to clarify it.

"Laugh?" he came back, uncertainly.

"Light!" I said it more clearly.

He looked confused. I made oval shapes in the air.

"Glow," I said.

He took out his hearing aid, and tried to resuscitate it with a rusty three-inch nail.

"Light!"

He looked perplexed—and quite deaf—as he asked, "Love?"

Zen has so much respect for human love that it rarely mentions it. But the stumbling speech of love—including our mishearings and our blank misunderstandings—stands timelessly open.

On being asked "What is the time?" an Australian child of fifty years ago might have said, looking down at her wrist, "A hair past a freckle." "A hair past a freckle" neatly encompasses past, present, and future. Even the less vivid, but more helpful, "Three thirty" cuts off all considerations of before and after.

THE FOURTH MODE: APPROACHING FROM TIME

Even though we have experienced timelessness, we don't throw away our watches. We still show up in difficult circumstances and are punctual. Punctuality is the courtesy of kings and queens, and the very least we can do for our fellow bodhisattvas.

The transformational process that we have associated with the corresponding mode in Dongshan's sequence of the essential and the contingent goes on in this sequence after we awaken to the timeless spring. This is change over time, surely, but it is now change informed by the unchanging. What is fleeting is, in the same breath, untrammeled and unbounded. Yet our only task is to attend to what is. We experience change over time, with its joys, its pain and loss, yet we take the moment neat. Our reflections on time and timelessness range widely, but the tasks are all in time.

The following verse by Wumen on Doushai's Three Barriers draws together the themes of time and timelessness that we are exploring here:

> One *nian* sees eternity;
> eternity is in the now;
> when you see through this one *nian*,
> you see through the one who sees.[104]

The Chinese word *nian* means "recollection, memory; to think on, reflect; repeat, intone; a thought; a moment." That thought, or that memory, is the wide-open experience of the universe appearing in the guise of our current joys and sorrows. That memory, with its inflection of remorse or regret, may be momentary, yet is, at the same time, timeless beyond reckoning.

Wumen presents the five positions of time and timelessness, in microcosm, in his verse on Doushuai's Three Barriers. The first and second lines present the first two positions: time within timelessness and timelessness within time. When we see into the moment, we see that time and the self are empty, corresponding to the third mode of arriving within the timeless. Yet the one who sees is unique, suggesting the fourth mode, approaching from time. When we see through that one *nian* we see that eternity is not other than this moment, or as Robert Aitken expresses it in his published version of Doushuai's verse, "Eternity is equal to now." This is expressive of the fifth mode, to which we now turn.

THE FIFTH MODE: ARRIVING AT THE CONCURRENCE OF TIME AND THE TIMELESS

Let's recall Dongshan's verse for the fifth mode:

> Everyone longs to leave the mundane stream, yet finally you return to sit in the charcoal heap.

Longing to leave the mundane stream is surely a deep motive for entering the Way. We long to step clear of the onrush, to experience timeless-ness and to redeem the swift passage of our days. We may yearn to step out of the mundane stream of time and change, but, as we have seen, the only way out is in. To encounter the timeless we must engage what is fleeting, for that is its home. Even our longing to leave the mundane stream itself is expressive of timelessness.

With our return to the charcoal heap, what looks and sounds like an ending is in fact the darkness and radiance of our present experience in timeless time. The concurrence of the timeless and the temporal means that they are none other than each other, even though we acknowledge them as distinct. Rumi seems to speak to this thought in a beautiful line about the aspects of a person: "The time part dies; the other is the good friend of together." From another perspective, the moment of death itself is unconfined and is none other than the good friend of forever.

We are confirmed in our evanescence, yet mysteriously touched by all that we have undergone. At the very last, the dialectic of the temporal and the timeless is forgotten, and the Way becomes our lives just as we find them. Just opening our eyes to the dawn conveys the timeless immensity, no less than closing our eyes last thing at night, to sleep.

24. Some Reflections on the Nature of the Five Ranks

The Five Ranks as a Philosophical Foundation of Zen

THE FIVE RANKS has been regarded as a philosophical foundation for the Zen Way, especially in Soto traditions. This isn't surprising, given the dialectical nature of the positions of the first cycle. However, understanding the Five Ranks in this way, we run the risk of reifying them into a rigid system. Our minds, hungry for order, find it everywhere. Fortunately, there are some considerations that urge caution against regarding the Five Ranks solely as a static and unconditional classification of the Way or as a fixed conception of the way things are.

Firstly, the relationship between the essential and the contingent is not fixed but is rather in constant, ever-changing mutual interpenetration, sometimes called "reciprocal interpenetration."[105] What this boils down to is that our experience of reality, in terms of the essential and the contingent, is always changing. Moreover, the dialectical terms of the Five Ranks—essential and contingent—cannot be statically identified with particular people, situations, or events.

Secondly, no matter how subtle and ramified the Five Ranks may be, ultimately, along with all other such systems, they are groundless, as shown in the following exemplary dialogue:

> Qingyuan Xingsi (660–740) asked Dajian Huineng (638–713), "How do I avoid becoming attached to ranks and stages?"
>
> "What have you been doing?" Huineng asked.

Qingyuan said, "I haven't even taken up the Four Noble Truths."

"Then, to what rank would you fall?" Huineng asked.

Qingyuan said, "I haven't even taken up the Four Noble Truths. What rank could there be?"[106]

Qingyuan's final words convey the empty realm where there are no ranks or stages. Fundamentally, the Way is without foundation, and to conceive a paradigm such as the five positions of the essential and the contingent as its ground, blocks the light, and stales its infinite variety. Better to regard the Five Ranks—including the dialectical captions ("the philosophy")—as a nest of koans. That keeps the Ranks—including its conceptual apparatus—alive and breathing with the spirit of Chan.

Centuries after Qingyuan and Huineng, Keizan Jokin (1285–1325), commenting on their dialogue, wrote:

> There is no trace in the way of flying birds, hither and
>   thither;
> In the subtle Way, how can ranks be sought?[107]

That very question conveys the inexpressible essence of the Five Ranks even as it deftly brushes them away. The notion of the Five Ranks being a philosophical foundation for Zen appears to depend on understanding the first Cycle of the Essential and the Contingent, alone, to be the Five Ranks. The second cycle, by contrast, has not drawn the same level of attention and has thus been spared a host of interpretations. When the two cycles are taken together—and I assume that this was Dongshan's intention—the story grows more complex, as it also involves cultivation and change over time. Seeing the Five Ranks thus, we will be less easily bewitched by the idea that they are a philosophical foundation for the Zen Way. Ultimately, we need to let go of such formulae and paradigms, helpful as they may be for equipping us with an intellectual overview of the path, and inspiring us to embark and endure on it. When all is said and done, the Five Ranks and its conceptual interlockings are readily subsumed in your breathing out or your adjusting your back when you are tired.

The Artistry of the Five Ranks

Dongshan elegantly and economically condenses the essence of his dialectic into captions, and these, in turn, counterbalance his allusive verses. The "dialogue" between these dialectical captions and poetic verses, for example, is a remarkable achievement, perfectly conveying the spirit of Chan as a subtle interplay of light and darkness, as well as of time and eternity.

For these reasons, the Five Ranks feel as if they were impelled by artistic concerns. This seems particularly evident in the elaborate inter-weaving of the Five Ranks with the "Song of the Precious Mirror Samadhi," the poem that may have served as womb for the Ranks, and in the evocative imagery of the verses. As with any other work of art, we can connect with the Five Ranks on a number of levels. Asking about the relevance of the Five Ranks feels rather like asking about the relevance of Bach's cello suites.

The Five Ranks as an Enactment of the Way

The Five Ranks shouldn't be regarded simply as an expedient teaching, in the way that we might regard the Four Noble Truths. I feel that Dongshan intended the modes to be pure, flavorless enactments of the Way: five dark, glittering manifestations of the void, which encapsulate each other, yet stand alone, like great cliffs fringed with stars. Like other mystical expressions, the Five Ranks tend to the condition of music. And like music, they are not a means to anything, even instruction. They are like Bach's music, which, being dedicated to the glory of God, is that glory.

Although they emerge from Buddhist traditions, the Five Ranks feel charged with the deepened significance that we attach to esoteric words and images associated with mystical experience. With their dazzling obscurity, they invite and challenge us to embark into the depths and to endure there, until we see through the one that sees and know beyond knowing the one who knows.

Having said all of this, the Five Ranks elude any final reckoning. As profound expressions of the nature of reality, they suggest sheer depths of the Way beyond personal awakening and challenge us to embark there. For any one of us, no matter how many years we have practiced, there is so much more to be discovered.

Path and No Path in the Five Ranks: Indivisible Reality

> I asked my old teacher Robert Aitken, "Are there levels of
> enlightenment?"
> "One level for all," he answered.

All the stages, ranks, hierarchies, and modes are completely empty. This matter is fundamental to the first cycle, the Cycle of the Essential and the Contingent, which is itself inherently without sequence or progression. On the other hand, the second cycle, the Cycle of Merit, presents the Way as a series of stages or levels. These two approaches are complementary: they depend on each other. There exists an important tension between these two approaches: the idea of the path as unfolding in time and the idea of the path complete in its silent immensity. Let's look more closely at this wide-ranging dialectic that plays out between the two cycles of the Five Ranks.

The path that unfolds in time corresponds to the mundane stream of birth, growth, maturity, and death. This is where we are formed as individuals and where over time we come to be seen and judged as people. When we experience the fleeting and evanescent as essentially timeless, we find a measure of ease and peace with whatever may befall us here: the seams are let out and we are no longer so confined by our ideas about who we think we are.

On the one hand, there is time, sequence, karma, and goals, but on the other, the path is timeless. And yet there's not a hair's breadth of difference between these. Considering the path as temporal in nature, we understand that it takes time and that we are changed over time.

We may awaken to the eternal in an instant—as when encountering the ancient mirror of the first cycle—but then spend a lifetime properly walking it into our lives. In terms of our lives, we are always at home, forever on the Way.

It is true that all the positions and stages are completely empty, but at the same time, and in perfectly ordinary ways, we can make sense of change and progress within the Way, and in fact we need to. Nothing is accomplished without aspiration, without commitment to practice over time, and without an acceptance of struggle and disappointment. Dongshan shows us some of the ways in which it is possible for us to awaken. He does this for its own sake, as an expression of awakening itself, and also to encourage us to awaken, and then to awaken more, and at greater depth. His composition of the Five Ranks is an intimate act of kindness.

We travel this Way, even as we are timelessly at rest. We express the mystery of our life in this place through our joys and struggles. Any point within the sequence of modes or stages—within the unfolding of our lives—opens into and is the breathing space of winter light, daydream, and the clouds banked on the horizon. We are launched toward death. Yet, in each moment, including that of death itself, we are home to the universe.

Confluence

The Five Ranks inspire us to embark on the Way; they illuminate the countryside of mature practice and are a means of refinement at the end of our journey, if indeed we can even consider the notion of an "end." However, regardless of their virtue and efficacy, the Five Ranks themselves are no substitute for practice and realization. Nor should we misleadingly attribute to the Five Ranks the changes—a more open heart, an ability to endure difficulty, and to find, even in that, a lightness of heart—wrought from years of practice. The Five Ranks are not a substitute for doing the hard yards of the Way.

With regard to the Five Ranks, we needn't undertake any kind of rush to relevance, either. The vivid, all-encompassing images of Huayan's fourfold dharmadhatu and of the Net of Indra, both of which prefigure and contextualize the Five Ranks, convey the interconnectedness of beings in an evolving universe even more readily than the formulations of the Five Ranks.

That being said, the theme of intimacy in the second mode of Dongshan's first cycle surely has implications for how we treat the planet and our fellow beings. Likewise, the stage of Service in his Cycle of Merit must be understood to include "service to all beings." Finally, the "lotus in the midst of fire" of the fourth mode of the first cycle is a memorably encouraging image for awakening oneself and others in the midst of the suffering world.

Back to the Source

In the piccaninny dawn, the tiny birds make up the whole chorus. Now the crows join them—raucous, mocking. To celebrate I put on an old record of Thelonius Monk playing Ellington. I'm stunned by the halting power that he brings to those ancient ballads, the ironic lilt he gives to "Solitude." It's said that he used to wear a chunky ring on the fourth finger of his left hand. When you looked at it one way up, it said "MONK." When you looked at it the other way, it said, "KNOW."

The truth is that we stand on the shoulders of giants, and it's good enough—yet not quite good enough—to say that everything we need is right here; that we needn't get to know those ancient teachers and their writings. Some nine centuries after Dongshan, Hakuin Ekaku rescued the Five Ranks from neglect and placed them at the heart of his teaching. He struggled for thirty years with them, and had at least one deep realization while meditating on them. On the occasions when an aspect of the Five Ranks clarified itself, he would say "the rhinoceros of my doubt fell down dead on the spot," and when confusion once again clouded the brilliance, "only to raise its head again." When they were finally clear to him, Hakuin used the unfolding structure of the Cycle of the Essential and the Contingent to systematize the hundreds of koans he had gathered, struggled with, and resolved over the years. His herculean labors to realize the Way at deeper and deeper levels for himself, and to find the best means to pass it on to his students, is an inspiration to all of us.

The Five Ranks are, as Hakuin knew, exemplary: They show us a path to awakening, its expression, and finally its transcendence and beyond. By reading and meditating on these verses, we learn their ancient song, and over time it becomes us. Almost without noticing it, we are changed and deepened. One brilliant corner darkens us, then another.

As we are released into our lives through our practice of the Way we may begin to fear death less, and to be less afraid of our lives, such that we are able to bless and to forgive, to love better and to have grace in the inevitable difficulties that we encounter. If our efforts with meditation and study bring no change at all—if it's the same old cuss haunting the marketplace—we might as well pack up and go home. Yes, let's. Let's.

APPENDICES

Appendix 1: Caoshan Benji (840–901):
Two Accounts of the Five Ranks

CAOSHAN'S FAME rests partly on his elaborations of Dongshan's Five Ranks.[108] His "Commentary on the Five Positions of Ruler and Minister," which follows, provides a useful introduction to the themes of Dongshan's Five Ranks. Here, following our translation of the title of the first cycle, I have rendered the title of Caoshan's work as "Commentary on the Five Positions of Ruler and Minister," rather than as it has been more commonly translated, "Commentary on the Five Ranks of Lord and Vassal."

Caoshan also introduced the use of circle diagrams into his expositions of the five positions. Circle diagrams were a device used at various times in the evolution of Chan. Before Caoshan, Guishan Lingyou (771–853) and Yangshan Huiji (807–883) had made use of a set of ninety-seven or one hundred circle diagrams, to which the key has been lost. Guifeng Zongmi (780–841) also employed circle diagrams, often in sets of ten. The most well-known set of circle diagrams is probably Kuoan Shiyuan's set of ten ox-herding pictures.[109] I have included Caoshan's diagrams, with their accompanying verses, under the title "Verses of the Five Features," below. There is extensive debate, even confusion, about how we are to interpret these diagrams, and I will not pursue these matters here.

Both of Caoshan's works to follow relate to Dongshan's first cycle: the five positions of the essential and the contingent, rather than to each other. The "Commentary on the Five Positions of Ruler and Minister" seems to be an elucidation of Dongshan's five positions. In it, Caoshan reorders Dongshan's positions to make the exposition clearer. The esoteric five features verses on the other hand employ

Dongshan's ordering, and treat the five positions in a way that is ornate and abstruse.

We can be grateful to Caoshan for his labors, which ensured that the Five Ranks became part of the teaching arsenal of the developing Chan tradition. As a consequence, the Five Ranks later entered the Soto and Rinzai streams of Zen in Japan, where they remain a significant in those traditions down to the present day. The themes of the first two modes of the essential and the contingent figure in the following memorable exchange, which reveals Caoshan to have been subtle and adroit in his teaching style:

> Caoshan asked Venerable Qiang, "The true Dharma body is like the empty sky. It manifests the form of itself as the moon reflects in the water. How do you explain the way it corresponds?"
>
> Qiang said, "It is like a donkey sees a well."
>
> Caoshan said, "That was nicely expressed, but it is only eighty percent."
>
> Qiang said, "How about you, Acharya?"
>
> Caoshan said, "It is like a well sees a donkey."[110]

Though Caoshan made a lasting contribution to the Zen heritage, his line of succession did not endure, and the Caodong line that comes down to us primarily as Japanese Soto does so through Dongshan's other chief successor, Yunju Daoying (d. 902). Ironically, Yunju evinced no interest in the Five Ranks.

CAOSHAN'S COMMENTARY ON THE FIVE POSITIONS OF RULER AND MINISTER[111]

There was a monk who asked about the fundamental points of the Five Positions of Ruler and Minister.

The master said, "The position of the essential is the realm of emptiness; originally, there is nothing.

"The position of the contingent is the realm of form; it has the images and shapes of myriad things.

"Contingent within essential turns its back on principle to accommodate phenomena.

"Essential within contingent forsakes phenomena to gain entry to principle.

"The concurrent responds silently to myriad conditions. It does not fall into affirming the various existences. It is not stained, not pure, not essential, not contingent.

"Therefore, we call it the empty, mysterious great Way— the genuine teaching of nonattachment. From earliest times, eminent masters have considered this position to be the most mysterious and profound."

"We should investigate these matters carefully and distinguish them clearly.

"Ruler refers to the position of the essential.

"Minister refers to the position of the contingent.

"Minister facing ruler is essential within contingent.

"Ruler watching minister is contingent within essential.

"The merging of the ways of ruler and minister is concurrence."

The monk further enquired, "What is the ruler like?"

The master replied, "Profound excellence is honored throughout the entire cosmos; lofty illumination lights up the great void."

The monk asked, "What is the minister like?"

The master replied, "The sacred way is broadened by inspired responsiveness; genuine wisdom benefits the many beings."

"How is it when minister faces ruler?"

"Without entertaining the various extraordinary sights, you focus your feelings in order to view the sacred countenance."

"How is it when ruler faces minister?"

"Even as the mysterious countenance does not move, its light shines impartially."

"How is it when the ways of ruler and minister merge?"

"Inchoate, without inside or outside; in complete accord, above and below are at ease."

And the master continued, "The reason for using the terms ruler and minister, and essential and contingent, is to avoid transgressing the center."

CAOSHAN'S VERSES OF THE FIVE FEATURES[112]

The first verse:
That the lay scholar in civilian attire must pay his
    respects
to the high minister is no surprising matter;
You who have descended from illustrious lineages of
    court officials
ought not to speak of the time when you were destitute.

The second verse:
On the stroke of midnight you ascend to the essential
    position,
but that illumination depends on both ruler and
    minister;
Before descending from the Tushita heaven,
the black hen walks on the snow.

The third verse:
Cold ice forms within the flame.
In the ninth month, willow blossoms take flight.
The clay oxen bellow on the water's surface,
and the wooden horse neighs while chasing the wind.

◯ The fourth verse:
In the royal palace, a newly setting sun
cannot be parted from the moon.
Having yet to attain the point of no-merit,
why tarry among humans or devas?

● The fifth verse:
Seemingly inchoate, it conceals principle and event;
signs and portents are finally difficult to discern.
The King with the awe-inspiring voice still
    does not know;
how could Maitreya remain in the dark?

Appendix 2: Linji Yixuan's (d. 866)
Four Measures

THE FIRST CYCLE of Dongshan's Five Ranks, the Cycle of the Essential and the Contingent, may be aptly compared with Linji Yixuan's Four Measures. Following this new translation of Linji's work, I will demonstrate how Linji's measures and Dongshan's modes correlate.

Linji and Dongshan were almost exact contemporaries. Dongshan and his disciple Caoshan initiated what became known as the Caodong School, and Linji initiated the school named after him. Centuries later, their schools became known in Japan and throughout the world as the Soto and Rinzai Schools, respectively.

Here, with our new translation of Linji's Four Measures, Peter Wong and I have included Linji's responses to questions about each statement, as well as Linji's own vigorous and inspiring conclusion to the dialogue.

LINJI'S FOUR MEASURES

In the evening gathering the master instructed the assembly, saying, "Sometimes I steal the person, but not the place; sometimes I steal the place, but not the person; sometimes I steal both person and place; sometimes I steal neither person nor place."

A monk then asked, "What is stealing the person but not the place?"

The master said, "With the warm sun, brocade carpets the earth;[113] an infant with hair hanging down as white as silk."

The monk asked, "What is stealing the place but not the person?"

The master said, "The rule of the sovereign prevails throughout the world; the general in the borderlands is unstained by smoke and dust."

The monk asked, "What is stealing both person and place?"

The master said, "Bing and Fen cease communication; one dwells alone."

The monk asked, "What is stealing neither person nor place?"

The master said, "The sovereign ascends the audience hall; an old man sings in the field."

Then the master said, "Students of the Dharma today ought to seek genuine insight. Once you have obtained it, then you are uncontaminated by birth or death, and you can freely come and go. Don't seek for the wonderful and the extraordinary, they will come of themselves. Those who belong to the stream of the Tao need only behave like those old worthies, who had their own ways to liberate people. All that this mountain monk teaches is not to be confused by others. If you wish to use it, then do. Never hesitate."

Linji's Four Measures Correlated with Dongshan's Five Modes

THE CYCLE OF THE ESSENTIAL AND THE CONTINGENT	LINJI'S FOUR MODES
2. The Essential within the Contingent	1. Sometimes I steal the person, but not the place.
1. The Contingent within the Essential	2. Sometimes I steal the place, but not the person
3. Arriving within the Essential	3. At times I steal both person and place.
5. Arriving at Concurrence	4. At times I steal neither person nor place.

Notes

1. "Wuwei junchen song" 五位君臣頌 (Jap. Henshō Gōi Shō). Although the terms "ruler" (*jun* 君) and "minister" (*chen* 臣) are clearly implied in the title "Gāthā of the Five Ranks, the Lords and Vassals" in William Powell's *The Record of Tung-shan* (Honolulu: University of Hawaii Press, 1986), 61, one notes that they are missing in the title given by Robert Aitken in *The Morning Star: New and Selected Zen Writings* (Washington, DC: Shoemaker & Hoard, 2003), 140, where the work is referred to as "The Five Modes of the Phenomenon and the Universal." Some Buddhist authors exclusively associate the imagery of "straight" (*zheng* 正) and "slant" (*pian* 偏) with Dongshan and attribute the imagery of "ruler" and "minister" to his successor Caoshan; c.f. *Foguang Da Cidian*, 《佛光大辭典,「洞山五位」》 北京:書目文獻出版社, 1989–93. Interestingly, this gatha is sometimes referred to in both editions of the Record of Caoshan as "Dongshan wuwei song" 洞山五位頌, or "Dongshan's Gatha on the Five Positions." Furthermore, we note that the imagery of "ruler and minister" does not explicitly appear in the text of the gatha itself. (See *Fuzhou caoshan yuanzheng chanshi yulu* 撫州曹山元證禪師語錄 [The Record of Caoshan Yuanzheng] T47n1987A, p0527 a10.)

2. The source of this text is *Ruizhou dongshan liangjie chanshi yulu* 瑞州洞山良价禪師語錄 [The recorded sayings of Dongshan Liangjie] (T47N1986B), edited and compiled by the Ming Chinese monk Yufeng Yuanxin 語風圓信 (1571–1647) and the layperson Guo Ningzhi 郭凝之 (n.d.). Our edition is found in *Dainippon Zokuzōkyō* 大日本續藏經 [The great Japanese supplement to the canon], Nakano Tatsue, ed. (Kyoto: Zōkyō Shoin, 1905–12). *Ruizhou dongshan liangjie chanshi yulu* also appears in an earlier collection entitled *Wujia yulu* 五家語錄 [Records of the Five Houses]. It should be noted that another Record of Dongshan exists, entitled *Yunzhou dongshan wuben chanshi yulu* 筠州洞山悟本禪師語錄 [The Record of Dongshan Wuben] (T47N1986A), proofed and compiled by the Japanese monk E-In 慧印 (1689–1764), and also collected in the *Dainippon Zokuzōkyō*. However, the "Gatha of the Five Ranks of Ruler and Minister" exists only as a title in the latter record, with a remark from the compiler saying that because it is found together with its commentary in *Fuzhou caoshan yuanzheng chanshi yulu* 撫州曹山元證禪師語錄 [The Record of Caoshan Yuanzheng] (T47N1987A), its content has been omitted.

3. *zheng zhong pian* 正中偏 (Jap. shō chū hen). The terms *zheng* 正 and *pian* 偏, for which "essential" and "contingent" are the proposed translation herein, are rich in connotation, and it is difficult to find a fully satisfactory translation. Literally, the terms mean straight (or upright) and slant (or askew), respectively. But they are also important terms in the ritual writings of Confucianism, where they could be taken to mean main or dominant and supporting or subordinate, respectively. More specifically, in terms of marital status, the main wife is zheng and concubines are pian. In terms of seating arrangements, the main seat at the table is zheng and the seats to the sides are pian. For its application in terms of the relative positions between ruler and minister, please see Caoshan's "Commentary on the Five Positions of Ruler and Minister" in Appendix I.

4. *pian zhong zheng* 偏中正 (Jap. hen chū shō)

5. *zheng zhong lai* 正中來 (Jap. shō chū rai)

6. There are competing versions for the title of the fourth position, *pian zhong zhi* 偏中至 (Jap. hen chū shō) [Approaching from the Contingent] and *jian zhong zhi* 兼中至 (Jap. ken chū shō) [Approaching Concurrence]. The former title appears in both editions of the Record of Caoshan, occurring three times in the *Fuzhou caoshan yuanzheng chanshi yulu* edition by E-in (T47 1987A), and once in the *Caoshan benji chanshi yulu* 撫州曹山本寂禪師語錄 [The record of Caoshan Benji] edition by Genkai 玄契 (T47 1987B)—though the latter also contains several mentions of the second title, "Approaching Concurrence." This latter version of the title is also found in *Ruizhou dongshan liangjie chanshi yulu* [The recorded sayings of Dongshan Liangjie] (T47 1986B). Among the commentaries collected in the canon, one finds both support for and rejections of both versions. For opinion in support of "Approaching from the Contingent," see the comment by Jiyin 寂音 in "Jiyin zheng wuwei zhi e" 寂音正五位之訛, published in 人天眼目 *Rentian yanmu*, vol. 3 (T48n2006). For an affirmation of "Approaching Concurrence" and a rejection of Jiyin's opinion, see Yongjue Yuanxian 永覺元賢, *Dongshang guche*, fascicle A, 洞上古轍卷上, published in *Yongjue Yuanxian chanshi guanglu*, 永覺元賢禪師廣錄, fascicle 27 (X72n1437-p0539b11(00)). Throughout our translation and commentaries below, both titles are employed because each provides important insights into the practice of the Way.

7. *jian zhong dao* 兼中到 (Jap. ken chū tō)

8. Gongxun Wuwei 功勳五位 (Jap. kōkun gōi). The sources for Dongshan's "Five Positions of Merit" are as follows: Compilation by E-in (pinyin: Hui Yin 慧印), *Yunzhou dongshan wuben chanshi yulu* 筠州洞山悟本禪師語錄 [Record of Dongshan Wuben], Taisho Tripitaka, vol. 47, no. 1986A. This source lists both verses and title. Compilation by Yufeng Yuanxing 語風圓信 and Guo Ningzhi 郭凝之: *Ruizhou dongshan liangjie chanshi yulu* 瑞州洞山良价禪師語錄 [Record of Dongshan Liangjie], Taisho Tripitaka, vol. 47, no. 1986B. This source lists the verses next to the Five Positions of Ruler and Minister but without a title.

The Chinese term *wu wei* for which we translate "Five Stages" in the Cycle of Merit and "Five Positions" in the Cycle of Essence and Contingent are in fact the same in the Chinese. We have chosen to translate it differently because of the different nuances detected in the two cycles.

9. *xiang* 向 (Jap. kō)

10. *feng* 奉 (Jap. bu)

11. *gong* 功 (Jap. kō)

12. *gong* gong* 共功 (Jap. gū kō)

13. *gong gong* 功功 (Jap. kō kō)

14. William Powell, *The Record of Tung-shan*, 3. For a more comprehensive biography of Dongshan, see also: *The Roaring Stream: A New Zen Reader*, Nelson Foster and Jack Shoemaker, eds. (Hopewell, NJ: Ecco Press, 1996), 115–16. This is a translation based on *Ruizhou donghsan liangjie chanshi yulu*.

15. Adapted from Powell, *The Record of Tung-shan*, 68. For another account, see Isshū Miura and Ruth Fuller Sasaki, *Zen Dust: The History of the Koan and Koan Study in Rinzai (Lin-Chi) Zen* (New York: Harcourt, Brace & World, 1966), 298.

16. Powell, *The Record of Tung-shan*, 54.

17. Anton Chekhov, *The Lady with the Little Dog, and Other Stories, 1896–1904*, trans. by Ronald Wilks (Penguin Books, London, 2002), 266.

18. Jay Garfield, *The Fundamental Wisdom of the Middle Way: Nāgārjuna's Mūlamadhyamakakārikā* (Oxford University Press, Oxford and New York, 1995), 296-8.

19. Ibid., 299.

20. Robert Aitken and Yamada Koun, trans., *Hekigan Roku (The Blue Cliff Record)* (unpublished manuscript, 1974), Case 95.

21. James Mitchell, *Sōtō Zen Ancestors in China: The Recorded Teachings of Shitou Xiqian, Yaoshan Weiyan, and Yunyan Tansheng* (San Francisco: Ithuriel's Spear, 2005), 19.

22. Chang Chung-Yuan, *Original Teachings of Ch'an Buddhism* (New York: Vintage Books, 1971), 42.

23. Robert Gimello, "Chih-yen and the Foundations of Hua-yen Buddhism," Ph.D. diss., Columbia University, 1976. ProQuest (7700252), 457–510.

24. I am indebted to Korin Charlie Pokorny for pointing out the relationship between the Ten Approaches and first cycle of the Five Ranks. Our analysis of the relationship between them differs, but without his discovery I could not have embarked into the foregoing analysis.

25. Robert Aitken and Yamada Koun, trans., *Shōyōroku* (unpublished manuscript, 1974), Case 79, slightly adapted.

26. Thomas Cleary and J. C. Cleary, trans., *The Blue Cliff Record* (Boulder: Shambhala, 1977), vol. 2, 467–8. Fenyang presented the Five Ranks in the order: 3, 1, 2, 4, 5—perhaps implying that emptiness is the source and origin of the other ranks.

27. Heinrich Dumoulin, *Zen Buddhism: A History (Japan)*, trans. James W. Heisig and Paul Knitter (Bloomington, IN: World Wisdom, 1994), 208–9.

28. Translated in Isshū Miura and Ruth Fuller Sasaki, *The Zen Koan* (New York: Harcourt Brace Jovanovich, 1965), 63–72. The books *Zen Dust* and *The Zen Koan*, both by Miura and Sasaki, have the first 122 pages in common. *Zen Dust* has a compendious set of notes extending for 390 pages. Wherever possible I will cite *The Zen Koan*, as *Zen Dust* is long out of print. I also draw on the translation of Hakuin's *Keiso Dokuzui* in Thomas Cleary, *Kensho: The Heart of Zen* (Boston: Shambhala, 1997).

29. Cleary, *Kensho: The Heart of Zen*, 69.

30. Adapted from Thomas Cleary, trans., *The Flower Ornament Scripture: A Translation of the Avatamsaka Sutra* (Boston: Shambhala, 1993), 321.

31. Foster and Shoemaker, eds., *The Roaring Stream*, 116.

32. I am grateful to Peter Wong for this explanation of the term *toujijie* 投機偈.

33. See Cleary and Cleary, *The Blue Cliff Record*, vol.2, ix–xi. Hakuin and his disciples developed this systematization of the koan path. It provides the paradigm for Miura's "Koan Study in Rinzai Zen" in Miura and Sasaki, *Zen Dust*, 37–72, in particular. Dongshan's ordering of the modes doesn't preclude other options. Caoshan, in his Commentary on the Five Positions of Ruler and Minister (see Appendix 1, pp. 266-68), ordered the five modes: 3, 4, 1, 2, 5—giving more than a passing nod to the Four Dharmadhatu by presenting the realms of emptiness and phenomena (in reverse order) as the first two stages. Later, Fenyang Shanzhao (947–1024), who introduced the Five Ranks into the Linji line, presented them in the order: 3, 1, 2, 4, 5—perhaps implying that emptiness is the source and origin of the other ranks. For his verses on the Five Ranks, see Cleary and Cleary, *The Blue Cliff Record*, 467–68.

34. I am indebted to Peter Wong for his elucidation of the Confucian senses of the terms *zheng* and *pian*, which I have adopted here.

35. E-mail correspondence with Mari Rhydwen.

36. Robert Aitken, trans. *The Gateless Barrier: Wu-Men Kuan (Mumonkan)*, (New York: North Point Press, 1991), 7.

37. *The Śūraṅgama Sūtra (Leng Yan Jing)*, trans. Upāsaka Lu K'uan Yü (Charles Luk) (London: Rider, 1966), 97.

   The Buddha replied [to Purnamaitrayaniputra]: "Although you have wiped out your troubles (kleśa), traces of your defilement still remain. I will now put some worldly questions to you. Have you not heard of (the madman) Yajñadatta of Śrāvastī who would look into a mirror and delight in seeing his eyebrows and eyes but when one morning he failed to see them in his own head, thought himself bedeviled? Do you think there was any valid reason for such madness?"

38. Yamada Koun and Robert Aitken, *Wumen-kuan* (unpublished manuscript), Case 32.

39. Aitken, *The Gateless Barrier: Wu-Men Kuan (Mumonkan)*, 4.

40. Buddhist Text Translation Society, *The Diamond Sutra*, chapter 18, last accessed December 10, 2013. www.buddhism.org.

41. I am indebted to Andy Ferguson and to Robert Aitken for their accounts of this celebrated story of Deshan's encounters with the Zen granny and with Longtan. The former can be found in Ferguson's *Zen's Chinese Heritage: The Masters and Their Teachings* (Boston: Wisdom Publications, 2000), p.196, and the latter in Aitken's *The Gateless Barrier*, pp. 177–79. I have slightly adapted Aitken's translation of this critical account of Deshan's awakening. It is difficult to better his wording.

42. Yamada Kōun and Robert Aitken, *Preliminary Notes on Henshō Gōi and Kokun Gōi* (unpublished manuscript).

43. Nyogen Senzaki and Ruth McCandless, *The Iron Flute* (Tokyo: Tuttle, 1964), 46, Case 36: "Where to Meet after Death." The northern and the southern branches have the primary sense of the northern and southern schools of Chan, but the reference is clearly richer than that.

44. See *Not Mixing up Buddhism: Essays on Women and Buddhist Practice*, ed. Deborah Hopkinson, Michelle Hill, and Eileen Kiera (White Pine Press: New York: 1986), 34–35.

45. *Kahawai Koans,* collected by women students of Robert Aitken, (unpublished manuscript).

46. Miura and Sasaki, *Zen Dust*, 69.

47. Cleary and Cleary, *The Blue Cliff Record*, 460.

48. Chang, *Original Teachings of Ch'an Buddhism*, 167.

49. Aitken and Yamada, *Shōyōroku*, Case 62.

50. See: Torei Enji, *The Discourse on the Inexhaustible Lamp of the Zen School* (Boston: Charles E. Tuttle, 1996), 285.

51. Don Paterson, *Rain* (London: Faber and Faber, 2009), 55.

52. Aitken and Yamada, trans., *Hekigan Roku (The Blue Cliff Record)*, Case 41.

53. Ibid., Case 43.

54. *The Vimalakīrti Nirdeśa Sūtra (Wei mo chieh so shuo ching)*, trans. Upāsaka Lu K'uan Yü (Charles Luk) (Berkeley: Shambhala, 1972), 90.

55. Aitken, *The Gateless Barrier*, 241: Case 40.

56. Retold from Zenkei Shibayama, *The Gateless Barrier: Zen Comments on the Mumonkan* (Shambhala, Boston, 2000), p.282.

57. See "Caoshan's Commentary on the Five Positions of Ruler and Minister" in Appendix 1.

58. *Kahawai Koans.*

59. Dogen, *Kyojukaimon,* trans. Robert Aitken, Diamond Sangha Jukai Ceremony.

60. Peter Wong: "I would tend to read *gongxun* as a bound term, which means 'merit.' That would be the primary meaning. In the dictionary, the term is glossed as 'merit and the fruit of labor (or service).' Our translation leaves out the sense that this term is normally applied to works of great importance that are in service to the state."

61. Powell, *The Record of Tung-shan*, 62.

62. In Australian parliamentary politics, a "Dorothy Dixer" is a rehearsed or planted question posed from the backbench of one's own party chamber during Parliamentary Question Time in order to "elicit" a typically self-serving rehearsed response.

63. See also Powell, *The Record of Tung-shan*, 62 for another translation.

64. Ibid., 52.

65. Chang, *Original Teachings of Ch'an Buddhism*, 51.

66. Adapted from Andrew Ferguson, *Zen's Chinese Heritage: The Masters and Their Teachings* (Boston: Wisdom Publications, 2000), 136–37.

67. *Kahawaii Koans,* adapted.

68. There are sixteen bodhisattva precepts comprised of the Three Vows of Refuge (taking refuge in the Buddha, Dharma, and Sangha), the Three Pure Precepts (renouncing evil, practicing good, and liberating manifold beings), and the Ten Grave Precepts (not to kill, not to steal, not to misuse sex, not to speak falsely, not to give or take drugs, not to discuss the faults of others, not to praise oneself while abusing others, not to spare the dharma assets, not to indulge in anger, and not to defame the Three Treasures).

69. Aitken, *The Morning Star: New and Selected Zen Writings*, 139.

70. In nineteenth century England a "sixpence" was the smallest coin minted. The saying "I felt as big as a sixpence" indicates an exceeding diminution, even as if unto death. The saying "I could have died of shame" is similar.

71. Aitken, *The Gateless Barrier*, 114.

72. Chang, *Original Teachings of Ch'an Buddhism*, 51.

73. Aitken and Yamada, *Hekigan Roku*, Case 27, "Yunmen's Golden Wind."

74. Aitken and Yamada, *Shōyōroku*, Case 65, "Shoushan's New Bride."

75. William Shakespeare, *Romeo and Juliet*. Act II, scene 2.

76. Cleary and Cleary, *The Blue Cliff Record*, 636: Case 100, "Pa Ling's Blown Hair Sword."

77. Cleary and Cleary, *The Blue Cliff Record*, 145.

78. Robert Aitken and Yamada Kōun, trans., *Denkōroku (The Transmission of the Light)* (unpublished manuscript, 1974), Case 41.

79. Powell, *The Record of Tung-shan*, 87, n. 174.

80. Aitken, *The Morning Star: New and Selected Zen Writings*, 161.

81. Cleary, trans., *The Flower Ornament Scripture*, 1489–90. (Slightly edited.)

82. If we regard the two cycles of the Five Ranks as having been written during the Song dynasty, rather than by Dongshan, we can't say which would have come first. I follow traditional ascription of the Five Ranks to Dongshan, and so consider them to be the older of the two works.

83. The ox-herding sequence may represent a Zen Buddhist interpretation of the ten stages experienced by a bodhisattva as outlined in various Mahayana sutras, most particularly the Avatamsaka Sutra. The Cycle of Merit also refers

to the Avatamsaka Sutra. The pictures and texts of the ox-herding sequence are believed to be based on the work of an earlier Taoist scholar.

84. I am grateful to Korin Charlie Pokorny for introducing me to the notions of "simultaneous" and "successive" causation through his notes on Chinese Buddhist philosophy.

85. Acharya (*ācārya*), according to *A Dictionary of Chinese Buddhist Terms*, compiled by William Edward Soothill and Lewis Hodous (Delhi: Motilal Banarsidass, 2000), is a Buddhist Sanskrit term meaning "a spiritual teacher, master, preceptor; a person of integrity, who is able to teach others."

86. Powell, *The Record of Tung-shan*, 27. Apart from changing to Pinyin, this is a literal account of Powell's exemplary translation. The gatha has been retranslated.

87. The exploration of the "Song of the Precious Mirror Samadhi" that follows was written while in weekly dialogue with Glenn Wallis, who teaches in New Zealand. Because I have found his approach to the Song to be cogent and incisive, I have included his perspectives at key points in my own exposition.

88. Miura and Sasaki, *The Zen Koan*, 63.

89. Powell, *The Record of Tung-shan*, 63.

90. See Whalen Lai, "Sinitic Mandalas: The Wu-wei-t'u of Ts'ao-shan," in *Early Chan in China and Tibet*, ed. Lancaster Lewis and Whalen Lai (Berkeley: Asian Humanities Press, 1983), 236–37, for an excellent account of Dongshan's reasons for choosing the Li hexagram to configure the five positions of the essential and the contingent.

91. Richard Wilhelm, trans., *The I Ching, or Book of Changes*, trans. English by Cary F. Baynes (London: Routledge, 1985), 118.

92. Ibid., 119.

93. Powell, *The Record of Tung-shan*, 88, n. 181.

94. The foregoing analysis is based on Chi-yin Huihung's exegesis of "Ranked in pairs they yield three; transformed they make five." See Alfonso Verdu, *Dialectical Aspects in Buddhist Thought in Sino-Japanese Mahāyāna Idealism* (Lawrence, KA: Center for East Asian Studies, University of Kansas, 1974), 132–33.

95. Retold from Norman Waddell, trans. and ed., *Hakuin's Precious Mirror Cave: A Zen Miscellany* (Berkeley, Counterpoint, 2009), 172; 175; 177.

96. I am grateful to Peter Wong for drawing my attention to the I Ching, and introducing the Way of the Center to me.

97. *Zhouyi yinde: fu biaojiao jing wen* 周易引得 ：附標校經文 [A concordance to Yi ching] (Taipei: Chengwen Publishing: Distributed by Chinese Materials and Research Aids Service Center, 1966), 19–20.

98. Roger T. Ames and David L. Hall, *Focusing the Familiar: A Translation and Philosophical Interpretation of the Zhongyong* (Honolulu: University of Hawaii Press, 2001), 89.

99. Powell, *The Record of Tung-shan*, 88, n. 186.

100. Ibid, 89, n. 187.

101. Miura and Sasaki, *Zen Dust*, 319, n. 164.

102. François Jullien, *Detour and Access: Strategies of Meaning in China and Greece* (New York: Zone Books, 2000), 307.

103. Aitken, *The Gateless Barrier*, 248: Case 47.

104. Ibid, 278. I am employing an earlier translation of this verse, with the Japanese transliteration transposed to Pinyin.

105. Miura and Sasaki, *Zen Dust*, 310, n. 129.

106. Aitken and Yamada, *Denkōroku*, Case 34.

107. Ibid.

108. For a comprehensive biography of Caoshan, see Foster and Shoemaker, *The Roaring Stream*, 132–33.

109. Jewel Mirror Samadhi Translation Study compiled by Korin Charlie Pokorny (unpublished manuscript, 2008), 92.

110. Aitken and Yamada, *Shōyōroku*, Case 52.

111. Caoshan's commentary on the Five Positions is found in both compilations of the Record of Caoshan. See *Fuzhoux caoshan yuanzheng chanshi yulu* 撫州曹山元證禪師語錄 (T47N1987A), compiled by E-in; and *Fuzhou caoshan benji chanshi yulu* 撫州曹山本寂禪師語錄 (T47N1987B), compiled by Genkai. However, we note that the latter compilation is in two fascicles, of which the first is actually attributed to Guo Ningzhi, the compiler. The present passage together with the following verses on the five features are found in fascicle 1.

112. Ibid. Caoshan's "Verses of the Five Features" are listed in the Record of Caoshan after his commentary on the five positions. There is an intervening passage between the two, which we have not translated.

113. *Pudijin* 普地錦, which translates as "brocade that carpets the earth," is also a common name for plants, one of which is a groundcover with small round leaves that is used in southern China as an ingredient in herbal remedies.

Selected Bibliography

A Source Book in Chinese Philosophy. Translated and compiled by Wing-Tsit Chan. Princeton, NJ: Princeton University, 1963.

Aitken, Robert. *The Morning Star: New and Selected Zen Writings.* Washington, DC: Shoemaker & Hoard, 2003.

Ames, Roger T., and David L. Hall. *Focusing the Familiar: A Translation and Philosophical Interpretation of the Zhongyong.* Honolulu: University of Hawaii Press, 2001.

Chang Chung-Yuan. *Original Teachings of Ch'an Buddhism.* New York: Vintage Books, 1971.

Chang, Garma C. C. *The Buddhist Teaching of Totality: The Philosophy of Hwa Yen Buddhism.* University Park: Pennsylvania State University Press, 1991.

Cleary, Thomas, and J. C. Cleary, trans. *The Blue Cliff Record.* Boulder: Shambhala, 1977.

Cleary, Thomas. *Entry into the Inconceivable: An Introduction to Hua-Yen Buddhism.* Honolulu: University of Hawaii Press, 1983.

———, trans. *The Five Houses of Zen.* Boston: Shambala, 1997.

———, trans. *The Flower Ornament Scripture: A Translation of the Avatamsaka Sutra.* Boston: Shambhala, 1993.

———*Kensho: The Heart of Zen.* Boston: Shambhala, 1997.

———, ed. and trans., *Timeless Spring: A Sōtō Zen Anthology.* New York: Weatherhill, 1979.

Dumoulin, Heinrich. *Zen Buddhism: A History* (Japan). Translated by James W. Heisig and Paul Knitter. Bloomington, IN: World Wisdom, 1994.

Ferguson, Andrew. *Zen's Chinese Heritage: The Masters and Their Teachings.* Boston: Wisdom, 2000.

Foster, Nelson, and Jack Shoemaker, eds. *The Roaring Stream: A New Zen Reader*. Hopewell, NJ: Ecco Press, 1996.

Gimello, Robert. "Chih-yen and the Foundations of Hua-yen Buddhism," Ph.D. diss., Columbia University, 1976. ProQuest (7700252).

James, William. *The Varieties of Religious Experience*. New York: New American Library of World Literature, 1958.

Jullien, François. *Detour and Access: Strategies of Meaning in China and Greece*. New York: Zone Books, 2000.

Kodera, Takashi James. *Dogen's Formative Years in China*. Boulder: Prajna Press, 1980.

Leighton, Taigen Dan. "Huayan Buddhism and the Phenomenal Universe of the Flower Ornament Sutra" *Buddhadharma: The Practitioner's Quarterly*, Fall 2006.

Luk, Charle. *Chan and Zen Teaching: Second Series*. London: Rider and Co., 1966.

Mitchell, James. *Sōtō Zen Ancestors in China: The Recorded Teachings of Shitou Xiqian, Yaoshan Weiyan, and Yunyan Tansheng*. San Francisco: Ithuriel's Spear, 2005.

Miura, Isshū, and Ruth Fuller Sasaki. *The Zen Koan*. New York: Harcourt Brace Jovanovich, 1965.

———*Zen Dust: The History of the Koan and Koan Study in Rinzai (Lin-Chi) Zen*. New York: Harcourt, Brace & World, 1966.

Pokorny, Korin Charlie. *Jewel Mirror Samadhi Translation Study*. Unpublished manuscript. http://zenstudies.wordpress.com/2011/02/05/jewel-mirror-samadhi-study/.

Powell, William. *The Record of Tung-shan*. Honolulu: University of Hawaii Press, 1986.

Sheng-yen. *The Infinite Mirror*. New York: Dharma Drum, 1990.

Suzuki, Daisetz Teitaro. *Essays in Zen Buddhism: Third Series*, edited by Christmas Humphreys. York Beach, ME: Samuel Weiser, 1953.

Tanahashi, Kazuaki. *Moon in a Dewdrop: Writings of Zen Master Dogen*. New York: North Point Press, 1985.

Torei, Enji. *The Discourse on the Inexhaustible Lamp of the Zen*

School: With commentary by Master Daibi of Unkan. Translated by Yoko Okuda. Boston: Charles E. Tuttle, 1996.

Waddell, Norman, trans. and ed. *Hakuin's Precious Mirror Cave: A Zen Miscellany.* Berkeley: Counterpoint, 2009.

Wu, John C. H. *The Golden Age of Zen.* Taipei: United Publishing Center, 1975.

Yu, Pauline. *The Reading of Imagery in the Chinese Poetic Tradition.* Princeton, NJ: Princeton University, 1987.

Zaehner, R. C. *Mysticism: Sacred and Profane.* London: Oxford University, 1980.

Index

Note: Page numbers in bold type indicate passages in Dongshan's or Caoshan's texts. Page numbers followed by "q" indicate quotations. Page numbers followed by "(2)" indicate two references.

About the Author

Photograph by Antoinette Carrier, Bayswater, Western Australia, 2013.

ROSS BOLLETER is a Zen teacher in the Diamond Sangha tradition. He trained with Robert Aitken and John Tarrant and received Transmission from them in 1997. He is also a composer with numerous CD releases, especially in the field of ruined piano. His book of poems, *Piano Hill*, was published by Fremantle Press in 2009. He teaches in Australia and New Zealand and has successors there. Ross has two grown-up children, Amanda and Julian, and is a grandfather twice over.

About Wisdom

WISDOM PUBLICATIONS is the leading publisher of contemporary and classic Buddhist books and practical works on mindfulness. Publishing books from all major Buddhist traditions, Wisdom is a nonprofit charitable organization dedicated to cultivating Buddhist voices the world over, advancing critical scholarship, and preserving and sharing Buddhist literary culture.

To learn more about us or to explore our other books, please visit our website at www.wisdompubs.org. You can subscribe to our eNewsletter, request a print catalog, and find out how you can help support Wisdom's mission either online or by writing to:

Wisdom Publications
199 Elm Street
Somerville, Massachusetts 02144 USA

You can also contact us at 617-776-7416, or info@wisdompubs.org.

Wisdom is a 501(c)(3) organization, and donations in support of our mission are tax deductible.

Wisdom Publications is affiliated with the Foundation for the Preservation of the Mahayana Tradition (FPMT).

Also from Wisdom Publications

The Heart of the Universe
Exploring the Heart Sutra
Mu Soeng
128 pages | $15.95

"Elegant, simple—and invaluable."—Mark Unno

Living by Vow
A Practical Introduction to Eight Essential Zen Chants and Texts
Shohaku Okumura
320 pages | $18.95

"An essential resource for students and teachers alike."
—Dosho Port, author of *Keep Me in Your Heart a While*

Dogen's Extensive Record
A Translation of the Eihei Koroku
Translated by Taigen Dan Leighton and Shohaku Okumura
Edited and introduced by Taigen Dan Leighton
824 pages | $26.95

"Taigen and Shohaku are national treasures."
—Norman Fischer, author of *Sailing Home*

The Clouds Should Know Me By Now
Buddhist Poet Monks of China
Edited by Red Pine and Mike O'Connor
Introduction by Andrew Schelling
224 pages | $15.95

"Here is a breathtaking millennium of Buddhist poet-monks."
—*Inquiring Mind*

Entangling Vines
A Classic Collection of Zen Koans
Translated and annotated by Thomas Yuho Kirchner
Foreword by Nelson Foster
352 pages | $28.95

"A masterpiece. It will be our inspiration for 10,000 years."
—Robert Aitken, author of *Taking the Path of Zen*